Helen Keller *Selected Writings*

Helen Keller

Selected Writings

Edited by

KIM E. NIELSEN

Consulting Editor: Harvey J. Kaye

Published in conjunction with the
American Foundation for the Blind

NEW YORK UNIVERSITY PRESS

NEW YORK AND LONDON

NEW YORK UNIVERSITY PRESS
New York and London
www.nyupress.org

All writings by Helen Keller courtesy of the American Foundation
for the Blind. Requests for permission for the use of these materials
should be addressed in writing to the American Foundation for the
Blind, 11 Penn Plaza, Suite 300, New York, NY 10001.

All photographs courtesy of the American Foundation for the Blind,
Helen Keller Archives.

Book design by Charles B. Hames

Library of Congress Cataloging-in-Publication Data
Keller, Helen, 1880–1968.
[Selections. 2005]
Helen Keller : selected writings / edited by Kim E. Nielsen.
p. cm. — (The history of disability series)
"Published in conjunction with the
American Foundation for the Blind."
Includes bibliographical references and index.
ISBN 0-8147-5829-0 (cloth : alk. paper)
1. Keller, Helen, 1880-1968.
2. Blind-deaf women—United States.
I. Nielsen, Kim E.   II. Title.   III. Series.
HV1624.K4A25   2005
362.4'1'092—dc22   2004028974

New York University Press books are printed on acid-free paper,
and their binding materials are chosen for strength and durability.

Manufactured in the United States of America

c 10 9 8 7 6 5 4 3 2 1
p 10 9 8 7 6 5 4 3 2 1

To Becky,

in celebration of our 40 years!

And to Helen Keller,

whom I grew to enjoy

far more than I ever imagined I would.

CONTENTS

THREE 1924–1945

All illustrations appear as inserts following p. 96, and p. 256.

ACKNOWLEDGMENTS

In August 1951, Helen Keller's dear friend Jo Davidson finished the book he'd been working on for years. She wrote to him with congratulations, "It delighted us to read the news that your autobiography has actually been finished and pushed out of the house into the hands of the publisher." In my case, many people helped to finish this project and push it out of the house into the hands of others. Eric Zinner shepherded the project. The American Foundation for the Blind and its staff members—especially Maureen Matheson, Natalie Hilzen, Regina Genwright, Helen Selsdon, and Daniel Cuff—assisted graciously, cheerfully, and with generosity. Staff at the Library of Congress, Perkins School for the Blind, and the Schlesinger Library helped in the early stages of this project. Paul Longmore and Lauri Umansky, as usual, performed intellectual and editing magic. Craig Jones of the Reader's Loft bookstore of DePere, Wisconsin found every out-of-print book I sought and made it look easy. My colleagues at the University of Wisconsin–Green Bay answered questions and gave much appreciated advice.

There are many others I could not do without. Cathy Kudlick and Georgina Kleege responded to numerous comments and questions about Helen Keller. Susan Burch provided cheerleading when I needed it. Becky Dale always asked how Keller and I were getting along. Ron and Kathie Nielsen model parenthood extraordinaire. Unbounded praise and appreciation goes to Nathan Tuff for cheerfully listening to more Helen Keller stories than any human being should ever have to endure, and for making everything else in life sweet. Morgan and Maya continue to make life chaotically wonderful.

INTRODUCTION

Throughout her entire life Helen Keller loved the written word. The world-famous deaf-blind woman born in 1880 realized at a young age that words held the power to transport her to other realms. Reading freed her and others from mental, physical, and spiritual impairments, as well as from disappointments and sorrows. As she wrote in *Midstream* in 1929, "More than at any other time, when I hold a beloved book in my hand my limitations fall from me, my spirit is free. Books are my compensation for the harms of fate. They give me a world for a lost world, and for mortals who have disappointed me they give me gods."[1] This continued to be the case until she died in 1968.

To Keller the written word was best when tactile. Her favorite way to read was by using braille, rather than having others finger-spell written material to her. Much-loved books grew flat and dirtied from frequent readings. Her Bible was the most frequently read: "I have read and reread it until in many parts the pages have faded out—I mean, my fingers have rubbed off the dots, and I must supply whole verses from memory, especially the Psalms, the Prophets, and the Gospels."[2] Good friends knew that having books new to her brailled was a special present, for books, newspapers, or letters from loved ones were best when brailled. She read brailled material alone and directly, without the intervention of an interpreter. As she wrote to Alexander Graham Bell, who had just learned the braille typewriter in 1900, "A letter always seems more truly my own when I can run my fingers over it, and quickly enter into the thoughts and feelings of my friends without an interpreter, even though the interpreter be the dearest and sweetest in the world."[3]

The written word could still be sublime, but reading via finger-spelling was second best. As she described her own finger-spelling, "I place my hand on the hand of the speaker so lightly as not to impede its movements. The position of the hand is as easy to feel as it is to see. I do not feel each letter any more than you see each letter separately when you read. Constant practice makes the fingers very flexible, and some of my friends spell rapidly—about as fast as an expert writes on a typewriter. The mere spelling is, of course, no more a conscious act than it is in writing."[4] Finger-spelling involved a third party. Who that was varied throughout Keller's life —perhaps father-figure Alexander Graham Bell, her teacher Anne Sullivan Macy, her mother Kate Keller, her mentor in religion John Hitz, friend Lenore Smith, editor and husband-of-Anne John Macy, dear friend Jo Davidson, or household companion Polly Thomson. No matter how cherished the finger-speller, no matter how impersonal or how intimate the written word, finger-spelling involved reading that was not private.

Throughout her entire life Keller also loved to produce the written word. Just as the words of others held the power to transport her, she learned that her own written words could contain tremendous power. Anne Sullivan sent the very first words she wrote to Michael Anagnos, director of the Perkins School for the Blind, who used them to quickly establish the eight-year-old and Perkins as world figures. The spectacular success of the twenty-three-year-old's 1903 autobiography, *The Story of My Life*, propelled her even further onto the international stage and led her to believe that she could make a living as a writer, supporting herself and Anne Sullivan, and creating for herself a career and purpose. Her own written word was a pivotal factor in the making of herself as a public figure.

This ability both cursed and blessed Keller. Once in her mid-twenties, and passionately interested in a variety of social, political, and theological issues, she wanted to write on subjects other than her own disability. Editors, however, only wanted to publish Keller's writings about herself, a subject on which she no longer cared to write. Though she had intense faith in the power of her own written words, and faith that what she had to say had merit, publishing all she wanted to write became difficult.

How did Helen Keller write? Her published material generally went through a process in which she typed and retyped drafts on the manual Hammond typewriter that accompanied her virtually everywhere. While John Macy served as editor, he read drafts and then made and/or suggested editorial changes which he finger-spelled to Keller, she rewrote the necessary changes as often as necessary, and together the pair polished the final version. In the case of *Midstream* (1929), friend and Doubleday employee Nella Braddy Henney read drafts to Anne Macy, whose eyesight made it impossible for her to read them. Henney and Macy then literally cut and pasted editorial changes, Henney read them to Macy again while Macy finger-spelled the drafts to Keller, and the process would start again. After Macy's death in 1936, this process continued in a similar fashion but obviously without Macy. Household companion Polly Thomson apparently never became involved in the editorial process of published material.

Publishing, however, was not the only purpose for which to write. Included in this collection is a large number of Keller's letters to loved ones and associates. Not intended for publication, many of these letters contain her unpublished (or unpublishable) thoughts, written without an editor.

The production process for letters differed. Keller knew her typewriter well and rarely made mistakes. She typed her own business letters and letters to dignitaries, and then had them proofed—first by Macy, then later in life Henney, Thomson, or others, who circulated in and out as household assistants. Letters to friends and family rarely included the proof-reading process, which meant that only Keller and the recipient knew of their content. Letters to friends and family was a largely private and unedited process.

Helen Keller: Selected Readings is a sampling collection of letters, articles, speeches, and book excerpts written during all periods of Helen Keller's life. Some were written for public consumption, others for private reflection. These writings are arranged in both a chronological and topical fashion. Some include important public matters that mattered to many; others include private elements that mattered to few, but contained joy or sorrow of immense personal importance.

Part One includes materials dated from 1889 to 1900 that reflect the changing concerns, realities, and goals of a young woman. Accompanied by an education, books, hopes of ice-skating, Anne Sullivan, philanthropists, her family, and the development of a Christian faith, the world-famous deaf-blind girl grew up.

Part Two covers Keller's adult life between 1900, when she started Radcliffe College, and 1924, when she became affiliated with the American

Foundation for the Blind. Part Two includes excerpts from Keller's books published in this period, both the wildly successful *The Story of My Life* (1903) and the not widely praised *The World I Live In* (1910). Since the material from the politically oriented *Out of the Dark* (1914) was published elsewhere before being collected in that volume, some it is included here in documents 13, 15, 16, and 17. The section on politics focuses on her public political life. Documents include published and nonpublished materials, addressing issues such as advocacy for blind people, socialism, venereal disease, and economic inequities. The last section reveals the emotional relationships and household matters that concerned Keller in this period. During these years she worked to create an adult relationship with her mother, who died in 1921; her dear friends Anne Sullivan and John Macy married and became estranged; she dreamed of and then failed to realize her dreams of supporting her household as a writer, simultaneously realizing the tenuous nature of her household income; and she both embraced and abandoned a public political life.

Part Three covers the period from 1924, when Keller became firmly and primarily identified with the issue of blindness, until 1945, the eve of the launching of her large-scale international career. Part Three provides excerpts from her published books: her 1927 explanation of Swedenborgianism, *My Religion*; the 1929 continuation of her autobiography, *Midstream: My Later Life*; and the very raw, but not widely read, *Helen Keller's Journal* (1938), that chronicles the approximately eighteen months after Anne Macy's death. The section on politics includes examples of her advocacy of people with disabilities and her opinions on issues that related to them: employment, state and federal funding, inequalities among people with disabilities, and veterans disabled by war. In the section on travel are letters showing Keller's increasing international interests, such as her 1937 visit to Japan, the growing strength of the Nazi regime, and World War II. The last section focuses on personal matters: concern for Anne Macy's eyes and eyesight, the pain of Macy's death in 1936, and the joys of friendships that developed in the 1940s.

Part Four covers the last years of Keller's life, which were increasingly devoted to international traveling and the advocacy of people with disabilities internationally. This part includes a chapter from Keller's last published book, the 1955 publication *Teacher* that she had been trying to write for nearly thirty years. The section on travel chronicles her international travels and sharp opinions of the postwar period, pertaining to places such as Greece, Japan, South Africa, France, Egypt, Syria, Lebanon, Jordan, Israel, India, and Chile. Finally, the letters in the last section provide glimpses into her friendships and the way those friendships supported and defined her.

Besides the topics that organize this book, several notable themes emerge in these documents from the eighty-seven years of Keller's life. One is her passionate knowledge of literature, poetry, and the Bible. She was highly familiar with and had memorized an immense amount of material. It was quite literally at her fingertips. Throughout her public and private, published and nonpublished, writings are excerpts, sometimes long and sometimes very brief, of poems, novels, biblical passages, and social commentary. Some are noted but others I've undoubtedly missed. Another repeated theme is her faith in God and its theological expression. From the time Keller embraced the Christian teachings of Emanuel Swedenborg as a young woman until her death in 1968, she believed passionately. This faith and its importance to her is reflected in the contents and tone of her private and public writings. It provided identity, purpose, intellectual activity, and comfort. Finally, Keller's love of dogs appears repeatedly in the documents (and photos) she left behind. Whether in Tuscumbia, Alabama, Wrentham, Massachusetts, Scotland, or Japan, dogs provided companionship, entertainment, and understood her oral speech without judgment.

Helen Keller: Selected Readings does not include excerpts from everything Keller published. Her private letters are far too numerous to include. Her published material varies dramatically in quality, some is simply bad, and some repeats earlier material. I selected material that I considered interesting, representative of a wide variety of topics and purposes, comprehendible, as well as simply what charmed or struck me strongly.

Those who wish to learn more about Helen Keller have many other opportunities to do so. The most recently published book is my biography of her, *The Radical Lives of Helen Keller* (2004). Others include Dorothy Herrmann's *Helen Keller: A Life* (1998) and Joseph Lash's *Helen and Teacher: The Story of Helen Keller and Anne Sullivan Macy* (1980). Keller's 1903 autobiography, *The Story of My Life*, remains widely available in numerous editions. The largest archival collections are available at the American Antiquarian Society, the American Foundation for the Blind, the Library of Congress, Perkins School for the Blind, and the Schlesinger Library.

When Helen Keller died in 1968 at the age of eighty-eight, she was one of the most widely known women in the world—as she had been since nearly the age of eight. The young girl, whose Tuscumbia, Alabama, parents had nearly given up in the early 1880s, when they saw little future for a deaf-blind girl, had literally and figuratively traveled far.

A Growing Up

1 I Learn Many New Words

November 10, 1889, letter from Helen Keller to William Wade, AFB.

From Perkins, nine-year-old Helen wrote this note of thanks to Pennsylvania philanthropist William Wade. The letter reflects the young girl's longing for home, still unaccustomed to being away from Tuscumbia and her family. Besides bestowing dogs on her, Wade provided funding for Helen's education from her years at Perkins through her college years at Radcliffe. See also document 23.

My dear Mr. Wade,

I have just received a letter from my brother, telling me that the beautiful mastiff puppy you sent to me had reached Tuscumbia safely. I thank you very much for the nice gift. I am very sorry that I was not at home to welcome her. But my mother and my baby sister will be very kind to her while her mistress is away. I hope she is not lonely and unhappy. I think puppies can feel very homesick as well as little girls. I should like to call her Lioness for your dog. May I? I hope she will be very faithful and brave too.

I am studying in Boston with my dear teacher. I learn a great many new and wonderful things. I study about the Earth and the animals, and I like arithmetic exceedingly. I learn many new words too. Exceedingly is one that I learned yesterday. When I see Lioness I will tell her many things which will surprise her greatly. I think she will laugh when I tell her that she is a vertebrate, a mammal, a quadruped, and I shall be very sorry to tell her that she belongs to the order Carnivora. I study French too. When I talk French to Lioness I will call her mon beau chien. Please tell Lion that I will take good care of Lioness. I shall be happy to have a letter from you when you like to write to me.

From your loving little friend,
Helen A. Keller
P.S. I am staying at the Inst. for the Blind.
H.A.K.

2 A Pleasant Christmas

December 28, 1889, letter from Helen Keller to Ethel Gray, AFB.

Helen's letter to her Tuscumbia friend Ethel Gray conveys the excitement of the nine-year-old about Christmas. This was likely the first Christmas Helen celebrated while separated from her sister Mildred, five years younger. The curriculum at Perkins included knitting and crocheting for young girls, and the results were often sold at fund-raising events.

Dear Ethel,

I did think you were never going to answer my letter. I was very glad to know that you have not forgotten me. Did you have a pleasant Christmas? I had a beautiful time. I had many pretty gifts, and it was such fun finding them on the tree. It was a queer looking tree with the strangest kinds of fruit growing upon it. I wish you could have seen it. I had a doll, a rocking-chair, building-blocks and many other things. What did you have? I like to knit and crochet too. I knit Mildred some mittens. With much love,
Helen A. Keller

3 Wishes for a Happy, Happy Christmas

December 21, 1893 [year uncertain],
letter from Helen Keller to John Hitz, AFB.

This letter, likely written the year Keller met Hitz, reveals her appreciation for the man who introduced and converted her to the teachings of Emanuel Swedenborg, a Swedish Christian mystic. Hitz first met Keller in his capacity as superintendent of the Volta Bureau in Washington, founded by Alexander Graham Bell (whose family is referred to in the letter). Until his death in 1908, he steadfastly provided Keller with literature, philosophy, theology and poetry in braille. For an account of Hitz and her conversion to Swedenborgianism, see document 38.

My dear Mr. Hitz,

Please accept the little gifts which I send you today with my love and kindest wishes for a happy, happy Christmas, and a brighter New Year. I think you will like my little present because I made it for you, and also because I have wrought into it my own thoughts and feelings. The poem as I call it, is a word picture of autumn as I see it with the eyes of my soul.

I wish you could be with us this Christmas. We would have such a happy time together. The approach of the glad Christmas tide always fills the heart with joy and hope, and quickens into sweet activity a thousand loving thoughts for others. Sometimes it seems almost as if it is wrong to feel so glad and happy when one knows there are so many of God's little ones friendless, and even cold and hungry, but if we are to let their misfortunes banish the gladness from our heart they would not be any happier, so I am sure it is right to be as happy as we can, and do whatever we may, be it ever so little, to make those around us happy and look forward hopefully to the beautiful time when Christmas shall bring to everyone joy untouched with sorrow.

Teacher sends you a great deal of love, and she joins me in wishing you every good wish. Please give our love to Mrs. Barton and to Mrs. Bell and Daisy and Elsie if you see them, and may the joy of Christmas Day linger like a blessing in the hearts of all. And may the whole year be gladder, sweeter, brighter.

Lovingly your friend,
Helen Keller

4 I Would Like Very Much to Learn How to Skate

February 10, 1895, letter from Helen Keller, New York, Wright-Humason School, to Kate Keller, AFB.

Hoping to improve Keller's oral speech, Anne Sullivan and Alexander Graham Bell persuaded Keller's parents to send her to Wright-Humason

School for the Deaf in the fall of 1894. The oralist school, founded by John D. Wright and Dr. Thomas Humason, included no other deaf-blind students.

My own dear Mother:

How did father enjoy his birthday? I hope he received the telegram I sent him wishing a happy birthday.

A week ago yesterday Teacher and I went with the others to the theatre to see the "Old Homestead." I only wish you could have been with us. We had anticipated the event with great pleasure; so our cup of joy was full to the brim when at last the curtain rose and revealed a happy peaceful farm-scene, though I think I liked the last scene best when the dear, kind old farmer and his son embraced each other after their long, unhappy separation. If you have never seen the play, I hope you will see it some day; for no words can give us most vividly the sweet, glad country-life of New England with its countless small joys and sweet content, and shows the kindness and shrewdness of the New England farmer.

What cold weather we have been having lately. Last week we had more than a foot of snow, and all the street-cars were delayed, and even comfortable people had much trouble in keeping their houses warm. I hope none of my friends at home have suffered severely from the cold. I suppose you have had snow too, as we saw in the paper that the thermometer dropped down to zero in Alabama.

I would like very much to learn how to skate. Would you and father be willing for me to do so? My friends say they think I can learn to skate, and every one who can do it seems to enjoy it so much.

Dr. Humason's brother and his wife came to see us several times last week. I liked them both very much. Mrs. Humason talked to me by means of the telegraph alphabet.

Yesterday Teacher, Mr. Wright and I went down-town to see if we could get a new typewriter for my own use. I agree with them that the "Remington" is the best writing-machine that is made, and dear Mr. Spaulding[1] has offered to pay for the typewriter we like best for us. But we found the store where the writing-machines are sold closed; so we went to the "Five Points," a place in this city which was once dreadfully dirty and poor; but which has been greatly improved, and to the "Tombs," the New York prison. We went into the court-house, which was Egyptian in style and very gloomy, with tremendous stone pillars. I was never so near a prison before, and I felt strangely and sad in the silent court-room.

Hoping to hear that all at home are quite well soon, I am,

Lovingly your child,

Helen Keller

5   Our Work Is Over for the Summer

July 9, 1897, letter from Helen Keller,
Wrentham, Massachusetts, to Kate Keller, AFB.

In her 1903 autobiography *The Story of My Life*, Keller wrote that "the thought of going to college took root in my heart and became an earnest desire."[2] Since prestigious Harvard denied entrance to women, she sought entrance to its counterpart Radcliffe College. In preparation, she and her sister Mildred enrolled at the Cambridge School for Young Ladies in October 1896, just two months after her father's death. This letter to her mother is written immediately after she took her preliminary examinations for Radcliffe, which undoubtedly had postponed the celebration of her June 27 birthday. She and Sullivan were enjoying the Wrentham farm of literary critic Joseph Edgar and Ida Chamberlin (whom Keller later referred to as "Uncle Ed" and "Aunt Ida"). The farm, a gathering place for literary figures, sat beautifully situated on the shores of King Josephs' Pond near Wrentham, where Keller would later live with John Macy and Anne Sullivan Macy. For a description of her later life on King Josephs' Pond, including canoeing, see document 39.

My precious Mother:

Here we are at last in Wrentham! And how good it is to feel that our work is over for the summer, and that we can do as we like, instead of being compelled to bend our wills to the demand, rules and obligations of school-life! I can now do many things which I longed to do during the winter, but could not on account of my work. I can for instance write to you regularly, and lower the pile of letters, which has been accumulating for several months.

But first of all, here is a piece of news which I know will make your heart glad. I have passed all my preliminary examinations, including advanced German!! The subjects I offered were elementary French and German, Greek and Roman history, Latin and English. It seems almost too good to be true, doesn't it? My brain and hands have worked very hard indeed ever since the latter part of May, the former acting as the dictator (you see, I like the authoritative Latin word) and the latter performing the clerk's functions: but, absorbed as I was in my work, I could not suppress an inward fear and trembling, lest I should fail, and now it is an unspeakable relief to know that I have passed my examinations with credit. But what I consider my crown of success is the happiness and pleasure that my victory has brought to dear Teacher. Indeed, the success is hers more than mine: for she is my constant inspiration. Then too the thought that you, dear mother, will rejoice, and be proud of your little girl, fills my heart with thankfulness.

Teacher and I came to Wrentham last Saturday, and received a loving welcome, as we always do. Mrs. Chamberlin's loving, motherly ways remind me of you, and make me feel myself a part of this sweet, friendly home life, which I find so seldom these days.

Of course we miss little sister very much. I thought she would be here this summer, and I had counted much upon the pleasant times we should have roaming the fields together. But I am glad she is with you. Beth is a dear, sweet little companion, and fills in some degree the great vacancy which Mildred's going left in my life. I needn't tell you that Mildred was a dear, good child, and that every one who knew her loved her. I received Mildred's letter, and will answer it soon.

Thank you so much for your dear letter with its birthday greetings. My seventeenth birthday was a happy one, though I could not help feeling a little sorry that my childhood had passed away so quickly. But still the future looks bright and full of promise, and I shall carry with me through all my life the memory of a happy childhood. I received several gifts, a pretty silk petticoat from Teacher, a lovely turquoise ring from Carrie, Hawthorne's "Twice-Told Tales" from Mrs. Hopkins[3] and a box of stationery from Mildred. At the dinner-table they surprised me with an angel cake, which was lighted prettily with seventeen candles.

What did Phillips do on his birthday? I can scarcely realize that he is six years old. It seems such a short time since I first met him, a tiny mite curled up in your arms!

I wish you and the children could be with us. Wrentham is a lovely place. How you would enjoy a ride in the canoe on a moonlight night! It is the crowning delight of a perfect day. What is so beautiful as the gleam of a golden moon in the bosom of a quiet lake? It draws one irresistibly into the Land of Dreams, and the spirit in ecstasy drinks "repose from the cool cisterns of the night."[4]

I suppose this letter will find you in Memphis. If so, please give my love to Uncle Fred and Aunt Nannie, and kiss the little ones for me. Poor little Louise, I feel so sorry for her. I am afraid the typhoid fever is very dangerous. It is a mercy that Baze was getting over it before Louise came down with it.

I have just finished reading "Nansen's Story." I hear that every one is talking about it, and no wonder: for it is as strange and wonderful as a fairy-tale. There is something new and startling on each page, and one is thrilled through and through with the bravery and daring of Nansen and his clever men.

I am now reading "The Lady of the Lake."[5] It is simply exquisite! Its verses, as my fingers run over them, pour out a stream of song and romance, and the easy, graceful flow of the poet's thoughts and his beautiful descriptions of Beauty, valor and martial Faith render it most charming. But I cannot help being glad that the poem belongs to the past, and not to the present: for I see through the shadowy veil, which Scott has drawn over those olden days, the ruin and desolation and sorrow, that were as much a part of the wars and struggles celebrated in the poem as the heroic exploits of Roderick Dhu and his warriors.

Now, ma chere mere, goodbye till next week. Teacher sends much love.

> Your affectionate child,
> Helen

6 How I Wish We Could Slip Away

February 3, 1899, letter from Helen Keller to John Hitz, AFB.

Finishing their time at Wrentham with the Chamberlins, Keller and Sullivan returned to Boston for Helen's private academic tutoring in order that she might enroll at Radcliffe. This letter reflects the stress both women felt as they sought to prove Keller's intellectual ability, and the anxiety caused by Sullivan's failing eyesight. Rarely did either woman acknowledge Sullivan's disability publicly at this time, and that Keller did so reflects her faith in Hitz's friendship. In June 1899, she passed her final examinations for Radcliffe and began coursework in the fall of 1900.

My dear Mr. Hitz,

Your letter, which came about two weeks ago, gave Teacher and me great pleasure. We wondered how you could write braille so well. It must be very hard for you to make the letters without using your eyes.

My teacher wants me to beg you to forgive her for not writing to you, but that I know is not necessary. You can easily understand why she does not write herself. She has been obliged to use her eyes more than usual. I have almost come to the end of my embossed text-books and she has to read most of my lessons to me. I really dread going to college next fall on her account. I cannot bear the thought of the constant and terrible strain upon her poor eyes, which I fear will come with our new studies. How I wish we could slip away, and live in the peaceful country for a year, at least, away from every one we know and just be happy, and free from care and anxiety! We could find a little house and make our rest there and do just as we please. We wouldn't let anybody except you and mother into our secret. You could come to see us once in a while; but no one else would know our hiding place. Perhaps her eyes could better there get well, and we would be quite ready for any amount of college work. But alas, we have not the means of carrying out this plan, so I suppose we must keep on until I take my "finals" in June. If you have any advice do not hesitate to give it. We should be happy if we could find a way out of this sad dilemma.

Few incidents of interest have occurred since we returned to Boston, the first week in January. However, I had an exceedingly interesting experience last Monday. A kind friend took us out in the morning to the Boston Art Museum. She had previously obtained permission from General Loring, Supt. of the Museum, for me to touch the statues, especially those which represented things away from the sanctuary of the Past, where they belong.

This afternoon, if the weather permits, I am going to the theatre with Beth Chamberlin to see the play "Love finds the way." I saw it in New York last spring, but I shall be glad to see it again, it is such a sweet, charming play.

But I must now silence these flippant keys; so good bye for the present. My Teacher sends her dearest love with mine.

Affectionately your friend,
Helen Keller

7 The Beautiful, Free Country

June 2, 1899, letter from Helen Keller to Alexander Graham Bell,
Alexander Graham Bell Family Papers, Library of Congress,
box 131. Copyright dedicated to the public.

Written less than a month before Keller's successful final examinations for Radcliffe, this letter reveals her delight in the rural joys of Wrentham, Massachusetts and the intellectual joys of literature. She thanks Bell for his continued financial support of her and Sullivan.

My dear, dear Dr. Bell;

My teacher and I received the check you sent us two days ago, and I cannot give you any idea how our hearts overflowed with gratitude to you for your thoughtfulness. Words are never warm and tender enough to express one's appreciation of a great kindness. One can only say "thank you," but I say it with all my heart. Not only have you made us both very happy indeed; but you have also enabled us to get away from the heat and fatigue of the city into the beautiful, free country earlier than we could otherwise have done; and you know, I delight in nothing more than in being close to Nature's heart.

We shall be at Wrentham tomorrow afternoon, and we shall stay in the little cottage, which my mother is to occupy this summer. We shall come to Boston several times a week for lessons; but you can think of me studying merrily under the trees, or on the shore of the lovely lake, which is only a few feet away from the cottage. Then, when my dear ones come, there will be but one drop left to fill my cup to the brim—if it is granted me by fickle Fortune, and that is success in my examinations!

Perhaps you would like to hear something of my work. My Greek progresses finely. I am reading the sixteenth book of the "Iliad," and also the "Odyssey." The "Iliad" is splendid; many of the descriptions are so vivid, one seems to hear the clash of spears and the shouts of the soldiers as they rush into battle. But I think I shall like the "Odyssey" best. The "Iliad" tells of almost nothing but war and the ruin, sorrow and cruelty that follows in its train; but the "Odyssey" tells of nobler courage—the courage of a soul, sore tried, but steadfast to the end. I enjoy Cicero too. His orations are wonderful! but they are very hard to translate, and I feel ashamed sometimes, when I make that eloquent man say what sounds absurd or insipid. But how is a school-girl to interpret such genius? Why, I should have to be Cicero, or talk like Cicero!

Some of my friends tell me that I am very foolish to give so much of my time to Greek and Latin; but I am sure they would not think so, if they knew what a wonderful, beautiful world of thought and experience Homer and Virgil have opened up to me.

I am very sorry indeed that my examinations will prevent me from going to Northampton this summer; but in future years I hope I can attend oftener the meetings of the Association, and do more towards promoting the welfare and happiness of the deaf, in whom I feel deeply interested.

My teacher joins me in sending love to dear Mrs. Bell, and Elsie and Daisy. We wish we did not live so far away; for then we could see more of you. With much love, and best wishes for a pleasant, restful summer, I am,

  Affectionately your friend,
  Helen Keller

8 Very Hard to Give Up the Idea of Going to Radcliffe

October 20, 1899, letter from Helen Keller to John Hitz, AFB.

Though Keller had already passed her Radcliffe entrance examinations, the opinions of others that a college education would be difficult and worthless for her continued to throw obstacles in her path. This letter discusses those obstacles as well as her vigorous curriculum. Though unable to enter Radcliffe yet, she obviously continued to enjoy life in rural Wrentham.

My dear Mr. Hitz,

You will probably be surprised to see that we are still at the Pines. Our plans for this winter are not yet settled, and anyway it is so lovely in the country now, we thought we would stay here as long as possible. Nearly all the people who come out here for the summer are gone, and the goldenrod, asters and the other flowers have all withered, and the leaves, which so lately made the woods and the shores of the lake seem all on fire with color, lie fading on the ground; but this place does not seem lonely or dreary; for there is a peace, and sweetness and quiet tenderness about these autumn days, which satisfies the spirit, and fills the heart with contentment. It has never seemed to me that autumn was a time for sadness. To me it is the season of fulfillment and promise. Nature's cup has been filled to overflowing, and in the divine order of things she empties the cup, only to fill it again.

I think I wrote to you last month about Mrs. Hutton's[6] coming to Boston. Well, she went to see Dean Irwin,[7] of Radcliffe, and told her how strongly I desired to take the regular college course; but Miss Irwin said she thought I ought not to attempt such a task, but to develop along the lines of study which would be of most interest and benefit to me. Finally we called upon her, and she persuaded me to take a special course, this year at any rate. She said that I had already shown the world that I could do the college work, by passing all my examinations successfully in spite of many obstacles. She showed me how very foolish it would be for me to pursue a four years' course of study at Radcliffe simply to be like other girls, when I might better be cultivating whatever ability I had in waiting. She said, she thought I had a "gift" and thus I could accomplish most by studying, and doing a great deal of translation and composition in the subjects I liked best—languages and literature. The arguments seemed so wise and practical that I could not but yield.

But I found it hard, very hard to give up the idea of going to Radcliffe. Ever since I was a little girl it has been my purpose to go to college, and I have always thought how splendid it would be to receive a college degree. So I could not help feeling a sharp pang. When we called again at Radcliffe last Friday, and found that Miss Irwin wished me to study with a young lady, not much older than myself, who is still in college. However, Teacher came to the rescue. A suggestion which Dr. Hale made long ago flashed across my mind—that I should take courses similar like those offered at Radcliffe under the direct tutelage of the professors in those courses. Miss Irwin seemed to have no objection to this proposal and kindly offered to see the professors and find out if they are willing to teach me, and if we can afford to pay them. I shall take the following courses, English, English literature of the Elizabethan period, Latin and German. So you see how matters stand. I will let you know the results when we are settled for the winter.

We intend to board in Cambridge with Miss Fosdick, the kind lady who was the chaperone at [indecipherable] House while we were there. Her house is very pleasant and home like, and I think we shall enjoy being there more than anywhere else.

I have already finished "The Ascent of Man,"[8] and am now reading it all through again. It is such a beautiful book, I want to impress upon my memory the great truths it teaches about nature, life and love. Have you read it yet?

You will be sorry to hear that Aunt Ida[9] has been very ill. She had another operation the last of September and we all feel very serious about her; now she is doing finely, and has been down on her piazza once or twice lately to enjoy the lovely air and warm sunshine. But they don't think she can move around much before Christmas, and she must be very careful of herself all winter.

With a great deal of love from Teacher, I am, dear Mr. Hitz,
      Affectionately your friend,
      Helen Keller

9 Almost Wholly a World of Books

March 9, 1900, letter from Helen Keller to Alexander Graham Bell,
Alexander Graham Bell Family Papers, box 131, Library of Congress.
Copyright dedicated to the public.

Still living with her numerous and disparate "book-friends,"
Keller clearly delighted in Alexander Graham Bell's effort to write her in
braille, while she continued her preparations for her fall 1900 entrance to
Radcliffe. Though she acknowledges Sullivan's visual disability, she does so
in less clear terms than she did to John Hitz in document 6. This 1900 discussion of South African politics contrasts strongly with Keller's views in
1951 (document 71).[10]

My dear Dr. Bell;

I was perfectly delighted to receive your letter and to be able to read
it myself. It seemed almost as if you had clasped my hand in yours and
spoke to me in the old, dear way. A letter always seems more truly my
own when I can run my fingers over it, and quickly enter into the
thoughts and feelings of my friends without an interpreter, even
though the interpreter be the dearest and sweetest in the world. It was
very kind of you to learn those queer little hieroglyphics and write to
me yourself; and nothing but unusually hard work has prevented me
from sending a more prompt rely. O yes, I could read every word you
wrote; indeed, I did not find a single mistake in the braille, and I
trust that, since your "first attempt" was such a wonderful success, I
shall receive many such "attempts."

I often think most lovingly of you and dear Mrs. Bell, Daisy and
Elsie, and wish, oh so earnestly, that I could see you all, if only for a
moment; but alas, hundreds of miles seem always to separate us, and I
must needs fall back upon the dear memories of the happy days we
have spent together. But there is mingled with these sweet memories
not a little sadness; for I cannot help feeling sometimes that the long,
long years are separating us more effectually than a continent and an
ocean thrown in could do.

I have had a very busy but pleasant winter. My little world is almost
wholly a world of books, and my life is lived more in the past than in

the present. My friends, many of them, like myself live in books; but I find them most companionable, witty, gay, sad, wise or foolish according to my mood.

My studies this year are languages, English history and literature. I have just finished "Macbeth." What a wonderful, terrible portrayal of the power of evil! How mysteriously and fearfully the chief characters in the drama develop after their natural bent! How graphic are the word-pictures of the worst passions of the human heart! How irresistibly Macbeth is borne on by the tide of evil to utter ruin! In French I have read "L'Avare" by Moliere, and "Horace" by Corneille, and am now reading "Andromaque" by Racine. I enjoy French plays so much, they are almost sure to be charming. But I enjoy nothing more than English history. I am also studying Horace's odes, Goethe's "Iphigenie" and "Prometheus Bound" in Greek. I think this is one of the most wonderful things I shall ever read; it is so mysterious and infinitely sad. Of course I admit Prometheus' crime; but I admire his high-spirited and generous soul, and feel deep gratitude to him for preserving our poor human race. You see, I am an optimist still, rejoicing in the good that comes out of evil.

I need not tell you that my dear teacher is ever at my side, ready to encourage and help me in my work. The only drawback to our complete happiness is her eyes. They trouble her constantly, and I cannot help worrying about them.

I have just written a paper on the South African question for Mrs. Hutton. I began by being strongly in favor of Great Britain; but after I had done all the reading required, I found myself in sympathy with the heroic Boers. Perhaps you do not take the same view of the subject as I do; but I feel very sorry for Great Britain. It seems to me, she has made a terrible mistake, and that from the seeds of discord and hatred which she is now sowing in her empire, she will some day reap a harvest of tares. However, I admit that it is possible that, if I could read more and make further investigations, I might arrive at a different conclusion.

Please give my love to Mrs. Bell, and Daisy and Elsie, and believe me, with kindest remembrances from my teacher,

      Affectionately your friend,
      Helen Keller

10 Only Love, Dearest Mr. Hitz

April 22, 1900, letter from Helen Keller to John Hitz, AFB.

Besides providing spiritual support, John Hitz clearly provided friendship to Keller. The brailled books he supplied consistently kept her intellectually entertained and would make much of college possible when she started in the fall of 1900. They also helped her master German while at Radcliffe. Keller's discussion of politics with Hitz is not unusual, but these 1900 opinions contrast sharply with her later opinions of South Africa (document 71).

The friendship of people such as Hitz also heightened Keller's awareness that her life was in sharp contrast to that of Laura Bridgman. When Boston reformer and Perkins School for the Blind director Samuel Gridley Howe brought seven-year-old Bridgman to Perkins in 1837, educating a deaf-blind child was considered impossible. Howe's success at teaching her language, and his perhaps even greater success at publicizing her, made Howe, Perkins, and Bridgman nearly world famous. Charles Dickens visited the child, chronicling her in *American Notes* (1842). Learning of Bridgman by reading *American Notes* prompted Keller's mother to seek an education for her daughter. For Keller's parents and for Alexander Graham Bell, the school where the by then elderly Laura Bridgman still lived was the logical place to seek an education for the young Helen. Unlike Keller, Bridgman remained at Perkins for the rest of her life, having little contact with life outside the institution.[11]

Only love, dearest Mr. Hitz, can say how deeply grateful I am to you for all that you have done to help me in my work! The German and French books you ordered for me came last week, and I am more glad than I can say to have them. Yes, my study-room is a perfect little library now, and I feel as proud of it as Boston is of her public library. Never did I dream that I should possess so many precious treasures of English and foreign literature. Poor Laura Bridgman, how narrow and monotonous her life was compared with mine, so rich with blessings—an immense capacity of enjoyment, books, and beloved friends, you among them without whom I could never, never know a moment of happiness. Most earnestly I pray the dear Heavenly Father that I may sometime make myself far more worthy of the love shown to me than I am now.

I was indeed delighted to get your German letter, and I only wish I could muster sufficient courage to answer it in German; but alas, I do not know how to write such letters. Perhaps, however, if you will write to me several times in German I can learn, and then I will try to answer them in that language. If I do, will you please correct any mistakes I may make?

How lovely it will be when you visit us at the Pines!

Teacher and I have just had a pleasant little vacation. We spent Easter as normal, with the Chamberlins. They are all well, Aunt Ida has improved wonderfully this spring, and looks as well as ever. It rained a good deal while we were there; but we seized every possible opportunity to wander about in the woods. We found song, fragrance and growth everywhere. We drank in the delicious air, as if we would drink in Wrentham, and our hearts simply ran riot with delight! Easter means a double resurrection—the rising again of the soul from the sickness and sorrow of past years and the renewal of the world.

I suppose Washington is quite a garden by this time. It is a joy to look out from our windows and see the trees budding and the lawns growing greener every day. They say tomorrow there will be ten thousand hyacinths in bloom in the Public Gardens. Don't you wish you could see such a resplendent display of color and beauty?

It is hard, very hard, to realize that in the midst of the universal gladness of nature, poor South Africa is groaning under man's cruel scourge. How is it possible that, while we see nothing but peace and beauty, a death-grapple should be at this moment going on between two [indecipherable] nations? My sympathies are intensely Pro-Boer; but I speak of this only to show you how much I am impressed by the stupendous contrasts of human life.

Now I must say auf weidersehen. With dearest love from Teacher, I am,

> Affectionately your friend,
> Helen Keller

TWO 1900–1924

A *Major Works*

11 Helen Keller, *The Story of My Life*

New York: Dover Publications, 1903.

Keller's 1903 autobiography *The Story of My Life* began as a college essay assignment, became a series of magazine articles, and was quickly transformed into a book. The autobiography (as much as one can write a life story at twenty-three years of age!) quickly became an almost unparalleled best seller. With this, she dreamt of almost unlimited opportunities and of supporting herself as an economically self-sufficient author. The book also brought John Macy into her life as editor, friend, and political intimate. By 1954, the book that has never gone out of print was not only being sold in what her editor referred to as "the regular foreign language translations," but also in Arabic, Assamese, Bengali, Burmese, Chinese, Debuano, Greek, Hiligayon, Hindi, Icelandic, Ilocano, Indonesian (just to name the first part of the alphabet). Chapter 1, included here, tells of Keller's family history and early life, largely before the illness at nineteen months left her deaf and blind.

Chapter I.

It is with a kind of fear that I begin to write the history of my life. I have, as it were, a superstitious hesitation in lifting the veil that clings about my childhood like a golden mist. The task of writing an autobiography is a difficult one. When I try to classify my earliest impressions, I find that face and fancy look alike across the years that link the past with the present. The woman paints the child's experiences in her own fantasy. A few impressions stand out vividly from the first years of my life; but "the shadows of prison-house are on the rest." Besides, many of the joys and sorrows of childhood have lost their poignancy; and many incidents of vital importance in my early education have been forgotten in the excitement of great discoveries. In order, therefore, not to be tedious I shall try to present in a serious of sketches only the episodes that seem to me to be the most interesting and important.

I was born on June 27, 1880, in Tuscumbia, a little town of northern Alabama.

The family on my father's side is descended from Caspar Keller, a native of Switzerland, who settled in Maryland. One of my Swiss ancestors was the first teacher of the deaf in Zurich and wrote a book on the subject of their education—rather a singular coincidence; though it is true that there is no king who has not had a slave among his ancestors, and no slave who has not had a king among his.

My grandfather, Caspar Keller's son, "entered" large tracts of land in Alabama and finally settled there. I have been told that once a year he went from Tuscumbia to Philadelphia on horseback to purchase supplies for the plantation, and my aunt has in her possession many of the letters to his family, which give charming and vivid accounts of these trips.

My Grandmother Keller was a daughter of one of Lafayette's aides, Alexander Moore, and granddaughter of Alexander Spotswood, an early Colonial Governor of Virginia. She was also second cousin to Robert E. Lee.

My father, Arthur H. Keller, was a captain in the Confederate Army, and my mother, Kate Adams, was his second wife and many years younger. Her grandfather, Benjamin Adams, married Susanna E. Goodhue, and lived in Newbury, Massachusetts, for many years. Their son, Charles Adams, was born in Newburyport, Massachusetts, and moved to Helena, Arkansas. When the Civil War broke out, he fought on the side of the South and became a brigadier-general. He married Lucy Helen Everett, who belonged to the same family of Everetts as Edward Everett and Dr. Edward Everett Hale. After the war was over the family moved to Memphis, Tennessee.

I lived, up to the time of the illness that deprived me of my sight and hearing, in a tiny house consisting of a large square room and a small one, in which the servant slept. It is a custom in the South to build a small house near the homestead as an annex to be used on occasion. Such a house my father built after the Civil War, and when he married my mother they went to live in it. It was completely covered with vines, climbing roses and honeysuckles. From the garden it looked like an arbour. The little porch was hidden from view by a screen of yellow roses and Southern smilax. It was the favourite haunt of hummingbirds and bees.

The Keller homestead, where the family lives, was a few steps from our little rose-bower. It was called "Ivy Green" because the house and the surrounding trees and fences were covered with beautiful English ivy. Its old-fashioned garden was the paradise of my childhood.

Even in the days before my teacher came, I used to feel along the square stiff boxwood hedges, and, guided by the sense of smell, would find the first violets and lilies. There, too, after a fit of temper, I went to find comfort and to hide my hot face in the cool leaves and grass. What joy it was to lose myself in the garden of flowers, to wander happily from spot to spot, until, coming suddenly upon a beautiful vine, I recognized tumble-down summer-house at the farther end of the garden! Here, also, were trailing clematis, drooping jessamine, and some rare sweet flowers called butterfly lilies, because their fragile petals resemble butterflies' wings. But the roses—they were loveliest of all. Never have I found in the green-houses of the North such heart-satisfying roses as the climbing roses of my southern home. They used to hang in long festoons from our porch, filling the whole air with their fragrance, untainted by any earthy smell; and in the early morning, washed in the dew, they felt so soft, so pure, I could not help wondering if they did not resemble the asphodels of God's garden.

The beginning of my life was simple and much like every other little life. I came, I saw, I conquered, as the first baby in the family always does. There was the usual amount of discussion as to a name for me. The first baby in the family was not to be lightly named, every one was emphatic about that. My father suggested the name of Mildred Campbell, an ancestor whom he highly esteemed and he declined to take any further part in the discussion. My mother solved the problem by giving it as her wish that I should be called after her mother, whose maiden name was Helen Everett. But in the excitement of carrying me to church my father lost the name on the way, very naturally, since it was one which he had declined to have a part. When the minister asked him for it, he just remembered that it had been decided to call me after my grandmother, and he gave her name as Helen Adams.

I am told that while I was still in long dresses I showed many signs of an eager, self-asserting disposition. Everything that I saw other people do I insisted upon imitating. At six months I could pipe out "How d'ye," and one day I attracted every one's attention by saying "Tea, tea, tea" quite plainly. Even after my illness I remembered one of the words I had learned in these early months. It was the word "water," and I continued to make some sound for that word after all other speech was lost. I ceased making the sound "wah-wah" only when I learned to spell the word.

They tell me I walked the day I was a year old. My mother had just taken me out of the bath-tub and was holding me in her lap, when I was suddenly attracted by the flickering shadows of leaves that danced in the sunlight on the smooth floor. I slipped from my mother's lap and almost ran toward them. The impulse gone, I fell down and cried for her to take me up in her arms.

These happy days did not last long. One brief spring, musical with the song of robin and mockingbird, one summer rich in fruit and roses, one autumn of gold and crimson sped by and left their gifts at the feet of an eager, delighted child. Then, in the dreary month of February, came the illness which closed my eyes and ears and plunged me into the unconsciousness of a newborn baby. They called it acute congestion of the stomach and brain. The doctor thought I could not live. Early one morning, however, the fever left me as suddenly and mysteriously as it had come. There was great rejoicing in the family that morning, but no one, not even the doctor, knew that I should never see or hear again.

I fancy I still have confused recollections of that illness. I especially remember the tenderness with which my mother tried to soothe me in my waking hours of fret and pain, and the agony and bewilderment with which I awoke after a tossing half sleep, and turned my eyes, so dry and hot, to the wall, away from the once-loved light, which came to me dim and yet more dim each day. But, except for these fleeting memories, if, indeed, they be memories, it all seems very unreal, like a nightmare. Gradually I got used to the silence and the darkness that surrounded me and forgot that it had ever been different, until she came—my teacher—who was to set my spirit free. But during the first nineteen months of my life I had caught glimpses of broad, green fields, a luminous sky, trees and flowers which the darkness that followed could not wholly blow out. If we have once seen, "the day is ours, and what the day has shown."

12 *The World I Live In*

New York: Century Company, 1908.

In 1929, Keller wrote, "I do not remember writing anything in such a happy mood as *The World I Live In*. I poured into it everything that interested me at one of the happiest periods of my life."[1] The book excerpts below are vivid and charming portrayals of her richly sensual life. Particularly interesting are her discussions of "the hand" and its importance in her tactile world.

The short preface to *The World I Live In* is contentious. Keller thanks her publisher, but expresses frustration that "while other self-recording creatures are permitted at least to seem to change the subject, apparently nobody cares what I think of the tariff, the conservation of our natural resources, or the conflicts which revolve about the name of Dreyfus." While she sought to make her living as a writer, all she could sell was material about herself. With both humor and irritation, she wrote, "But until they give me opportunity to write about matters that are not-me, the world must go on uninstructed and unreformed, and I can only do my best with the one small subject upon which I am allowed to discourse."

IV: The Power of Touch

Some months ago, in a newspaper which announced the publication of the "Matilda Ziegler Magazine for the Blind," appeared the following paragraph:

> Many poems and stories must be omitted because they deal with sight. Allusion to moonbeams, rainbows, starlight, clouds, and beautiful scenery may not be printed, because they serve to emphasize the blind man's sense of his affliction.

That is to say, I may not talk about beautiful mansions and gardens because I am poor. I may not read about Paris and the West Indies because I cannot visit them in their territorial reality. I may not dream of heaven because it is possible that I may never go there. Yet a venturesome spirit impels me to use words of sight and sound whose meaning I can guess only from analogy and fancy. This hazardous game is half the delight, the frolic, of daily life. I glow as I read of splendors which the eye alone can survey. Allusions to moonbeams and clouds do not emphasize the sense of my affliction: they carry my soul beyond affliction's narrow actuality. Critics delight to tell us what we cannot do. They assume that blindness and deafness sever us completely from the things which the seeing and the hearing enjoy, and hence they assert we have no moral right to talk about beauty, the skies, mountains, the song of birds, and colors. They declare that the very sensations we have from the sense of touch are "vicarious," as though our friends felt the sun for us! They deny a priori what they have not seen and I have felt. Some brave doubters have gone so far even as to deny my existence. In order, therefore, that I may know that I exist, I resort to Descartes's method: "I think, therefore I am." Thus I am metaphysically established, and I throw upon the doubters the burden of proving my non-existence. When we consider how little has been found out about the mind, is it not amazing that any one should presume to define what one can know or cannot know? I admit that there are innumerable marvels in the visible universe unguessed by me. Likewise, O confident critic, there are myriad sensations perceived by me of which you do not dream.

Necessity gives to the eye a precious power of seeing, and in the same way it gives a precious power of feeling to the whole body. Sometimes it seems as if the very substance of my flesh were so many eyes looking out at will upon a world new created every day. The silence and darkness which are said to shut me in, open my door most hospitably to countless sensations that distract, inform, admonish, and amuse. With my three trusty guides, touch, smell, and taste, I make many excursions into the borderland of experience which is in sight of the city of Light. Nature accommodates itself to every man's necessity. If the eye is maimed, so that it does not see the beauteous face of day, the touch becomes more poignant and discriminating. Nature proceeds through practice to strengthen and augment the remaining senses. For this reason the blind often hear with greater ease and distinctness than other people. The sense of smell becomes almost a new faculty to penetrate the tangle and vagueness of things. Thus, according to an immutable law, the senses assist and reinforce one another.

It is not for me to say whether we see best with the hand or the eye. I only know that the world I see with my fingers is alive, ruddy, and satisfying. Touch brings the blind many sweet certainties which our more fortunate fellows miss, because their sense of touch is uncultivated. When they look at things, they put their hands in their pockets. No doubt that is one reason why their knowledge is often so vague, inaccurate, and useless. It is probable, too, that our knowledge of phenomena beyond the reach of the hand is equally imperfect. But, at all events, we behold them through a golden mist of fantasy.

There is nothing, however, misty or uncertain about what we can touch. Through the sense of touch I know the faces of friends, the illimitable variety of straight and curved lines, all surfaces, the exuberance of the soil, the delicate shapes of flowers, the noble forms of trees, and the range of might winds. Besides objects, surfaces, and atmospherical changes, I perceive countless vibrations. I derive much knowledge of every-day matter from the jars and jolts which are to be felt everywhere in the house.

Footsteps, I discover, vary tactually according to the age, the sex, and the manners of the walker. It is impossible to mistake a child's patter for the tread of a grown person. The step of the young man, strong and free, differs from the heavy, sedate tread of the middle-aged, and from the step of the old man, whose feet drag along the floor, or beat it with slow, faltering accents. On a bare floor a girl walks with rapid, elastic rhythm which is quite distinct from the graver step of the elderly woman. I have laughed over the creak of new shoes and the clatter of a stout maid performing a jig in the kitchen. One day, in the dining-room of a hotel, a tactual dissonance arrested my attention. I sat still and listened with my feet. I found that two waiters were walking back and forth, but not with the same gait. A band was playing, and I could feel the music-waves along the floor. One of the waiters walked in time to the band, graceful and light, while the other disregarded the music and rushed from table to table to the beat of some discord in his own mind. Their steps reminded me of a spirited war-steed harnessed with a cart-horse.

Often footsteps reveal in some measure the character and the mood of the walker. I feel in them firmness and indecision, hurry and deliberation, activity and laziness, fatigue, carelessness, timidity, anger, and sorrow. I am most conscious of these moods and traits in persons with whom I am familiar.

Footsteps are frequently interrupted by certain jars and jerks, so that I know when one kneels, kicks, shakes something, sits down, or gets up. Thus I follow to some extent the actions of people about me and the changes of their postures. Just now a thick, soft patter of bare, padded feet and a slight jolt told me that my dog had jumped on the chair to look out the window. I do not, however, allow him to go un-investigated; for occasionally I feel the same motion, and find him, not on the chair, but trespassing on the sofa.

When a carpenter works in the house or in the barn near by, I know by the slanting, up-and-down, toothed vibration, and the ringing concussion of blow upon blow, that he is sawing or hammer-ing. If I am near enough, a certain vibration, traveling back and forth along a wooden surface, brings me the information that he is using a plane.

A slight flutter on the rug tells me that a breeze has blown my pa-pers off the table. A round thump is a signal that a pencil has rolled on the floor. If a book falls, it gives a flat thud. A wooden rap on the balustrade announces that dinner is ready. Many of these vibrations are obliterated out of doors. On a lawn or the road, I can feel only running, stamping, and the rumble of wheels.

By placing my hand on a person's lips and throat, I gain an idea of many specific vibrations, and interpret them: a boy's chuckle, a man's "Whew!" of surprise, the "Hem!" of annoyance or perplexity, the moan of pain, a scream, a whisper, a rasp, a sob, a choke, and a gasp. The utterances of animals, though wordless, are eloquent to me—the cat's purr, its mew, its angry, jerky, scolding spit; the dog's bow-wow of warning or of joyous welcome, its yelp of despair, and its con-tented snore; the cow's moos; a monkey's chatter; the snort of a horse; the lion's roar, and the terrible snarl of the tiger. Perhaps I ought to add, for the benefit of the critics and doubters who may peruse this essay, that with my own hand I have felt all these sounds. From my childhood to the present day I have availed myself of every opportunity to visit zoological gardens, menageries, and the circus, and all the animals, except the tiger, have talked into my hand. I have touched the tiger only in a museum, where he is as harmless as a lamb. I have, however, heard him talk by putting my hand on the bars of his cage. I have touched several lions in the flesh, and felt them roar royally, like a cataract over rocks.

To continue, I know the plop of liquid in a pitcher. So if I spill my milk, I have not the excuse of ignorance. I am also familiar with the pop of a cork, the sputter of a flame, the tick-tack of the clock, the metallic swing of the windmill, the labored rise and fall of the pump, the voluminous spurt of the hose, the deceptive tap of the breeze at door and window, and many other vibrations past computing.

There are tactual vibrations which do not belong to skin-touch. They penetrate the skin, the nerves, the bones, like pain, heat and cold. The beat of a drum smites me through from the chest to the shoulder-blades. The din of the train, the bridge, and grinding machinery retains its "old-man-of-the-sea" grip upon me long after its cause has been left behind. If vibration and motion combine in my touch for any length of time, the earth seems to run away while I stand still. When I step off the train, the platform whirls round, and I find it difficult to walk steadily.

Every atom of my body is a vibroscope. But my sensations are not infallible. I reach out, and my fingers meet something furry, which jumps about, gathers itself together as if to spring, and acts like an animal. I pause a moment for caution. I touch it again more firmly, and find it is a fur coat fluttering and flapping in the wind. To me, as to you, the earth seems motionless, and the sun appears to move; for the rays of the afternoon withdraw more and more, as they touch my face, until the air becomes cool. From this I understand how it is that the shore seems to recede as you sail away from it. Hence I feel no incredulity when you say that parallel lines appear to converge, and the earth and sky to meet. My few senses long ago revealed to me their imperfections and deceptivity.

Not only are the senses deceptive, but numerous usages in our language indicate that people who have five senses find it difficult to keep their functions distinct. I understand that we hear views, see tones, taste music. I am told that voices have color. Tact, which I had supposed to be a matter of nice perception, turns out to be a matter of taste. Judging from the large use of the word, taste appears to be the most important of all the senses. Taste governs the great and small conventions of life. Certainly the language of the senses is full of contradictions, and my fellows who have five doors to their house are not more surely at home in themselves than I. May I not, then, be excused if this account of my sensations lacks precision?

B *Politics*

13 Our Duties to the Blind

Presented at the annual meeting of the Massachusetts Association for Promoting the Interests of the Adult Blind, January 5, 1904, Boston. Out of the Dark *(New York: Doubleday, Page and Company, 1914).*

When Keller graduated from Radcliffe in the spring of 1904, she had already addressed both the Massachusetts and New York legislatures on behalf of bills funding manual training for blind people. Like other young female college graduates she believed the purpose of her education to be service. She imagined her most viable and important form of service to be advocacy for deaf and blind people. Critics of all sorts disparaged her entry into politics in the first decades of the century, just as critics had debated her intellectual capacities prior to and during her enrollment at Radcliffe. According to detractors and sometimes according to well-intentioned supporters, her blindness and deafness rendered her politically disabled and thus incapable of independent and reasoned political opinions. This essay thus begins with Keller's justification of her own opinions.

After attempting to legitimate herself, she goes on to advocate that Massachusetts and civic entities help blind people by establishing employment agencies and work training programs. She recognized that idleness (as she characterized the lack of wage work) was not a privilege for people with disabilities, but a highly stigmatized status that undermined social legitimacy and cast people with disabilities as second-class citizens.

The annual meeting of this association gives us another opportunity to discuss among ourselves, and to present to the public, the needs and interests of the adult blind, and I am glad to avail myself of the opportunity. This question of helping the blind to support themselves has been near to my heart for many years, since long before the formation of this society. All I have learned on the subject in the books I have read, I have stored up in my mind against the day when I should be able to turn it to the use of my blind fellows. That day has come.

I have heard that some people think the views I am expressing on this subject, and indeed on all subjects, are not my own, but Miss Sullivan's. If you please, I do very often express Miss Sullivan's ideas, just as to the best of my ability I express ideas which I have been fortunate enough to gather from other wise sources—from the books I have read, from the friends with whom I talk, even from the poets, the prophets, and the sages. It is not strange that some of my ideas come from the wise one with whom I am most intimate and to whom I owe all that I am. I rejoice for myself and for you if Miss Sullivan's ideas are commingled with mine. The more on that account ought what I say to receive your respectful consideration; for Miss Sullivan is acquainted with the work of the blind and the work for the blind. She was blind once herself, and she spent six years in the Perkins Institution. She has since proved a successful teacher of the blind. Other teachers from all over the world have sought her out and exchanged views with her. So Miss Sullivan's ideas on the matter we have to consider are those of an expert. But may I venture to protest I have some ideas of my own? It is true I am still an undergraduate, and I have not had time to study the problems of the blind so deeply as I shall some day. I have, however, thought about these problems, and I know that the time is ripe, nay, it has long been ripe, to provide for the adult blind the means of self-support.

The blind are in three classes: first, blind children who need a common school education; second, the aged and infirm blind, who need to be tenderly cared for; third, the able-bodied blind, who ought to work. For the first class, blind children, this state has splendidly provided in that great two-million dollar school, the Perkins Institution. The second class, like all other people who are invalid and infirm, must be sheltered in the embrace of many public and private charities. For the third class, healthy adult blind, nothing adequate has been done in this state. They do not want to go to school and read books. They do not want to be fed and clothed and housed by other people. They want to work and support themselves. The betterment of this class is the object of our association. We ask that the State give the adult blind opportunity to earn their own living. We do not approve any system to pauperize them. We are not asking for them a degrading pension or the abstract glories of a higher education. We want them apprenticed to trades, and we want some organized method of helping them to positions after they have learned these trades.

Consider the condition of the idle adult blind from the point of view of their fellow-citizens, and from their point of view. What sort of citizens are they now? They are a public or a private burden, a bad debt, an object of pitying charity, an economic loss. What we ask for them, in the name of Christian philanthropy, we ask equally on the ground of economic good sense. If there are three thousand adult blind in this Commonwealth who could be taught to work, and who are not working, to keep them alive means a burden of ten or twelve thousand dollars every seven days. If each of the three thousand could be taught to work and earn three dollars a week—surely a low figure—the State would obviously be twenty or twenty-five thousand dollars a week richer. At present the adult blind form a large class who are unremunerative and unprofitable.

Such they are from the point of view of the thoughtful citizen. What are they from their point of view?

Not merely are they blind—that can be borne—but they live in idleness, which is the cruelest, least bearable misery that can be laid upon the human heart. No anguish is keener than the sense of helplessness and self-condemnation which overwhelms them when they find every avenue to activity and usefulness closed to them. If they have been to school, their very education makes their sorrow keener because they know all the more deeply what they have lost. They sit with folded hands as the weary days drag by. They remember the faces they used to see, and the objects of delight which made life good to live, and above all they dream of work that is more satisfying than all the learning, all the pleasures gained by man, work that unites the world in friendly association, cheers solitude, and is the balm of hurt minds. They sit in darkness thinking with pain of the past, and with dread of the future that promises no alleviation of their suffering. They think until they can think no more, and some of them become morbid. The monotony and loneliness of their lives is conceivable only to those who have similar deprivations. I have enjoyed the advantages of the blind who are taught. Yet, I used to feel unhappy many times, because it seemed as if my limitation would prevent me from taking an active part in the work of the world. Never did my heart ache more than when I thought I was not fit to be a useful member of society. Now I have found abundant work, and I ask for no other blessedness.

I have talked with blind students at the institution for the blind, and I remember the distress and perplexity with which they considered how they should shift for themselves when they graduated. Many of them left school only to go back to poor, bare homes where they could find no means of self-support. For seven, ten or fourteen years they live in the midst of refined surroundings; they enjoyed good books, good music, and the society of cultivated people. When their school days are over, they return to homes and conditions which they have outgrown. The institution that has educated them forgets them, unless, perchance, they have sufficient ability to fight their life-battle single-handed and come out victorious. Institutions are proud of successful graduates. Let us not forget the failures. What benefit do the graduates who fail in the struggle of adult life derive from an education which has not been of a kind that could be turned to practical account? From an economic point of view has the money invested in that education been invested wisely? To teach Latin and Greek and higher mathematics to blind pupils, and not to teach them to earn their bread, is to build a house entirely of stucco, without stones to the walls or rafters to the roof. I have received letters from educated blind people, who repeat the cry, "Give us work, or we perish," and their despair lies heavy on my heart.

It is difficult to get satisfactory statistics about the blind after they graduate from the institutions where they receive a book education, because little or no interest is shown in them after they leave school. It is still harder to get information about the blind who have lost their sight when they are too old to go to the existing institutions. But it is evident that only a small portion of the blind now support themselves. A prominent teacher of the blind is reported to have said that less than 8 per cent. of the entire blind population of the United

States, even those who have been to schools for the blind, are self-supporting, and the percentage for the whole country will be higher than the percentage for this State; for Massachusetts is behind some states in industrial education for the blind. Others will give you the exact figures. But whether there are in Massachusetts one thousand or five thousand adult blind who might be taught to work, they are too many for us to have neglected so long.

It is difficult to understand how a State which was a pioneer in the education of the blind, and which boasts the Perkins Institution, could have so conspicuously failed to turn their education to account. Surely it is only an accidental division which has left one side of the education of the blind in the sunlight where Doctor Howe placed it and has left the other side in the dark. In spirit, all aspects of the education of the blind are one, and we can be sure that Doctor Howe, had he lived, would have been the leader of this movement, in which we are doing our little best. Indeed, I believe that he would long ago have rendered our labours unnecessary. Let us gratefully and lovingly render, in company with those who survive him, the honour that is his due. But since he is dead and cannot lead us, let us push forward, guided by what light we have. Wisdom did not die with Solomon. All knowledge about the needs and capabilities of the blind did not die with Doctor Howe. There is much to do which he did not live to achieve, or, it may even be, which he had not thought of.

The important fact remains that nothing of consequence has been done for the adult blind in Massachusetts since Doctor Howe's day. It was he who established the workshop for the adult blind in South Boston, in connection with the Perkins Institution, and that remains much as he left it. Two or three years ago, the State appropriated a small sum of money—five thousand dollars, I think—for traveling teachers, who visit the homes of blind persons too old to go to the Perkins Institution. This was a step in the right direction, but it was inadequate, and it is not altogether practical. I have known old ladies who have told me how glad they were to learn to read the Lord's Prayer with their fingers. They looked forward to the weekly lesson with joy; it was a bright spot in the monotony of their life. But, after all, this is not so important as it is to teach younger and stronger men and women to earn their living. The needs of the adult blind cannot be covered by an extension of this appropriation or by a development of this kind of teaching. Something new is necessary. Either the scope of the workshop at South Boston must be greatly enlarged, or new ones, independent of it, must be established. It would have been no argument against founding the Massachusetts Institute of Technology to say that there was already a good college across the Charles. He who is content with what has been done is an obstacle in the path of progress.

Up! Up! Something must be done. We have delayed too long. If you want to know how long we have delayed, listen to what the Bishop of Ripon said recently at the Institution for the Blind in Bradford, England. Speaking of a time thirty years ago, he said: "The workhouse and the charity of the passer-by in the street were the only hope of the blind. All that has been changed. The blind have been taught useful occupations, and have been enabled in many cases to earn sufficient to maintain themselves in comfort, so that it has come to be a reproach that a blind man or woman should beg in the streets." This is the change in England in thirty years. There has been no such change in Massachusetts. Something must be done, that is clear. What shall we do?

There are two things to do which work together and become one. First, let the State establish by an adequate appropriation an agency for the employment of the blind. This agency should be in Boston. At the head of it should be a competent man, whose sole duty should be to study all occupations in which the blind can engage, to exhibit the work of the blind, to advise and encourage them, and to bring employers and blind employees together without expense to either. This bureau should do for the blind of Massachusetts what is done by the employment bureau of the British and Foreign Blind Association in England, namely, provide a place in the busiest part of the city, where blind workers and their patrons can be brought together and where articles made by the blind can be advantageously exhibited. The agent should advertise to the public that they can get blind piano tuners, notepaper embossers, shampooers, masseurs, chairmakers, brushmakers, tutors, singers, church organists, tea tasters, and other useful blind people.

Then there is the second part of the work—to increase the variety and efficiency of those other useful blind workers. This means industrial schools; that is workshops, with all possible machinery and appliances which the blind can profitably handle. To every blind person should be given opportunity to serve an industrial apprenticeship. After he has learned this trade, or that mechanical process, he would go to the agent at the employment bureau, or the agent would go to him, and the agent would then offer to employers the services of a blind workman. In each of the large manufacturing towns—Brockton, Lowell, Taunton, Lawrence, Worcester—there should be a branch of the agency. The head of each branch bureau should know all the industries peculiar to his locality, and should know the employers of the neighbourhood.

Suppose at the age of thirty a man loses his sight, and that means that he must give up his work, let us say, as a salesman in a dry-goods house. He goes to the nearest agent of the Massachusetts Industrial Bureau for the Blind. The agent knows every occupation in the State which it is profitable for a blind man to engage in, and he tells this man that the best occupation near his home is running a machine of a certain kind. The man then goes to the Industrial School for the Blind and learns to run that machine; in other words he serves an apprenticeship in a free state school, and incidentally learns the other things which a blind man must learn in order to adapt himself to the new conditions of his life; that is, he gets the experience of being blind. At the end of the apprenticeship the agent, knowing what the man can do, goes to a manufacturer and asks that he give the man a chance. The agent stands behind the man during his period of probation, until the employer is convinced that his blind workman understand his business.

Am I dreaming dreams? It is no untried experiment. It is being done in Great Britain. Remember that to educate a blind man so that he becomes a competent workman is no magical and mysterious process. A blind man can do nothing less and nothing more than what a person with five senses can do, minus what can be done only with the eye. Remember, too, that when a man loses his sight he does not know himself what he can do. He needs some one of experience to advise him. The other day the commission listened to a blind man, forty years old, who lost his sight at the age of thirty-six, four years ago. Before he became blind, he had been a lithographer, and was for eight years a foreman. He testified that he was determined not to be a quitter, and that he had tried one and another kind of work, only to fail in each. "What," asked one of the commissioners, "do you think you can learn to do?" "I do not know," replied the man. Do we need a stronger argument for an industrial agency than this answer? Although intelligent and industrious, this man had struggled wildly in the dark for four years, trying in vain to discover what kind of work he had best apply himself to. Think of it! In four years he had had no one to tell him what it was best for him to try to learn to do.

Now who shall change all this? Who shall establish the Massachusetts Industrial Bureau for the Blind? Surely the State—Massachusetts, in whose watchtowers burn continuously the beacons of sympathy and love; Massachusetts, to whom every State in our country turns for example and guidance in education and philanthropy; Massachusetts, in whose beneficent institutions the deaf have learned to speak, the blind to read the printed page, the idiot clay to think. Surely Massachusetts will not now turn a deaf ear to the cry of the helpless adult blind. Has she not lovingly nurtured and abundantly provided for the Perkins Institution and the Kindergarten for the Blind? Once the people learn what should be done, we need not fear that those whose authority is law and those whose authority is loving charity will neglect the sacred duty to raise the adult blind from dependence to self-respecting citizenship. Therefore I have complete faith in the ultimate triumph of our cause.

14 A Fair Chance to Be Independent and Self-Respecting and Useful

February 18, 1905, letter from Helen Keller to Mrs. Elliot Foster, Secretary of the Board of Education of the Blind, Hartford, Connecticut. Legislation: State, General, AFB.

In this letter Keller protested state efforts to classify the Connecticut Institute for the Blind with charity institutions rather than educational institutions. By insisting on this, she reinforced her belief that states should provide education to blind children and adults that could lead to wage employment. Economic independence she insisted, was essential to a complete and adult life; distinguishing blind adults from "the feeble minded, the degenerate, the blind, the criminal, and the pauper." Here, as elsewhere, she disparages the "mentally blind," who failed to agree with her.

My dear Mrs. Foster,

I am pleased to have this opportunity to write a protest against the classification of the Connecticut Institute for the Blind with penitentiaries and asylums for paupers. I have followed with deep interest the noble, disinterested, efficient work of the institution and I honor the courage with which its directors have continued their efforts in the face of prejudice, poverty and indifference. I only regret that I cannot come and with my own voice help you to show the Connecticut Legislature the true educational character of the institution.

It is logically right and necessary that the school for the blind should be classified with the educational institutions of the state. It is not a charitable institution for the care and support of a dependent, pauper class, but it is a school that gives the blind the instruction which the state owes to all its children, it is a school which tries to place the blind on a level with the seeing. Blind children are not, or ought not to be, dependent on charity any more than the pupils of the neighboring public school. It is true that the blind need a great deal of public and private aid, but it is equally true of their seeing fellows. The only difference between the two classes is that it takes more time and effort, and so costs more, to give the blind an education and teach them to work; for the blind must use the sense of touch, while other people use their eyes. It is to meet the peculiar limitations of the blind that special institutions are established for their instruction.

If the Connecticut Institute is intended to educate the blind so that they may think intelligently and work like their fellow citizens, it ought to be under the supervision of the State Board of Education. It is to be presumed that a board which is interested in all educational matters is more competent to visit, inspect and report upon a school for the blind than the best board of charities in the world. The blind child demands an education from the state as his right, and not as a charity. A state that puts any branch of its education on other than an educational basis is un-American. Justice requires the change of the status of the Connecticut school and sentiment demands it too. To class able-bodied, active blind pupils with the feeble minded, the degenerate, the blind, the criminal, and the pauper robs the blind of their sense of equality as citizens, and adds to their burden of darkness the more intolerable humiliation of inferiority and dependence. Thus the intelligent blind who can work come to be disparaged and lose the dignity and self respect which is the right of their manhood and womanhood. I cannot sit still while they suffer from this glaring injustice. I protest against it, and the directors of schools for the blind all over the country have protested against it, and public opinion has echoed their protest. Massachusetts, New York and seventeen other states regard the work of educating the blind and the deaf as an essential part of the great educational system which each commonwealth has built up and of which each is so justly proud. I am blind and deaf too, and I owe all I have, all that I am, to the generosity, kindness, patience, self-sacrifice of others; but I refuse to be regarded as an object of charity and I resent the insult which the Hartford *Courant* has seen fit to print. What strange blindness has befallen the eyes of editors who cannot see that three hundred dollars spent to educate a blind child is precisely like three hundred dollars spent to educate a seeing child, that money appropriate to teach the blind is not different from money spent for a normal school, an art school, a college of agriculture. There are none of us so blind as seeing people who will not see, and I find that the Hartford *Courant* and the Springfield *Republican* have more than their share of the mentally blind who try to give advice about the instruction of the physically blind. But we whose eyes are closed to the light refuse to be led by those who, having their eyes open, yet see not. The blind person of spirit, whose lot it is to live in a just and intelligent community, stands up, undismayed by his limitations, and says, "I am a man. I have both mind and strength. I [undecipherable] to work as becomes a man, and the state shall not repent the dollars that my education has not cost her."

How I wish I could be with you, dear Mrs. Foster! It is a great disappointment to me not to be able to speak in a cause that is so near to me. But I am with you in your work, and your success will be precious to me. Succeed you must, sooner or later; for no one appeals to the instinct of people to help more strongly than does the brave, upright blind man who asks of his fellowman no boon of charity, but only a fair chance to be independent and self-respecting and useful to his Commonwealth.

Yours very sincerely,
Helen Keller

15 The Truth Again

Ladies' Home Journal, *vol. 26, January 1909*. Out of the Dark
(New York: Doubleday, Page and Company, 1914).

In the first decade of the century, at least two-fifths of all blindness in the United States was due to opthalmia neonatorum, a highly treatable infection of newborns caused by the mother's venereal disease. Because of what Keller called "false modesty—the shame that shelters evil," few doctors, public health officials, or legislators were willing to confront, much less discuss, the issue. This refusal infuriated her. She acknowledges in this article that "the subject was one of which a young woman [such as herself] might be supposed to be ignorant," but called for all American women (as well as churches, schools, and the press) to demand that federal funds and education ensure that all children received the cheap preventive eyedrops at birth.

Ladies' Home Journal editor Edward Bok received praise for the courage required to publish this article, but it includes conservative elements. Keller blamed "licentious men" entirely for the spread of venereal disease. She explained women's infection by stating that "previous to the child's birth she has unconsciously received it through infection from her husband. He has contracted the infection in licentious relations before or since marriage." Looking back in 1938, she referred to the forthrightness of this article with pride.[1]

A year ago I wrote about the prevention of blindness. I wrote guardedly and with hesitation; for the subject was new to me, and I shrank from discussing before the general public a problem which hitherto had been confined to conferences of specialists. Moreover, the subject was one of which a young woman might be supposed to be ignorant, and upon which, certainly, she would not be expected to speak with authority. It is always painful to set one's self against tradition, especially against the conventions and prejudices that hedge about womanhood. But continuous study of blindness has forced upon me knowledge of this subject, and, if I am to stand as an advocate of the work for the sightless, I cannot, without accusing myself of cowardice, gloss over or ignore the fundamental evil.

Once I believed that blindness, deafness, tuberculosis and other causes of suffering were necessary, unpreventable. I believed that we must accept blind eyes, deaf ears, diseased lungs as we accept the havoc of tornadoes and deluges, and that we must bear them with as much fortitude as we could gather from religion and philosophy. But gradually my reading extended, and I found that those evils are to be laid not at the door of Providence, but at the door of mankind; that they are, in large measure, due to ignorance, stupidity, and sin.

The most common cause of blindness is ophthalmia of the new-born. One pupil in every three at the institution for the blind in New York City was blinded in infancy by this disease. Nearly all of the sixteen babies in the Sunshine Home in Brooklyn, one fourth of the inmates of the New York State Home for the Blind, six hundred sightless persons in the State of New York, between six thousand persons and seven thousand persons in the United States, were plunged into darkness by ophthalmia of the new-born. The symptoms of the disease appear in the infant's eyes soon after birth. The eyelids swell and become red and about the second day they discharge whitish pus. At this stage the eyes can be saved by the simplest prophylactic care. That such care is not always exercised is due to the fact that one half of the cases of childbirth in America are attended by midwives, many of whom are ignorant and incompetent. In this country very little has been done to secure the proper education and examination of midwives; and they and the equally ignorant parents resort to poultices, nostrums, and domestic remedies.

There is a remedy for ophthalmia neonatorum. This is an instillation of nitrate of silver solution into the eyes of the child. It is efficacious if promptly and skillfully applied. It is not, however, infallible, and in unskillful hands it may do great harm. The mother who sees in the eyes of her baby the symptoms which I have described should lose no time in summoning the assistance of an intelligent physician.

Let no one suppose that this is idle advice. In France and Germany the laws require that the eyes of every child shall be treated with nitrate of silver solution as soon as it is born, and in those countries there has been a considerable decrease in blindness resulting from the scourge of ophthalmia neonatorum. And what do the wise lawmakers of America do? A bill for the prevention of blindness introduced recently in the Illinois Legislature failed to pass because it was argued that this was only another scheme of doctors to provide fees for themselves! But, at best, the law is concerned only with the remedy. The people themselves, and only they, can wipe out the cause.

What is the cause of ophthalmia neonatorum? It is a specific germ communicated by the mother to the child at birth. Previous to the child's birth she has unconsciously received it through infection from her husband. He has contracted the infection in licentious relations before or since marriage. "The cruelest link in the chain of consequences," says Dr. Prince Morrow, "is the mother's innocent agency. She is made a passive, unconscious medium of instilling into the eyes of her new-born babe a virulent poison which extinguishes its sight."

In mercy let it be remembered, the father does not know that he has so foully destroyed the eyes of his child and handicapped him for life. It is part of the bitter harvest of the wild oats he has sown. Society has smiled upon his "youthful recklessness" because Society does not know that "They enslave their children's children who make compromise with sin."[2]

Society has yet to learn that the blind beggar at the street-corner, the epileptic child, the woman on the operating-table, are the wages of "youthful discretion." To-day science is verifying what the Old Testament taught three thousand years ago, and the time has come when there is no longer the excuse of ignorance. Knowledge had been given us; it is our part to apply it.

Of the consequences of social sin, blindness is by no means the most terrible. The same infection which blots out the eyes of the baby is responsible for many childless homes; for thousands of cases of lifelong invalidism; for 80 per cent. of all inflammatory diseases peculiar to women; and for 75 per cent. of all operations performed on mothers to save their lives.

The day has come when women must face the truth. They cannot escape the consequences of the evil unless they have the knowledge that saves. Must we leave young girls to meet the danger in the dark because we dare not turn the light upon our social wickedness? False delicacy and prudery must give place to precise information and common sense. It is high time to abolish falsehood and let the plain truth come in. Out with the cowardice which shuts its eyes to the immorality that causes disease and human misery! I am confident that when the people know the truth the day of deliverance for mother and child will be at hand.

We must look to it that every child is protected before his birth. Every child has a right to be well born. Every child has a right to be told by his parents and teachers about his birth and his body; for in such knowledge lie true innocence and safety. Civilization is menaced by an insidious enemy. It must learn that only one cure is sure and cheap: right living, which God gives free to all. And right living depends on right knowledge.

We must set to work in the right direction the three great agencies which inform and educate us: the church, the school, and the press. If they remain silent, obdurate, they will bear the odium which recoils upon evildoers. They may not listen at first to our plea for light and knowledge. They may combine to baffle us; but there will rise, again and again, to confront them, the beseeching forms of little children: deaf, blind, crooked of limb, and vacant of mind.

This is not faultfinding. I am not a pessimist, but an optimist, by temperament and conviction. I am making a plea for American women and their children. I plead that the blind may see, the deaf may hear, and the idiot may have a mind. In a word, I plead that the American woman may be the mother of a great race.

Throw aside, I beseech you, false modesty—the shame that shelters evil—and hasten the day when there shall be no preventable disease among mankind.

16 The Enfranchisement of Women

Published in the Manchester (England) Advertiser, *March 3, 1911.*
Out of the Dark *(New York: Doubleday, Page and Company, 1914).*

Keller argued in numerous places that women's rights were part of the larger issue of social justice for everyone. As with the rest of her political views, the inequalities of class permeated her analysis. For example, just as she declared herself "indignant" at the imprisonment and forced feeding of British suffragists, so was she "indignant when the women cloakmakers of Chicago are abused by the police." The economic, political, and social tyranny of a few, she reasoned, caused both "indignities." When she declared herself a "militant suffragette" in 1913, she explained she did so because she believed female suffrage would lead to socialism.[3]

I thank you for the copy of "Votes for Women." Mr. Zangwill's address interested me deeply. You ask me to comment on it, and though I know little, your request encourages me to tell you some of my ideas on the subject.

I have thought much lately about the question of woman-suffrage, and I have followed in my Braille magazines the recent elections in Great Britain. The other day I read a fine report of an address by Miss Pankhurst[4] at a meeting in New York.

I do not believe that the present government has any intention of giving woman a part in national politics, or of doing justice to Ireland, or to the workmen of England. So long as the franchise is denied to a large number of those who serve and benefit the public, so long as those who vote are at the beck and call of party machines, the people are not free, and the day of women's freedom seems still to be in the far future. It makes no difference whether the Tories or the Liberals in Great Britain, the Democrats or the Republicans in the United States, or any party of the old model in any other country get the upper hand. To ask any such party for women's rights is like asking a czar for democracy.

Are not the dominant parties managed by the ruling classes, that is, the propertied classes, solely for the profit and privilege of the few? They use us millions to help them into power. They tell us like so many children that our safety lies in voting for them. They toss us crumbs of concession to make us believe that they are working in our interest. Then they exploit the resources of the nation not for us, but for the interests which they represent and uphold. We, the people are not free. Our democracy is but a name. We vote? What does that mean? It means that we choose between two bodies of real, though not avowed autocrats. We choose between Tweedledum and Tweedledee. We elect expensive masters to do our work for us, and then blame them because they work for themselves and for their class. The enfranchisement of women is a part of the vast movement to enfranchise all mankind. You ask for votes for women. What good can votes do you when ten elevenths of the land of Great Britain belongs to two hundred thousand, and only one eleventh to the rest of the forty millions? Have your men with their millions of votes freed themselves from this injustice?

When one shows the masters that half the wealth of Great Britain belongs to twenty-five thousand persons, when one says that this is wrong, that this wrong lies at the bottom of all social injustice, including the wrongs of women, the highly respectable newspapers cry, "Socialist agitator, stirrer of class strife!" Well, let us agitate, let us confess that we are thoroughgoing Social Democrats or anything else that they please to label us. But let us keep our eyes on the central fact, that a few, a few British men own the majority of British men and all British women. The few own the many because they possess the means of livelihood of all. In our splendid republic, where at election time all are "free and equal," a few Americans own the rest. Eighty per cent Of our people live in rented houses, and one half the rest are mortgaged. The country is governed for the richest, for the corporations, the bankers, the land speculators, and for the exploiters of labour. Surely we must free men and women together before we can free women.

The majority of mankind are working people. So long as their fair demands—the ownership and control of their lives and livelihood—are set at naught, we can have neither men's rights nor women's rights. The majority of mankind are ground down by industrial oppression in order that the small remnant may live in ease. How can women hope to help themselves while we and our brothers are help-less against the powerful organizations which modern parties repre-sent, and which contrive to rule the people? They rule the people because they own the means of physical life, land, and tools, and the nourishers of intellectual life, the press, the church, and the school. You say that the conduct of the woman-suffragists is being disgrace-fully misrepresented by the British press. Here in America the lead-ing newspapers misrepresent in every possible way the struggles of toiling men and women who seek relief. News that reflects ill upon the employers is skillfully concealed—news of dreadful conditions under which labourers are forced to produce, news of thousands of men maimed in mills and mines and left without compensation, news of famines and strikes, news of thousands of women driven to a life of shame, news of little children compelled to labour before their hands are ready to drop their toys. Only here and there in a small and as yet uninfluential paper is the truth told about the workman and the fearful burdens under which he staggers.

I am indignant at the treatment of the brave, patient women of England. I am indignant when the women cloakmakers of Chicago are abused by the police. I am filled with anguish when I think of the degradation, the enslavement and the industrial tyranny which crush millions, and drag down women and helpless children.

I know the deep interest which you and your husband always took in God's poor, and your sympathy invites me to open my heart to you and express these opinions about grave problems.

17 Their Cause Is My Cause

Letter written to the strikers at Little Falls, New York, November 1912.
Out of the Dark *(New York: Doubleday, Page and Company, 1914).*

When workers struck, Keller quickly supported them and through her strike activism became involved with the radical Industrial Workers of the World (IWW or "Wobblies"). The IWW sought to unite all workers, skilled and unskilled, in the overthrow of capitalism via strikes, direct ac-tion, propaganda, and boycotts. Inspired by the massive and successful

IWW strike in Lawrence, Massachusetts, she joined 1912 strike efforts in Little Falls, Massachusetts, by sending a letter of encouragement and $87 to striking workers. John Macy read aloud the message at a strike meeting while strike leader Big Bill Haywood praised her actions. Keller called the cause of the strikers, seventy percent of them female, "my cause. If they are denied a living wage, I also am denied. While they are industrial slaves, I cannot be free."

I am sending the check which Mr. Davis paid me for the Christmas sentiments I sent him. Will you give it to the brave girls who are striving so courageously to bring about the emancipation of the workers at Little Falls?

They have my warmest sympathy. Their cause is my cause. If they are denied a living wage, I also am defrauded. While they are industrial slaves, I cannot be free. My hunger is not satisfied while they are unfed. I cannot enjoy the good things of life which come to me, if they are hindered and neglected. I want all the workers of the world to have sufficient money to provide the elements of a normal standard of living—a decent home, healthful surroundings, opportunity for education and recreation. I want them to have the same blessings that I have. I, deaf and blind, have been helped to overcome many obstacles. I want them to be helped as generously in a struggle which resembles my own in many ways.

Surely the things that the workers demand are not unreasonable. It cannot be unreasonable to ask of society a fair chance for all. It cannot be unreasonable to demand the protection of women and little children and an honest wage for all who give their time and energy to industrial occupations. When indeed shall we learn that we are all related one to the other, that we are all members of one body? Until the spirit of love for our fellowmen, regardless of race, colour or creed, shall fill the world, making real in our lives and our deeds the actuality of human brotherhood—until the great mass of the people shall be filled with the sense of responsibility for each other's welfare, social justice can never be attained.

18 Blind Leaders

Outlook, *vol. 105, September 27, 1913*.

Keller begins this essay once again feeling that she must defend her capacity to form opinions before she gives hers. Many considered that blindness and deafness rendered her politically disabled and thus incapable of independent and reasoned political opinions—unfit for civic life. Here Keller denies these accusations, claiming that her reliance upon "the eyes of the mind" made her better fit to form opinions than "blind leaders," who ignored social inequalities.

This essay includes many sharp political statements, including Keller's insistence that "I am the determined foe of the capitalist system, which denies the workers the rights of human beings. I consider it fundamentally wrong, radically unjust and cruel." She lists poverty, working conditions, child labor, and unequal distributions of wealth, as "glaring evils" ignored by those with "spiritual blindness." Yet, she remains adamant that "the deaf, blind, dumb multitude shall find its soul, shall find its tongue!"

In this period Keller frequently used disability as a metaphor of obtuseness about injustice, echoing biblical metaphors, in an effort to explain social *ills* to others. She frequently argued that those indifferent to the problems of modern society were the truly blind. On the vaudeville circuit she combined humor with the same thread, stating that she had a "fellow-feeling" for President Harding, for "he seems as blind as I am."[5] This commonplace rhetorical use of disability bought into an understanding of disability as both debilitating and dehumanizing. That rhetorical move also narrowed the possibilities of her own political expression, leaving her again unable to claim disability as a legitimate political class or as the base for legitimate political interests.

When Mr. Booth [a literary adviser and friend—The Editors] read my essay "Blind Leaders," he said to Mrs. Macy, "It's all right. But people won't believe that Helen Keller wrote it. I have heard men say, 'How can she know about these things? How can one deaf and blind from infancy know about life, about people, about affairs? It is impossible for her to have a first-hand knowledge of what is going on in the world. She is only a mouthpiece for somebody else.'"

I must plead guilty to the charge that I am deaf and blind, although I forget this fact most of the time. Occasionally I come into sharp collision with the stone wall out in my back field, and for a second or two there is not the slightest doubt in my mind that I am blind. When my friends tell me they cannot hear me speak because a freight train is passing, I realize that I'm deaf. But I do not feel so very sorry; for it is not pleasant to have one's thoughts disturbed by the noise of a freight train.

As for the other charges, they are groundless, they are ridiculous. My blindness does not shut me out from a knowledge of what is happening about me. True, I did not witness the recent dreadful wreck at Stamford; neither did most people in the United States. But that did not prevent me, any more than it prevented them, from knowing about it. To be sure, I cannot hear my neighbors discuss the events and questions of the day; but, judging from what is repeated to me of those discussions and all that they say is often repeated conscientiously—I feel that I do not miss much.

I prefer to use the eye and the ear of the world which the printed page makes mine. I prefer to read the opinions of well-informed persons, clear thinkers like Alfred Russell Wallace, William Morris, Bernard Shaw, Sir Oliver Lodge, H. G. Wells, William English Walling, Judge Lindsey, Robert Hunter, Karl Kautsky, Herbert Spencer, Darwin, and Marx. You say, "But what do you know about life that enables you to judge of the competency of such men to give an opinion?" If books are not life, I do not know what they are. In the writings of poets, sages, prophets, is recorded all that men have seen, heard, and felt. Having all this in the grasp of my two hands, my means of observing what is going on in the world is not so very limited, after all. I have all the keys to the doors of knowledge. I am benefited by every observation made by scientist, philosopher, prophet. The eyes of the mind are stronger, more penetrating, and more reliable than our physical eyes. We can see a lot of things with a little common-sense light to aid our perceptions.

I have never been a captain of industry or a strike-breaker or a soldier; neither have most people. But I have studied about them, and I think I understand their relation to society. At all events, I claim my right to discuss them. I also know something about gambling. For I gambled once, in stocks and bonds—once only; for I lost all I had in that one venture. But if I did not win, somebody else did, and I had a good deal of "first-hand experience."

I have worked for the blind. I have come into contact with them. I have taken an active part in meetings and spoken before legislatures in their behalf. I have studied their problems, and in order to understand them fully, I found it necessary to study the problems of the seeing among whom the blind live and work. I have found that the needs and difficulties of the sightless are similar to the needs and difficulties of all who are handicapped in the struggle for a livelihood, for education, for equal opportunity. If this work for the blind is not "first-hand experience," I do not know where you or I can get it.

Finally I have visited sweat-shops, factories, crowded slums of New York and Washington. Of course I could not see the squalor; but if I could not see it, I could smell it. With my own hand I could feel pinched, dwarfed children tending their younger brothers and sisters while their mothers tended machines in near-by factories.

Besides the advantages of books and of personal experience, I have the advantage of a mind trained to think. In most people I talk with thought is infantile. In the well educated it is rare. In time their minds become automatic machines. People do not like to think. If one thinks, one must reach conclusions, and conclusions are not always pleasant. They are a thorn in the spirit. But I consider it a priceless gift and a deep responsibility to think. Thought—intelligent thought—gives new eyes to the blind and new ears to the deaf.

I do not doubt that many persons who read what I am going to write will say to themselves: "She is indeed blind. She is so blind she imagines everybody else to be blind." As a matter of fact, I have been thinking for a long time that most of us are afflicted with spiritual blindness. Certainly, very few people open fresh, fearless eyes upon the world they live in. They do not look at anything straight. They have not learned to use their eyes, except in the most rudimentary ways. They will usually see a lamp-post—if it is a large one—and sometimes they are able to read the danger signal on a railway crossing, but not always. Most of the time they expect some one else to see for them. They often pay fabulous sums to lawyers, doctors, ministers, and other "experts" to do their seeing for them; but, unfortunately, it frequently happens that those hired guides and leaders are also blind. Of course they deny that their sight is imperfect. They claim to have extraordinary powers of vision, and many people believe them. Consequently, they are permitted to lead their fellows. But how often do they steer them to their destruction!

When we look about us with seeing eyes, what do we behold? Men and women at our very doors wrung with hard labor, want or the dread of want, needing help and receiving none, toiling for less than a living wage! If we had had penetrating vision, I know that we could not, we would not, have endured what we saw—cruelty, ignorance, poverty, disease—almost all preventable, unnecessary. Our blind leaders whom we have sent away told us that the poverty and misery of mankind were divinely ordained. They taught us that the words, "Ye have the poor always with you," mean that Christ sanctioned poverty as necessary and irremediable. Now we read the Gospel with our own eyes, and we see that Christ meant no such thing.

Much poverty is abominable, unnecessary, a disgrace to our civilization, or rather a denial that we are civilized. Let us try to understand poverty. What is the cause of it? Simply this: that the land, the machinery, the means of life, belong to the few, while the many are born and live with nothing that they can call their own except their hands and their brains. They live by selling their hands and their brains to the few; and all the work they do makes the rich more rich, and gains for the workers a mere livelihood, or less than a livelihood. The ownership of the world by a small class is the main cause of poverty. Strange that we could not see it before, and that when we did see it we accepted it in blind contentment! Our blind guides consoled us by saying that there was much charity, and that the rich were generous and gave to the poor. We now see that what the rich give is only a small part of the money which is made for them by the labor of the poor! They never stop to think that if the workers received an equitable share of their product, there would be no rich, there would be little need of philanthropy. Charity covers a multitude of sins. It does something worse than that. It covers the facts so that they cannot be seen. It covers the fact that the property of the few is made by the labor of the many. The rich are willing to do everything for the poor but to get off their backs.

Our blind leaders used often to blame the poor for their poverty. They declared that the workers did not work enough, were not thrifty enough, squandered their wages. Now we stop and think. We remember that if the workers do not work enough, they do all the work that is done. They make every house that stands, every yard of cloth, every loaf of bread. All that we have we owe to them. If the worker is not thrifty, does not save, it is as often as not because a large part of what he produces goes to some one else, and some one else does the saving. If one man has without producing, it is only because another man produces without having, and that is the trouble in a nutshell.

We never used to ask ourselves why we were well dressed, well housed, why we had time for study and self-improvement, why some of us who talked about the worker's lack of thrift had abundance to squander and waste. Nor did we ask why thousands live in poor houses, eat poor food, wear shabby clothes, and are overworked, and have nothing to look forward to all their lives but monotonous days of toil and poverty. Those two questions answer each other. It is the labor of many poor, ignorant people which makes it possible for us to be refined and comfortable. The employers own what the workers make, and that means that they own the workers. Think of it! The employers own the workers, their time, their strength, their brains, the houses in which they live. They own them really as if they were actual slaves. But the eyes of the owners are veiled. They do not see that to own the worker's tools is to own the worker. In "The Merchant of Venice" Shylock cried, "You take my life when you do take the means whereby I live." It was a moneylender who said that. A workman can say it with better justice and with warmer appeal to our sympathies. But the masters are blind, they are insensible.

We used to walk through dark, dirty streets; we saw debased men and women, stunted children, blind beggars, brutalized young men, and our curiosity was not aroused to ask the cause of these things. Our blind leaders told us that that was human nature. Poor human nature! When human nature plays with matches and sets fire to our house, shall we sit down and say, "How human!" or shall we try to put out the fire? We want to turn the intelligence and goodness of human nature against the ignorance and evil of human nature. I believe we can do this, and that is why I am not a pessimist. When I talk about poverty and ignorance and misery, I know that I am not drawing a beautiful picture of the world. Yet I am no pessimist. The pessimist— another kind of blind leader—says, "Man lives by darkness and in darkness he shall die." I do not believe it. Man was intended for the light, and he shall not die. In light I would have every one live and see clearly to dispel all darkness. The diagnosis of evil is the beginning of cure. I am no prophet of evil. I find much to love in this world of ours. It is a good world—or it will be when we all use our eyes to make it more as it should be. It is a better world than it was ten centuries ago. It is a better world than it was last year. We lose nothing that man has gained by the sweat of his brow or the genius of his brain. We are every day gaining a little more love, light, and knowledge. We are not becoming blind, we are widening our vision. We are not losing our freedom, because we never had it. Freedom is an ideal. Because it is an ideal I want to make it clear that most of us are not free. If we understand that we are not free, we can work towards our freedom. We cannot be optimists until we have an ideal. We cannot seek intelligently for good until we know evil. We cannot be free until we know the nature of our bondage and examine the chains that bind us.

Our blind leaders used to stand in the high places and harangue about our freedom. The truth is, there never was a free nation, there never was a good government. Since the slaying of Abel there has never been a brother-loving period. We still have to say with Mark Twain: "The brotherhood of man is the most precious thing in the world—what there is of it." From times immemorial men have bowed to the will of masters. Each day they have gone, some to do battle, some to hunt, some to dig and delve, some to spin, all striving to win the bread of life. Ever have the toilers tilled and planted, and been hungry. Ever have the mighty rejoiced and feasted. Never have men labored with glad confidence, glorying in the work of their hands. Ever have some stronger, fiercer brothers robbed them of a portion of their labor.

We remember to have heard our blind leaders say that the people were free men, that if they did not like a "job" they could go wherever they pleased. But where can they go? To some other mill, to some other master. When they stop work, go on strike, society is up in arms against them. Idle workmen make the owners indignant. Why? Because when the workman puts his hands in his pockets the employer's profits are cut off.

Again and again our blind leaders have discoursed on the value of gold and silver. But they never answer the vital question, "Why, after centuries of growth, of education, of intervention, in an age of great plenty, are the majority of men still poor and ignorant?" What a contradiction is this—abundance increasing manifold side by side with increasing poverty, constant improving of labor-saving machinery, but the laborer still without salvation! Worried, puzzled, he knows not how long he shall eat or drink, how he shall stand or sit, wherewithal he shall clothe himself honestly by the work of his hands. But, lo! there is much charity.

From our all-knowing blind leaders we learned that this strange state of things was a result of overproduction. Now let us open our eyes and face this absurdity. How can there be over-production when many men, women, and children are cold and hungry and scantily clothed? The trouble is not over-production or under-production as a whole. As a matter of fact, the worker produces too little for himself and too much for others. There is enough of everything in the world; but it is not intelligently distributed. Some people are obliged to be idle and have not enough; some people are enabled to be idle and have more than enough. Hundreds of people own more than one house. Thousands of people own no house. Hundreds of people have good incomes, whether or not they contribute one thought or motion of the hand to production. Thousands of men work hard and are underpaid. Women and children are bound to machines in unclean workrooms to eke out the small earnings of the men.

Where, then, is the freedom of the people—I mean, the great majority of the people?

Our blind leaders were wont to vaunt of the great prosperity of the country. They talked so loudly that we failed to hear the protest of the workers. They boasted that "America lifts up the manhood of the poor," that we care for the child and give woman a position of dignity. When we tear away the veil which they so skillfully wrapped about our eyes, what do we see? A dwarfed humanity, stunted in body and mind, at war with each other and with the forces of life; the multitudes of mankind ill fed, ill clothed, living in noisome habitations, working at deadly occupations, dulled to joy and the spirit. Our blind guides wring our hearts with details of the tragic fate of the Titanic. But they never told us about the far greater wreck of human lives in the industrial world, or the heroism of men who grapple with wheel, shuttle, and drill. And yet cotton lint, flint of the quarry, dust of flour, cause more havoc than the slaughter in the Balkans. Gas, steam, deadly vapors, white lead, phosphorus, chlorine from the bleaching-room—these are only a few of the horrors that the workman must face hour after hour every day. When we look into mine and factory for ourselves, what do we see? Little children whose souls are quenched out like a flame in joyless toil—little beings freighted with the bud and sap of divine beginnings bent and stunted, stupid and grown old before their time! Does not all that is kindest in us cry out that they were happiest who went first? For what is there in life for those pinched little ones to grow up for? Sooner or later the giant hands of the machines will seize them and hold them, taking all, giving nothing!

And what about the dignity of womanhood? Only a small part of the millions of workingwomen receive enough pay to maintain a decent home and give their children proper care and education. What dignity do women have as citizens when they may not even elect those who shall decide for them vital questions affecting food, clothing, shelter, education? What do we do to save mothers from the necessity of working at machines until they are unfit to become mothers and they bring feeble children into the world? Eight million women and children are in the factories of this country, and three million men are out of work! Blind indeed must be those who do not see that there must be something wrong when such a state of things exists.

I speak from no personal "grouch" or disappointment. For me life has been one long caress of gentle words and gentle hands. I love all men—rich men, poor men, beggar men, thieves. Millionaires have been among my nearest, kindest friends. Henry Rogers was one of the noblest men that ever lived, in spite of his millions. Kindness and consideration have followed me all the days of my life. But I have seen the exaggerated inequality in the conditions of men, and I have studied the cause of this inequality. I am a child of my generation. I am alive to new forces in the world. Disturbing ideas of dynamic power have penetrated the closed doors to my mind, and awakened in me a social conscience. Not the stream which has passed, but that which is passing, turns the wheel of the mill.

When we inquire why things are as they are, the answer is: The foundation of society is laid upon a basis of individualism, conquest, and exploitation, with a total disregard of the good of the whole. The structure of a society built upon such wrong basic principles is bound to retard the development of all men, even the most successful ones, because it tends to divert man's energies into useless channels and to degrade his character. The result is a false standard of values. Trade and material prosperity are held to be the main objects of pursuit, and consequently the lowest instincts in human natures—love of gain, cunning, and selfishness—are fostered. The output of a cotton mill or a coal mine is considered of greater importance than the production of healthy, happy-hearted, free human beings.

This unmoral state of society will continue as long as we live under a system of universal competition for the means of existence. The workers cannot lift up their heads so long as a small favored class in each generation is allowed to inherit the accumulated labor of all preceding generations, and the many who produce the wealth inherit nothing. (We often forget what wealth is. It is the stored-up labor of men, women, and little children. Money does not create anything. Money is about as productive as a wheel revolving in a void. It has value only in proportion to the toil and sweat of human hands that went into the getting of it.)

During the past century man has gained greater mastery over the forces of nature than he ever had before. Consequently the wealth produced in the world has increased a hundredfold. With the help of the machines he has invented, man can produce enough to provide necessaries, comforts, and even some luxuries for every human being. But in spite of this enormously greater productive power the condition of the workers has not essentially improved. Because the industrial system under which we live denies them the fruits of their labor, they have not received their fair share in the products of civilization.

As a matter of fact, machinery has widened the gulf between those who own and those who toil. It has become a means of perpetuating man's slavery, because it may be run by unskilled laborers who receive low wages, which of course increases the profits of employers and stockholders. So the workers become part of the machines they manipulate; but the machine is expensive, while human life is cheap. When the workers can no longer live, they go on strike, and what happens? The masters evict them from the hovels that they called home; the police and militia break up their protest-meetings, imprison their leaders, and when they can, drive them out of town. This appalling condition of things exists in many different parts of our county at this moment. For even the Constitution does not safeguard the liberties of the workers when their interests are opposed to those of the capitalist. Our administration of justice, which blind leaders used to tell us was a splendid inheritance from our fathers, is grossly unequal and unjust. It is based on a system of money fees. It is so encumbered at every step with technicalities that it is necessary to employ experts at great cost to explain and interpret the law. Then, too, all petty offenses are punishable by fine or imprisonment. This means that the poor will always be punished, while the rich are usually allowed to go free.

We cannot longer shut our eyes to these glaring evils. They divide the world into economic classes antagonistic to each other. It is because of all these undeniable evils that I am the determined foe of the capitalist system, which denies the workers the rights of human beings. I consider it fundamentally wrong, radically unjust and cruel. It inflicts purposeless misery upon millions of my fellow men and women. It robs little children of the joy of life, embitters motherhood, breaks the bodies of men and degrades their manhood. It must, therefore, be changed, it must be destroyed, and a better, saner, kinder social order established. Competition must give place to co-operation, and class antagonism to brotherhood. "Each for all" is a far more stimulating and effective doctrine than "each for himself." Private ownership of land and the means of production and distribution of the necessaries of life must be replaced by public ownership and democratic management.

Oh, no, it is not human nature that we have to change. Our task is not so difficult as that. All that is necessary to make this world a comfortable abode for man is to abolish the capitalist system. In the words of Sir Oliver Lodge, "we have entered upon the period of conscious evolution, and have begun the adaptation of environment to organism."[6] In other words, we have learned to curb and utilize the forces of nature. The time of blind struggle is drawing to a close. The forces governing the law of the survival of the fittest will continue to operate; but they will be under the conscious, intelligent control of man.

In all my reading I am conscious of a multitudinous discontent. Slowly man is waking up. He is rubbing his eyes and muttering to himself: "There's something wrong with the world. Considering how hard I work I get mighty little in return. I don't see that with a hundred steel plows I get more bread than my forbears who used a wooden plow. I am no better clad, since one machine does the work of a thousand hands, than my ancestors who wore homespun garments. There's a public school in every city and town, but I don't see that my children are the better taught. We have many things that don't count—cheap ornaments, tawdry clothes, patent medicines, and food made to sell, not to eat. This is not reasonable. I will arise and find out why things are as they are." That is what all the "noise" is about. The people—the great "common herd"—are finding out what is wrong with the social, political, and economic structure of the system of which they are a part. The workers—the producers of all the wealth in the world—are chafing at the narrow bounds of their lives. They fret and fume like hounds, and strain at the leash of industrial bondage. They are weary of old trammels, old burdens, creeds outworn, tired of feasting on emptiness and digesting in imagination. The masters find the aroused workman a loud, egotistical animal, a "paid agitator." This is not a time of gentleness, of timid beginnings that steal into life with soft apologies and dainty grace. It is a time of loud-voiced, open speech and fearless thinking, a time of striving and conscious manhood, a time of all that is robust and vehement and bold, a time radiant with new ideals, new hopes of true democracy. I love it, for it thrills me and gives me a feeling that I shall face great and terrible things. I am a child of my generation, and I rejoice that I live in such a splendidly disturbing age. Through the centuries, in spite of hindrances, persecutions, obloquy, "what is to be picks its way" without apology, without fear. Without asking your leave the new order emerges from the old. To the powerful this condition of things is too absurd for patience—the opposition of unreasoning iconoclasts to the traditions of the fathers and the sacred rights of private property; and so they reinforce the police department and call out the militia. In their blindness they think that they can stay the onward march of that dynamic power, silence the voice of God in the land. Those blind ones are but hastening the day when every yoke shall be broken from the necks of men. Crushed, stupefied by terrible poverty, the workers yet demand that they shall have some of the beauty, some of the comforts, some of the luxuries which they have produced. They shall demand, and neither courts, legislatures, nor armies shall prevent the millions from slowly regaining that which the millions have created.

The young generation is beginning to realize this, and new ideas about the workers of the world, about women and children, are "flashing meteor-like through the darkness where we live." Sophistication and greed are instilled characters, and are fortunately not transmitted to offspring by inheritance. The sun of brotherhood is emerging from the eclipse. It is this light that has waked us. It is showing us what we should see in our fellow-men. We are finding out that workmen are not mere machines, they are Men and Women. Imagination, sympathy, and growing knowledge compel us to share in their suffering and in their desires. We are uniting our senses, our hands, and our feelings to end cruel conditions under which millions live, work, and die.

Already thousands of earnest men and women have their faces turned towards this light, and by it they are daily guided in their lives, their thoughts, their work. Steadily, surely, the new light is growing, spreading like the morning upon all lands, broad and broader it glows, and it shall glow until it shines upon all the dark days of humanity. It is a light coming to those who looked for light and found darkness, a life to them who looked for the grave and were bitter in spirit. It shall open all blind hearts, and it shall make evident to every human soul our close dependence upon one another in all the changes, the joys, the sorrows of the world. It is a light which shall banish the cloud of ignorance and the shadow of man-wrought death. At last the deaf, blind, dumb multitude shall find its soul, shall find its tongue! Erect and proud shall all men earn their bread and eat it; for the stigma of labor shall be clotted out forever. The workers shall be no more parts of machines, but masters of them. We shall all stand together; we shall look to each other always for aid and joy, and no one shall be told, "Every man for himself." The hands of all men shall support all men, and we shall dwell in safety. We shall know happiness not bought at the cost of another's misery. We shall be "fellow-workers unto the kingdom of God."[7]

19 The Persecution of Those Who Uphold Their Downtrodden Brethren

December 12, 1917, letter from Helen Keller
to President Woodrow Wilson, AFB.

Without hesitation, Keller here claims sympathy and affiliation with political radicals and International Workers of the World activists Arturo Giovannitti, Elizabeth Gurley Flynn, and Carlo Tresca. In September 1917 the three, along with 166 others, had been indicted for violation of the Espionage Act, though charges were later dropped. Through John Macy, Keller had known Giovannitti and his family for several years. After reading one of her essays in 1913, Giovannitti had praised her with humor to his good friend: "She has grasped the full meaning of the socialist movement as well as any grizzled strategos of the class war. . . . none of us will contend any more that she does not deserve to go to jail."[8]

Dear Mr. Wilson,

Again I enter your presence through the medium of a letter. I am aware that it may be almost an inexcusable intrusion. But I have more than ordinary confidence in your kindness, patience and forbearance. I have read with eager interest a good deal that you have written. Many of your splendid utterances have become an integral part of my thoughts and aspirations. That is what gives me courage to write to you about matters that multiply perplexities and wring my heart.

Some friends of mine are soon to be arraigned with many others in Chicago for alleged violation of some recently enacted statutes abridging freedom of speech and of the press. I cannot plead for them without attempting to make you understand why I sympathize with them, and why I feel with them that they are the victims of intolerance and persecution. Although we are living in a time of intolerance, suspicion and force rather than of forbearance, confidence and compassion—a time when men's thoughts grow confused, and their sense of fairness is well nigh stifled in the smoke of battle—a time when all sorts of prejudiced, self-appointed persons sit in judgment upon the words and acts of others—a time when the most fatuous utterances in the name of patriotism are hailed with unchallenged reverence, yet even in such a time I shall not believe that the humanity and kindliness in your great heart are dormant.

I do not imagine that I even begin to know what you know about the situation. I only wish to speak out what is in my mind because similar thoughts are in the minds of a great many people who are feeling their way through a darkness of conflicting duties and beliefs. We sincerely wish to be loyal to our country. But we must also be true to our consciences and ideals. We are perplexed because they often seem to conflict. Still, when I feel most depressed, most under the spell of fear, I think of your sincerity and wisdom, and a groping warmth steals into my heart.

The danger from Prussian militarism is as clear, as intolerable to my friends and myself as it is to you or to any one fighting in France. It is because we think a similar despotism is beginning here that we are troubled. Rights we had thought ours forever—rights hallowed by the blood and fortunes of our fathers—rights we had been taught were the very bulwarks of our liberties—rights guaranteed to us by the Constitution of the United States, are being openly violated every day. The voice of authority commanding silence has downed the voice of justice. Meetings of protest are forcibly broken up; newspapers expressing the opinions of radicals are debarred from the mails; individuals are threatened and clubbed for speaking their minds; many of them have been imprisoned, and excessive bails demanded. The intolerance of the newspapers amounts to fanaticism. Ministers of the gospel of Christ find humor in the flogging of Herbert Bigelow.[9] A high government official condones the murder of Frank Little by a mob, thereby upholding mob rule and lynching.[10] If such a state of affairs continues, our prisons will become holy shrines where thoughtful men will go and pray.

When they hung John Brown, Emerson said, "They have made the gallows as holy as the cross."[11] Beware, lest the avenging hand of remorse be laid upon our generation for the persecution of those who uphold their downtrodden brethren.

Because the Kaiser is destroying freedom in Europe to preserve autocracy, must we destroy it here to preserve democracy? Is there no democratic way of accomplishing the noble enterprise we have undertaken? We want America safe for democracy, no matter what happens in Europe. We want peace and freedom for the world, and we believe that this can be attained only by substituting an industrial democracy for the present economic system. When we emphasize this phase of the world-struggle, we meet with opposition, intolerance and persecution.

It takes courage to uphold opinions opposed by all the forces of a strong government. It may require a Bolsheviki mind to do that. Perhaps you think that is the sort of mind I have. I have. For to me the Russian Revolution seems the most wonderful thing that has happened in two thousand years. It is like a conscious sun bursting upon a gloomy, disastrous world—a sun which shall heal the nations. Yet the *New York Times* characterizes it as "a wreck and ruin, not ameliorated by anything admirable, but attended with every circumstance of shame and disgrace from cowardice to treachery." What shall bridge the gulf between a Bolsheviki mind and a capitalist mind?

Now my friends, among them Arturo Giovannitti—a maker of plays, Elizabeth Gurley Flynn, who is beloved by the struggling workers, and Carlo Tresca are victims of this angry intolerance. They seem to have been arrested because they are associated with the Industrial Workers of the World.

As a matter of fact, since America entered the war, Arturo Giovannitti and Miss Flynn have taken no part in propaganda directed against the war policy of the nation. Mr. Tresca, one of the kindest, sweetest, most lovable of men, is the editor of "L'Avenire": an Italian paper opposed to militarism. His opposition to war, like my own, is based not only on humanitarian grounds, but also on the conviction that wars are disastrous to the welfare and happiness of the working-people, their struggles, their aspirations and their liberties.

But I am come to plead for these friends, not to praise them. True; they are honest exponents of a social revolution which they believe will overthrow the present economic system. Their crime is, that they see the evils of their time and speak out against them, not always wisely or well. They are more or less erratic. But they follow their ideals, and the way is one of self-denial and danger. Faith alone lights that path. All through the ages idealists have followed a course opposed by majorities and governments. Despots are impotent before this divine urge. A nation is civilized or not according to the number of those who follow that light, that urge. Nay, while the accumulated growths of civilization are being destroyed at this time, they are sowing the seeds from which the future will be fructified. I am bound to these thinkers by many holy interests, affections, hopes, visions, and desires. We hope that some day mankind will be free and wise and happy in a world where there shall be no want or fear, but bread and work and joy for every human being; and even if that wondrous day should never dawn, to have hoped and worked for it cannot be wrong. We believe in the oneness of humanity. We believe in peace and brotherhood. We believe in the elimination of poverty, ignorance and oppression by one or by many. We believe in industrial democracy as a solution of the economic problem. We grope for the wall—the wall that shall support our weakness; we grope as those who have no eyes; we stumble at noon-day as in the night; therefore is understanding far from us, and justice doth not overtake us.

I also venture to assert that if conditions in this country were quite what they should be, there would be no Industrial Workers of the World in America. They are victims caught in a maddening maze of wrong economic and industrial conditions. They have endured cumulative wrongs and injuries until they are driven to rebellion. They have proclaimed defiance to the ruling classes and avowed their intentions of attempting to overthrow all existing social conditions. They consider they have a world to win.

But in spite of the affiliation of my friends Arturo Giovannitti, Miss Flynn and Mr. Tresca, with the Industrial Workers of the World.

they [*sic*] have individually, and in conscious deference to the war policy of the nation, committed no seditious act, and have not been connected with any illegal propaganda. Does not a sense of fair play dictate that they should be tried separately, instead of collectively?

We look to you, our president whose name shall not be writ in water, you whose sincerity, wisdom and strength we rely upon in these disastrous days—we look to you to befriend the weak and the misrepresented against those who are guided solely by general rules which seek a short cut to justice, without the trouble of exerting patience, discrimination, impartiality. Your far-seeing statesmanship, your wisdom, your idealism are our national honor. You are our beacon in the multitudinous darkness of war.

With cordial assurances of appreciation and esteem, I am,

Sincerely yours,

Helen Keller

20   I Am for You

*July 27, 1924, letter from Helen Keller to Wisconsin Senator
and U.S. presidential candidate Robert La Follette, AFB.*

In 1924, Wisconsin Senator Robert La Follette received the presidential nomination of the Farmer-Labor ticket. A month later Keller publicly released this letter to him, apologizing for her tardiness, but explaining that she had hesitated to write. She feared what newspapers opposed to him would say about his political movement and its manipulation of her if she endorsed him publicly. Despite this, she figured publicly in the La Follette campaign by serving as "colonel" of the New York City "Fighting Bobs" (La Follette's campaign team)—a task that included numerous public appearances. She corresponded with both Robert and his wife Belle La Follette throughout the fall and spoke at La Follette events at least three times. After the La Follette campaign, however, her public activism on a wide range of issues diminished almost entirely. The frustration she felt was very real. Her detractors and political opponents succeeded in doing what her blindness and deafness had not. They robbed her of her political voice, denying her the full expression of citizenship.

Dear Senator Robert M. La Follette,

Unto you greetings and salutations and fealty! My congratulations are somewhat delayed; but if you know how my heart rejoiced when I heard of your nomination, my silence would not seem to you like indifference.

I have hesitated to write to you because I know that the newspaper opposed to the Progressive movement will cry out at the "pathetic exploitation of deaf and blind Helen Keller by the 'motley elements' who support La Follette." It would be difficult to imagine anything more fatuous and stupid than the attitude of the press toward anything I say on public affairs. So long as I confine my activities to social service and the blind, they compliment me extravagantly, call me "archpriestess of the sightless," "wonder woman" and "a modern miracle." But when it comes to a discussion of poverty, and I maintain that it is the result of wrong economics—that the industrial system under which we live is at the root of much of the physical deafness and blindness in the world—that is a different matter! It is laudable to give aid to the handicapped. Superficial charities make smooth the way of the prosperous; but to advocate that all human beings should have leisure and comfort, the decencies and refinements of life, is an Utopian dream, and one who seriously contemplates its realization must indeed be deaf, dumb and blind. As political speeches and editorials of our "best" papers are transmitted to me, I am amazed at the power which stops the ears and clouds the vision of society.

Please pardon this long personal preamble. It is rather out of place in a congratulatory letter, but it explains my silence on subjects which are of vital interest to me. Opposition does not discomfort me when it is open and honest. I do not mind having my ideas attacked and my aims opposed and ridiculed, but it is not fair fighting or good argument to find that "Helen Keller's mistakes spring out of the limitation of her development."

For years I have followed your public efforts with approval and admiration. I have often wished to write and express my interest in what you were doing, but have refrained for the reasons given above. Recently Mr. Leffingwell, a son of Wisconsin and an enthusiastic friend of yours, happened to be calling here. When it was revealed that I was a La Follette woman, Mr. Leffingwell urged me to write to you. I am emboldened to follow his suggestion because of God's commandment to "bring forth the blind people that have eyes and the deaf that have ears."

I rejoiced that a sufficient number of thinking Americans have come to the conclusion, after many trials and tribulations, that you are the man of the hour—the man most capable of breaking the power of private monopoly and leading the people to victory. Your nomination at Cleveland was in the nature of a gesture toward the readoption of the Declaration of Independence. The revolt of thoughtful Democrats and Republicans against innumerable blunders and obvious incompetence of their own parties is the sure sign of a new spirit in the nation. I believe we have heard the swan song of the old parties. The muddling of their leaders has brought the world to the brink of chaos. The progressives insist upon taking matters into their own hands. They see that the government must be revitalized.

I am for you because you have courage and vision and unyielding determination to find a sensible, just way out of the evils which threaten this country. I am for you because you have a forward-looking mind. You are alive, and have a grip on live issues. When I think of you, I do not need to go back to dead statesmen for inspiration or dig out of books ideals for which I am willing to make sacrifices. You have principles you are ready to fight for, to risk your life for. Your golden age is not behind you, but just ahead of you, and to be reached in the future.

I am for you because you stand for liberty and progressive government. You know that a constitution, however admirable, cannot be final as an effectual guide to conduct in the ever shifting circumstances of a rapidly developing nation which is ever touching elbows with the rest of the world.

I am for you because you believe that the people should rule, and that the voters should have assured and effective freedom of choice of those who make and execute the laws. I am for you because you believe that labor should participate in public affairs. The aim of all government should be to secure for the workers as large a share as possible of the fruits of their toil. For is it not labor that creates all things?

I am for you because you have held fast to the three elements of human liberty—free speech, a free press and freedom of assemblage.

You understand that to sweep away the right of the people by legislation and force is not progress, is not justice, but is decadence.

I am for you because you have discernment, and perceive that the ills from which America is now suffering are economic rather than political. You realize that the curtailment and limitation of wealth and special privilege are essential to the building up of honest government.

I am for you because you represent the spirit of kindly consideration by every American toward all his fellow men. You believe in peaceable methods of settling differences—in open discussion and the method of friendship as opposed to intolerance, hatred and violence. You stand for an enlightened world policy, for international cooperation and amity.

  Sincerely yours,
  Helen Keller

C Friendships, Intimacies, and the Everyday

21 Again in Working Order

December 7, 1901, letter from Helen Keller to John Hitz, AFB.

Once Keller enrolled at Radcliffe, John Hitz clearly continued to provide household assistance to Keller and Sullivan. He also continued to serve as an audience for her concerns about Sullivan's eyes and her joys about college. The article Keller refers to is most likely the initial piece that grew to be the 1903 *Story of My Life*.

Dear Mr. Hitz,

The watches came two days ago, and we thank you ever so much for having them fixed. It is *good* to have them again in working order. Will you please send the watch maker's bill?

We are delighted to hear that you are so well, and we do hope you will keep as well through the winter.

Another pleasure has lately found its way into our little home. Teacher has rented a piano and a pianola! Isn't that lovely? She will now have something to enjoy in the long evenings, when she cannot use her eyes. I can play the pianola a little myself, and we have great fun with it.

I am still in the throes of completing the "article," so I will make this note very short. With dear love from us both, I am,

Affectionately your friend,
Helen Keller

22 Some Nice Young Men

March 3, 1902, letter from Helen Keller to Kate Keller, AFB.

Keller savored the friends she made while at Radcliffe. Never before, at home in Tuscumbia or in Boston at Perkins, had she developed intimate friendships outside of Anne Sullivan (with whom she was still in the process of becoming a compatriot rather than a pupil). These included Harvard geology student Philip Smith and his wife Lenore. Keller particularly appreciated Lenore because she could finger-spell proficiently and would occasionally provide respite for Sullivan. This couple figured even more prominently in Keller's future because they shared a boarding house with John Macy, and introduced the man who would become Anne Sullivan's husband and Keller's editor to the already-famous duo.

This 1902 letter also reflects Keller's pride and frustration at writing what would become her incredibly successful autobiography, as she became increasingly aware that she and Sullivan would and did need economic sustenance of some kind. As she became an adult and philanthropists grew less likely to support her, economic tensions would continue to exacerbate.

Dearest Mother;

Yes, I neglect my home letters sadly; but the fret and worry that the "Home Journal" article has caused us all has made me feel quite disinclined to write. Except for the prospect of getting enough money to have you and the children with me in a cosy home, I should quit the whole business. I have succeeded in covering the period of my life up to the year 1892, in four articles; but there are two or three more to write, and I dread "tackling" them because an account of studies with set tasks that everybody is familiar with sinks too easily into commonplace, and I haven't the gift of keeping the reader's interest from flagging. But this is a work of love, and the thought of the good that may come out of it gives me courage to go on to the end. Do you realize that I am receiving five hundred dollars for each additional article? I got $1000 for the first, you know, and if there are seven articles in all, I shall receive four thousand dollars—think of that!

Did Phillips get my letter? Well, the dog I told him about has been extremely troublesome. He is not trained, and his frolics are little better than horse-play. The other day he got out and killed four of Mr. Coolidge's hens! We are obliged to keep him chained, and that makes the poor fellow sad. He needs a doghouse; but when it comes, I hope we can manage him more easily. His heart is all right, but it is his utter want of education that makes all this trouble.

I told you, did I not, that Lenore and Phil Smith live near here. We see them often, and they are so happy and full of fun, it is good to be with them. They have brought some nice young men to see us. I like best Mr. Arnesberg, a neighbor of Mr. Wade's, who is very jolly, and yet is more like a girl than a man—in his gentleness, I mean, and Mr. Whitson, who has a fine tenor and sings with great animation. But I like none half as much as Mr. John Macy, Phil's dearest friend. He is one of the noblest men I ever knew—his nature is much the same as Dr. Bell's. He has been helping with my literary work since Christmas. He was an instructor in the English department at Harvard, and he is very bright; so in most cases we hearken to his advice as to an oracle. I think he enjoys our society, and I know we have every reason to be fond of him. I'll tell you more of him sometime.

We have had several parties, and have been out sleighing repeatedly. One night I invited the young people I just mentioned to ride with me, and a more gay time I never had! The moon was full, the air fresh and crisp, not too cold, and I enjoyed the crunch of the snow as the sleigh ran over it. Another time I rode with Mr. Brown, and we were pelted until the sleigh was nearly filled up with snowballs.

We think our investment will prove valuable. All the shares in the Boston Coal and Fuel Company have been sold, and they say that at the end of the year our stock will be as good as diamonds. So cheer up, mother mine, and do not let the boarding-house matter prey upon your mind. The lot will yet fall unto you in pleasant days. Mr. Brown has done a great deal for us. His own mine, the Fanny Maria gold-mine, is not paying yet; but he gave us each two thousand shares in it, and that will be valuable too by and by. And that is not all. He put in the five hundred dollars I received from the "journal" people a short time ago, at one dollar per share, when the price was one dollar and a half. In order to satisfy our friends, and to avoid all risks, he promised that he personally would pay back our money in case the mine proves unsuccessful. He has also had a telephone put in for us. Now; is Mr. Brown not lovely?

I am sorry Uncle Cranworth is not well, but it surprises me that Aunt Corinne should need you, and you so busy too. Are not her little boys well?

I am much excited over the battle of Klerkedorp. I admired the Boers, but now I marvel at their heroism!

Well, I must stop;

> for every one business and desire,
> such as it is, and for my own poor part,
> look you, I will so write![1]

Affectionately your child,
Helen Keller

23 I Am Very Sorry, Dear Mother

May 12, 1902, letter from Helen Keller to Kate Keller, AFB.

Keller's family obviously did not respond favorably to what was said about them in the articles that became *The Story of My Life*. In this letter Keller responds with sadness and defensiveness to what was obviously a strong scolding from her mother. She speculates that perhaps philanthropist William Wade was behind her mother's complaints (see also document 1). This document provides a unique perspective on the best-selling autobiography and its content, including her stories about Martha Washington.

Dearest Mother;

We came home last night from a visit to a friend at Northampton, very tired indeed, and I found your letter awaiting me. It distresses me terribly to know that I have written anything in my biography to pain you, dear mother. I did not know that I had said a word which would lead anybody to think that my family were unkind to me, or that I was denied any privilege in my father's house. I thought I had made it plain that you were my refuge in those dark days. I recall vividly the unhappiness of my early years—an unhappiness which no tenderness could alleviate, except through the medium of language, which opens a world of love and teaches us to dwell in the shadow of God's wing and find it a sweet heaven of content.

I remember distinctly many naughty things I did of which I have said nothing. I remember how I pinched my dear grandmother's arm whenever I came near her; but I did not mention it because I feared it would hurt you. I also remember how I used to break things when I was in a temper, especially my dolls and the dishes; and how, when my teacher first tried to give me lessons, I kicked and scratched her like a veritable little savage. I have not forgotten the day I broke the little table in our room all to pieces, and do you not remember that you whipped me for it? I am glad you did. And have you forgotten the day I struck my teacher and broke her tooth! I recall all these things perfectly. Indeed, there is nothing in the articles which you or Aunt Ev or Cousin Leila has not told me many times. But I am very sorry, dear mother, that these memories distress you. I do not think, however, it would have been right to leave them all out of my story.

Of course I invented slight details of description. I gave the little negro girl I used to play with Martha Washington because I could not remember her real name, and that seemed a characteristic name for a darky.

I have not seen the first article since before Christmas; so I do not understand what you mean by saying that I make Mildred so much older than she is. Of course I have not forgotten her birthday, or dear little Phillip's existence. We had nothing at all to do with the illustrations, which explains his picture not being out with mine. You must know, mother, that the articles are hurriedly written, in the midst of my other work, and it is natural that I should make many slips; but they will be carefully revised before they go into the book.

My heart is heavy. I wish I had not undertaken to write the articles at all. I did so in the hope that some day I should be able to repay you in a small part for the love and tenderness you lavished upon me in the days since your cup of sorrow was full to overflowing. And in your last letter you made me glad by saying, "It was worth all the suffering of those days to have you speak so lovingly of me." What has changed you?

I cannot help thinking that Mr. Wade has been writing to you about the matter of making the task of teaching deaf and blind children harder by telling the difficulties that beset my early education. It seems to me, Mr. Wade is as wrong in this as in many other things. He is no true educator, in fact, he knows nothing about education, and those who know the difficulties of teaching the deaf laugh at his ignorance. But I will not write any more now, my heart is so sad.

Your loving child,
Helen Keller

24 I Shall Not Lose Her, and I Shall Gain a Brother

April 7, 1905, letter from Helen Keller to Alexander Graham Bell.
Alexander Graham Bell Family Papers, Library of Congress,
box 131. Copyright dedicated to the public.

In this letter from Wrentham, Massachusetts, Keller shares her joy at the upcoming May marriage of Anne Sullivan and John Macy with her long-time counselor Alexander Graham Bell. Though the marriage would deteriorate completely within ten years, Keller is optimistic that it would bring only happiness to all three of them. They purchased land and settled in Wrentham near the cottage that Keller and Sullivan had been renting sporadically for several years. In her 1929 book *Midstream,* Keller recalled these early years at Wrentham with incredible fondness despite its eventual sadness: "I can never quite accustom myself to the vicissitudes of life, but, despite the shadows upon it, both my teacher and I feel that all that was loveliest in the Wrentham days is ours forever."[2] For her further reflections on the early marital years at Wrentham, see document 39.

Dear Mr. Bell,

I know you are wondering how I like the new turn our affairs have taken. I am delighted that Teacher is to be married, and to such a dear, good friend as Mr. Macy too. I have always wanted just this thing to happen to her. But she has often said, "I shall never marry," and laughed to think I should entertain such idle hope. Like Benedick she did not know what the future held in store for her when she declared that she would die a maiden. But now the long wished-for happiness has come, and I never cease to rejoice with her. I am very fond of John (that is Mr. Macy). He is kind and helpful to every one, and has a personal care of me which I love. Besides, he is cheery and good-natured, and home is most truly home when he returns from town of evenings full of news.

Teacher will be married on May 3rd, and Dr. Edward E. Hale is to perform the ceremony. It will be a quiet wedding. They decided not to send out invitations because there would be so many people to ask, and Teacher has no one to help her out with a large affair, and if she undertook it herself, she would be worn out. So only Mr. Macy's family, my mother and a few of Teacher's dearest friends are to be present. I suppose I shall "give away" the bride. You see, she belongs to me more than to any one else in the world. But I shall not lose her, and I shall also gain a brother, and thus I shall be twice blest in giving and in receiving.

Please give my love to Mrs. Bell and Daisy. We are delighted to know of her new happiness, and our warmest wishes for a life rich in everything good and precious are hers. I should not have filled this letter with ourselves, except that I want you to understand what a beautiful joy has come to me.

Affectionately your friend,
Helen Keller

25 To Fight My Battles Without Further Help

December 14, 1910, letter from Helen Keller to Andrew Carnegie, AFB.

Keller valued her wage work as a writer and public speaker. Like other advocates for blind people throughout the twentieth century, she sought to refute the biases that blind people were incapable of paid employment and therefore incompetent for full citizenship. Increasingly she argued that work was essential for herself and other people with disabilities if they were to advance personally and as a group, though she focused almost exclusively on blind people. Work was their salvation. Work would raise blind people from dependence to usefulness. By this argument, she distinguished herself from the many unemployed blind people, devalued by society as unproductive and dependent.

When Andrew Carnegie offered her a regular pension income in 1910, she turned him down, clearly hoping that she, John, and Anne Macy could support themselves despite continued economic difficulties. Perhaps she was uneasy accepting cash from one of the nation's wealthiest industrialists while she attacked capitalism. She had joined the Socialist Party the year before and increasingly targeted capitalism. Perhaps she was uneasy with the dependence and all it might demand. She wrote to Carnegie that she needed to make it on her own and hoped that the self-made industrialist would understand. Keller wrote fairly extensively about this in *Midstream* (1929), chapter 9.

Dear Sir:

I am deeply touched by the generous offer which you and Mrs. Carnegie have made to me through Mrs. Fuller. I appreciate the beautiful spirit in which you have done this for me. Your sympathy is most precious, and it fills me with tender pride to know that I have won your respect. Your belief that the highest worship of God is service to man I shall make my own, and I shall count it a very precious gift indeed. I have read much and heard much from my friends of your munificent endowments of institutions for the advancement of the human spirit, and the thought that you regard me as an instrument in the work which you are doing brings me sincere happiness.

This sense of happiness triumphs over the grief that I feel because I must tell you that I cannot accept your gift. It is a grief because my acceptance would fulfil your pleasure, and because my refusal will give pain to my dear friend Mrs. Fuller.

I have known her since I was a little girl. She has been my teacher's staunch friend and admirer. She has stood by us in our triumphs and our failures. Recently she came to our house, and she seems to have been impressed by the lack of certain advantages which she thinks we should have. She declared that she would do something for us, and silently she has carried out her plan. I did not dream of her writing to you or to any one else in my behalf.

Your kindness gives me the right to explain to you my circumstances. I realize that a large sum of money would broaden my work and increase my pleasures. But my kind friends have given me the necessary equipment—education, books and a house to live in. I lack no essential comfort. There are many things which I should be happy to do for others if I had more money. But is this not true of most human beings, that they wish for what they have not? Are there not millions of deserving people who would like just a little more, so that they might increase the joy in the lives of their dear ones? But we millions cannot have this little more. I hope to enlarge my life and work by my own efforts, and you, sir, who have won prosperity from small beginnings will uphold me in my decision to fight my battles without further help than I am now receiving from loyal friends and a generous world.

I rejoice to hear how nobly you are promoting the cause of peace in the world. My life lives in the happiness of those who shall benefit by the growing, warm-hearted peace which fosters and develops. My joys and sorrows are bound up indissolubly with the joys and sorrows of my fellowmen, and I feel far more blessed to see them receiving new opportunities, better tolls with which to do their work, than I could feel if I received more for myself when I already have a fair share, and millions have less than their rightful portion.

With sincere messages of [undecipherable] to you and Mrs. Carnegie.

Helen Keller

26 To Enliven Things a Bit

January 24, 1911, letter from Helen Keller to Kate Keller, AFB.

While the trio of John Macy, Anne Sullivan Macy and Keller continued life at Wrentham, Keller continued her efforts to support the household by writing. Publishers generally wanted nothing but her reflections on disability, while she sought to write on a variety of political and social topics. This newsy note to her mother gives a glimpse into the daily life of the household, but ignores the growing tensions between Anne and John.

Dearest Mother:

I've been so distraught with work that two or three weeks have passed without my writing to you. But I'm all right, I don't feel any the worse for the rush. Indeed, I feel better than I have since I left college.

I've looked over and sent off the greater part of the matter for the April number of the Ziegler magazine.[3] Then the literary work which I'm trying to do has proved something of an elephant on my hands.

What do you think? A minister, who was a friend of Dr. Hale's, has just written to ask me for "a history of the stone wall!"[4] He wants to know where it was built, and when the Puritans built it, and whether it is a wall surrounding a church. Did you ever!

We're trying to enliven things a bit. Maude and Teacher invite each other to card-parties now and then. We had one here last Saturday night, and about thirteen people came. We had ordered some beer; but it didn't make its appearance. There was a lot of jollying over it. Mr. Farrington said he'd go home. So when everyone had come, Teacher exclaimed, "Now I wish we had sold the house." Mr. Blatchford was among the guests. We're going to have another party tomorrow night, and beer too, or nothing. Tonight Miss Proctor and Mr. Weaver are going to sup with us. We all intend to go to the theatre Saturday afternoon. About two weeks ago Teacher, John and Maude went to see "The Return of Peter Grimm," in which Mr. Warfield had the chief part, I think. I couldn't go out that day: but they told me it was a dear, touching little play.

Really this weather is preposterous. One day the thermometer drops to zero, and the next it jumps up to forty or fifty. Sometimes we walk as far as the Pond woods. They are really beautiful in sheltered spots. The pines are just as green as in summer. We gather handfuls of bright laurel and moss which have lived bravely through the season.

Yesterday Teacher was in Boston, and she saw a fine market—a regular spring in advance. There were new vegetables, tomatoes, strawberries, melons, and all kinds of lovely flowers. I wish you could have been there too.

When are you ever coming back? You say "very soon"; but it seems to me that like Mr. Micawber[5] you're waiting infinitely for something to turn up.

With dear love from us all, I am,
  Your affectionate child,
  Helen Keller

27 Blundered So Grievously as to Love Me

October 5, 1912, letter from Helen Keller to Anne Sullivan Macy, AFB.

In the fall of 1912, Anne Sullivan Macy underwent major surgery and hospitalization considered life-threatening.[6] Though she and John were already separated, he joined her in the hospital. Keller stayed with her dear friends Philip and Lenore Smith. While she wrote cheerfully to Anne, the separation between the two was rare and undoubtedly caused stress heightened by her concern for Anne's health. Additionally, the Smiths considered Keller's socialist convictions, the expression of which were at their height in this period, quite mistaken and this frustrated Keller.

Clearly, Keller felt herself a burden to the Smiths, though they welcomed her. She drew comfort from R. L. Montgomery's *Anne of Green Gables* (1908), in which she saw the main character Anne as "such a splendid mirror in which to see myself as I shouldn't be" and found "wiser counsel in meeting the trials and discouragements I run up against."

Dearest Teacher:

Let me try to give you some idea of what is going on here just now. We're all in a perfect whirl, as Lenore is getting ready for the winter.

A man and a woman have come to help clean up, and such bustle and helter-skelter activity as this is really amusing. All windows are flung open, and everything that has been put away is being brought out again. Rolled-up rugs are lying around, making a sort of obstacle race in every hall and room. Furniture which has been repaired and polished is being carried upstairs, and Lenore is exulting over her success in getting it fixed so nicely. I know her walnut bureau and bedstead, which she sent to be made over, are handsome! Their beautiful browns are brought out well, she says, and the new gray paper on the walls renders the effect still more pleasing. The silver is being put back in the sideboard, and Lenore is putting up portieres and sewing on silk curtains. And every time she begins to do something, the phone rings. She can't speak to me or sit down to eat or give orders or rest a minute but that little demon of a bell sends her flying down-stairs or across the hall from the farthest part of the house. The floors are being waxed, and chairs, tables and ornaments are finding their way gradually into the house. It will soon be easy for me to go about the house alone, as there will be things all around to guide me.

Dear me! I am interrupted in every sentence that I write you this morning. Here is Lenore telling me that we are to go automobiling with a friend of hers, Mr. Fenning tomorrow afternoon. Gracious, here she comes again with a telephone message from Miss Marion Campbell URGING me to come to the last meeting of some kind of congress for the study of speech in deficient children. Miss C. wants me to come tomorrow afternoon. I reply no, with sincere regrets. I really know nothing about the matter, and they didn't make arrangements for me to go in time. I don't say this of course; but Miss C. explains that she sent me that long telegram a week ago in a rush because they had had much trouble in arranging the programme. So now, we've a little peace, I hope.

Ah no! There they are once again! This time it is a Dr. Roberts telephoning that I must come this afternoon or to the meeting "just to show myself." Of course it is impossible for Lenore to go, and I say no most positively. Now he has talked steadily to her for ten minutes, and hardly let her go even though she is so terribly busy. Why, while she stood listening to him, in came a man with the silver from storage, and another man with furniture and another with questions about what to do next, and she could scarcely hear them. And all her trouble is on my poor account. She's just as sweet, jolly and communicative as can be, and her kindness in looking out for me is so touching, my eyes fill with tears. No matter how great the confusion may be, she runs in just to let me know "what's up," and I haven't asked her a single question either. Indeed, I'm studying how not to bother her. But alas! The more I do that, the more I seem to get in people's way. I'm a perpetual stumbling-block, a handicap, a hindrance, a hanger-on. Worse still, I'm a disturber of the peace, an upsetter of plans, "a tremendous burden," as you say, and the next thing I hear, I shall be a forlorn ghost crossing your path wherever you go. Don't you think you and my friends had better get together and decide in committee how to remove this human incubus?

Seriously, Lenore is as good and thoughtful of my happiness as you can wish. She is like mother, sister, companion and friend in one. She is eyes and ears for me, and I haven't asked a single thing of her. She thinks of what I want before I realize that I want it. It's wonderful, isn't it, to be so well loved, so well understood by those on whom one has no claim?

I've borrowed some books from the reading-room for the blind in the Congressional Library. Among them is "Anne of Green Gables" by R. L. Montgomery. Mark Twain said that Anne was the most lovable character in American fiction. Well, well, I agree with him that it is the most delightful book; but what do you think? I can't well join in saying such pleasant things about Anne. Can you ever guess why? Because she is—or I think she is my duplicate in many ways! I recognize in her nearly all my faults and deficiencies, most of my moods, impulses and secret thoughts. She is a great trial to others in the same way that I am, speaking in large terms. Like me she takes the joys and sorrows of life tremendously, and like me she has a passion for everything which "gives scope for imagination." Since you and John have blundered so grievously as to love me, you'd better read this book. It is amazing how many of my words and sentiments jump out of it and confront me, as it were. I have never had such a splendid mirror in which to see myself as I shouldn't be, nor have I found wiser counsel in meeting the trials and discouragements I run up against.

Goodnight to my dearest treasures upon earth.

Your and John's loving Helen

28 Perhaps a Little Bit Crestfallen

April 21, 1913, letter from Helen Keller
to Mr. and Mrs. Andrew Carnegie, AFB.

Money matters did not disappear and 1913 was a difficult year. Keller found it "a marvel" to live with her two fiercest critics—the married

John and Anne—to aid her in putting together a collection of political and social commentaries. *Out of the Dark* (1913), however, made little money. Critics panned the book and questioned her ability to develop valid social observations on her own. On top of everything else, the Macy marriage grew worse and John fled to Europe.

The need for money created a consistent tension between Keller's economic reliance on philanthropists and her personal desire for independence. Though she largely solicited for others rather than herself, tension always remained in between her lifelong appeals to wealthy philanthropists and her political critiques of capitalism. Her disability made class security slippery, so did her gender and Anne Macy's. By this point in their lives, neither could rely on a husband for money. Her political analysis included a critique of the poverty that accompanied capitalism, but she left no record of analyzing her own tenuous economic stance and the reasons for it. Her own claims to civic participation generally built on her ability to be economically independent, but this was undermined by the fact that she was not as economically self-sufficient as she desired and claimed to be.

Sometime during the spring when this letter was written, Carnegie, Macy, and Keller met for tea. He asked her it if was true that she had become a socialist. When she admitted it, he threatened to lay the thirty-three-year-old woman across his knees and spank her if she did not come to her "senses."[7] She received a Carnegie pension for decades but never wrote about her feelings on the matter.

Dear Mr. and Mrs. Carnegie,

I am writing to you both; for you are so intermingled in my thoughts that what I have to say goes by right to you both.

This is what I want to tell you. I have changed my mind about accepting your gift. I have just been through an experience which shows me how much I need help. When I first refused to let you help me, I was filled with the idea that I could succeed with such aid as I had received from other friends. I was ambitious to earn my own living and to make things easier for those that I love. But I did not understand until now that in order to carry out this idea I should have to lay another burden upon the dear shoulders of those who were already heavily burdened. The experience which I had last Thursday has opened my eyes to my true position. Each new experience in life is an encounter. There is a struggle—a cloud of dust, and we come out of it wiser, and perhaps a little bit crestfallen. I hope I have come out of this tussle a wiser woman.

Last Thursday my teacher and I lectured in Bath, Maine. After the lecture Mrs. Macy was taken ill. There was no one to help us in that dismal hotel, not even an intelligent maid. It was a disconcerting experience. An overpowering sense of my helplessness came over me. I understood then why our friends had insisted that we should have a competent woman with us. The time seems far distant when we shall be able to employ such an assistant without your help. When I reached home, I found an accumulation of letters which Mr. and Mrs. Macy had to read to me and answer. I was startled to find out how much they both had had to do for me all these years. I felt, as I had never felt before, the necessity of having a secretary to help me with some of my work. Our last words, as we were leaving your house, came back to me with a sense of great relief. "Remember," you said, "that we are your friends, and that we shall always be ready to help when you need us." I need your help now. It must needs be that I have a staff for my groping feet.

I have great faith in the genuineness of your kindness. Faith, you know, is the evidence of things unseen, though in this case I have had much to inspire it. You have been so wise and clear-seeing in many things, I am sure that you will be equally wise and clear-seeing in your interpretation of this letter. Already my burden is lighter. I feel anew the capacity to rise and meet my life. The staff has begun to put forth flowers. [You have been so wise and clear-seeing in many things, I am sure that you will be equally wise and clear-seeing in your interpretation of this letter.[8]]

Please tell Miss Margaret that her sweet note has made me happy.

With cordial messages from my teacher and myself, I am,

Sincerely yours,
Helen Keller

29 Have You Forgotten All

January 15 (possibly 25), 1914, letter from Helen Keller,
Appleton, Wisconsin, to John Macy, AFB.

From 1913 through 1920, Keller and Anne Sullivan Macy traveled almost constantly. Sometimes their new household companion Polly Thomson joined them, at other times they were accompanied by Keller's mother. Across the nation they went—in this case, Appleton, Wisconsin—attempting to raise funds by making public appearances and lectures for pay.

Keller's personal struggles with economic independence and her political identity occurred simultaneously with major household transitions. In 1914, John and Anne separated permanently. It was a lengthy process of counteraccusations that Helen characterized as Anne's "greatest sorrow." Understandably, no one dealt well with the locked rooms, tears, and innumerable letters, accusations, and counteraccusations flying among the *three* of them. Everything about the situation pained Keller. Anne, she wrote later, wept "as only women who are no longer cherished weep."[9] The lengthy and convoluted letters she wrote to John, such as the one below, in which she referred to his marriage while speaking fondly of the days in which "*we three* [italics added] seemed to feel in each other's handclasp a bit of heaven," probably did not help. This letter, in which she refers to herself using the nickname "Billy," makes clear that even Keller's mother Kate became involved in the marital debates.

Dear John,

Mother has read your letter to her to me from beginning to end. It has amazed me and filled my heart with sorrow. If you ever loved Teacher or me, I beseech you to be calm, fair, kind, to consider what you have said in that letter.

You are wrong, John, in thinking that Teacher has tried to influence me against you. She never has. She has always tried to make me see how very good and helpful you have been to us both. She has impressed it upon me that very few men would have endured my foolish tears, my fussy and exacting ways as you have all these years, and I love you for it. She never told me that she thought you pushed me out of my place at the table one night at the apartment until mother read it in your letter! I know you put me in a seat away from you: but I thought it natural that you should have Mrs. White beside you, as she was a guest, and I think so now. But it hurt Teacher to think that you would have any one else in my seat when I was to be home only a few days.

As to my voice, you know, John, and every one else knows that for twenty years we worked hard together to make it better. She never claimed to know anything about the science of the voice. She simply tried, as you yourself used to try, in every way possible to help me speak better, and I love her for it. Mr. White has often expressed to me in glowing words the warmest enthusiasm for her work, and his indignation that some people did not give her the credit for it. She gives him full credit in every lecture as a fine voice teacher, and she loves to do it. No, there has not been any "unintelligent nagging" or nagging of any kind about my voice. Please, please be fair, be just.

You say you can "never explain to me what your life with Teacher has been." I remember that in spite of many hard trials in the past we have had happy days, many of them, when we three seemed to feel in each other's handclasp a bit of heaven. Have you forgotten it all, that you should say such bitter things about my teacher, about her who has made my darkness beautiful and rent asunder the iron gates of silence. Have you forgotten all the sunshine, all the laughter, all the long walks, drives and jolly adventures, all the splendid books we read together. Have you forgotten how exultantly you used to say, after you had helped me with a difficult task; "There! We are happy now because we have a piece of faithful workmanship to show." Have you forgotten that at times, when we had all been impatient, you would say to me; "If we were not a trouble to each other, we could not love as we do."

I know how imperious, changeable and quick-tempered Teacher is. I have suffered just as much from those failings as you have: but my love for her has never wavered, never will. Perhaps she owes her success to some of those very failings. You know—you have often told me as much—that the education of a deaf blind child is a tremendous strain upon the faculties and the health of the teacher, and that only a few can stay with such a child more than a year or two. Only Teacher's splendid vigor has made it possible for her to stick to her colossal task during twenty-six years. Think of it!

You say that she "has never been a wife to you, or done any of the things that a woman might be expected to do." You know, we have shared everything we had with you. You have helped us in all our literary work, and all that has come from it has belonged to you as much as to us. You know, too, that you have dictated as freely as we have what ought to be done with any gains we have from our work, and we have looked up to you in all our problems, all our difficulties, all our undertakings. Do you remember that I refused to take lessons from Mr. Devol years ago because you so evidently disapproved of the plan. If you still think I am "dominated" by Teacher, this proves that you yourself have done it, and I love you none the less for it.

Again; Teacher does not like the lecturing: but she was glad to do it last year when she thought that some money would take you to Italy and give you the chance you desired. I copied all the letters she wrote to you last summer, often with her tears running over my hand. She really felt that she was doing and saying things to make you happy and bring you back to us again well and strong. And now you say that "she has played a game"—that she has been untrue to you!

Be careful, John, what you say. If you love me, as you tell mother you do, be careful. The world before which we three stand will certainly judge what we do and say, and I believe that the world will judge fairly of us, as it always has.

I know that in the past year Teacher has changed in some essential respects. By talking with her daily I have learned that you have helped her to see the world, the workers and economic, social and moral conditions as she never saw them before. Living so close to her as I do, I can prove, absolutely prove, that she has new aims, a new conviction, a new vision of life, a new ideal and a new inspiration to service, and you will know it too some day. Believe me, John, from this work the great jury of the world will pass its verdict upon her actions and sentiments, and upon yours. They will also say that this trouble is my affair; Teacher is my affair; you are my affair, just as all suffering humanity is my affair.

Now, dear, you have every one of Teacher's failings, as I can show you from my experience with you: and your letter has proved that you have more grievous ones than she has, and I still cherish you. When I first heard your letter, I thought you had destroyed my love for you.

Once you said you were a sworn foe to all who brought such charges against Teacher, and I thought I was too. But now I know you have not killed my love, and you never can. Does not love—true love—suffer all things, believe all things, hope all things, endure all things. Love suffers long and is patient. It gives without stint, without measure and asks for nothing in return. It expects only good from the dear one through all trials and disillusionments.[10] With such a love I cling to you, as I cling to Teacher. You and I are comrades journeying hand in hand to the end. When the way is dark, and the shadows fall, we draw closer.

Of course I do not ask you to give Teacher what you cannot give. Why should I. Why should any one. It is something over which you have no control. But you certainly did give us something better when you were in New York in December. You did more for us unexpectedly in little ways than ever before, and I knew then that you had a new, nobler feeling. Oh, John, recall that feeling, foster it more and more, give up everything for it, and believe me, undreamed sweetness and peace shall come into your life. It shall no longer seem to you "a poor life." I have lived to know that love which is love indeed casts out the ghosts of dead affections, dead hopes, wasted years and disappointed ambitions. Let your heart speak for "my Helen" as you so fondly call me, prompt you to exceed what you have thought you could do, match my love with your own for us both, as you once said you would. I have unfaltering faith in you. One day you asked me to trot in the same team with you, and now I ask you. Whether you choose to or not, I promise that you shall find me unchanged.

Affectionately,
"Billy"

30 Your Unkind and Altogether Unbrotherly Note

March 4, 1914, letter from Helen Keller to John Macy, AFB.

Throughout 1914, John and Anne Macy's marital debates and antagonisms continued, as did the interventions of Keller and her mother.

Keller clearly missed John. He was her friend, political conversant, and a much-needed editor. She described him as, next to Anne, "the friend who discovered most ways to give me pleasure and gratify my intellectual curiosity."[11] She clearly missed the connections he provided for her to the larger world of political radicalism—in this case, Industrial Workers of the World strike organizer and hero Arturo Giovannitti.

This letter is notable also for its mention of Peter Fagan. Employed in 1914 as John Macy's secretary, the finger-spelling socialist went on to make secret but unsuccessful plans with Keller to marry in November 1916 (see also document 39).

Dear John,

In Salt Lake City they were to pay us sixty percent of the gross receipts of the tickets and the cash got balled up somehow, and did not balance. After eleven o'clock last night Mr. Graham, the manager, came to our room with his troubles. He seemed to think Teacher ought to take less than the tickets showed she was entitled to. She refused, and suggested that he pay her the full amount subject to modification later. This he did: but he gave us a personal check because of course the banks were all closed, and we had to leave early in the morning before they opened. So Teacher sent the check and explanations to Mr. Glass. The amount paid was seven hundred and two dollars and ninety cents. These percentages are very annoying, and cause us much irritation.

I am writing on the train in the middle of a vast desert. There is nothing as far as the eye can see but yellow sand and sedge-grass and blue sky. It is as warm as summer, and the sand is sifting in the cracks and crevices. I shall be glad when we get out of Utah!

I have not written to you since I received your unkind and altogether unbrotherly note in St. Louis because my work was very hard, and I tried to keep unpleasant thoughts out of my mind all I could. Both mother and I feel that you are harsh and unreasonable, and unjust too.

You know, John, that you took that apartment in Boston because YOU wanted it, not because we did. You knew that we could not be in the apartment more than two weeks at the most: and yet you talk about "a scale of living based upon the fact of our being together!"

Your mind does not seem to be as honest and just as it used to be, or you could not write in that way.

You had no business to call me "a fook" [*sic*] as you did in your last letter to mother. You know that I am not a fool, and that it was directly in answer to what you said about Teacher's being ungenerous that I brought up the subject of money. You know me well enough to realize that I do not value money any more than you say you do. I have always been willing, glad to share with you, evenly or any way that pleased you, all I had. But do you think it is fair or generous or consistent to say you "hate our money," and in the very same letter to tell us that you deposited a thousand dollars of that "hated" money for yourself? It is all right for you to have the money. But it is mean thus to insult me.

You say "it was Annie, and not I, that wrecked us." If it was she, you DROVE her to it. Your first letter to mother showed that you did, and when the facts are known, everybody else will see it. You know also, I believe, that Teacher left the apartment that night because she had to in order to fulfill her contract. You are not, then, playing fair to lay all the blame upon her and take advantage of the necessity which forced her to go away that time. Apparently you are making circumstances fit in with your wishes. I imagine it is possible for a woman to tell her husband that she thinks they had better separate, without wishing to "leave his domicile."

As to your helping me in the future, how do you think we could work together with advantage when you keep saying that Teacher is dishonest, that you cannot be harassed by a woman whom you cannot trust, that she has lied and deceived you? Can you not see, John, that it was you who wrecked us? You are certainly not yourself, or you could not have brought yourself to write as you have, even if we had been in the wrong. Teacher has many faults, so have I, and so have you. But we are not irredeemable, I hope. I pity your blindness, and I suffer on.

This is intended to be my last letter on the subject of your relations to Teacher. Please do not think that she or mother wants me to write it. They do not.

I have not heard for many weeks about matters on which you always used to inform me so particularly—correspondence, opportunities to help in a good cause, Arturo's books and so forth. I understand that you have taken Mr. Fagan as secretary to attend to my correspondence.

Well, if you do not want to write yourself, why not let him write the home news, and so help me straighten out the many details which always come up when I return home? I love to be of use to others, and I do not let any one spare me in my tasks, and I never shall.

Lovingly,
Helen

31 How Alone and Unprepared I Often Feel

January 30, 1917, letter from Helen Keller to Anne Sullivan Macy, AFB.

Tumult was the norm for Keller and Macy in 1916. Keller's February donation and letter of support to the National Association for the Advancement of Colored People caused a public upheaval and family discord. In addition, Anne Macy suffered ill health, made worse by the continued marital discord and a relatively unsuccessful 1916 Chautauqua tour for the student and teacher duo. Doctors advised her rest, which she took alone in Lake Placid, New York, and then Puerto Rico. With Macy gone, Keller planned to spend several months with her widowed mother in Alabama, perhaps smoothing over their relationship. Before leaving, however, her relationship and intended marriage with Peter Fagan became public. Her extended family vigorously squashed the relationship with forced midnight train trips out of town, an angry and gun-waving brother, and drama worthy of a bad novel. All felt adamantly that marriage and child-bearing were not options for a deaf-blind woman. With this pressure she apparently acquiesced to the belief. Peter Fagan disappeared from her life.

While Anne Macy attempted to find solace in Puerto Rico, Keller found herself isolated in her mother's new community of Montgomery, Alabama. Everyone around her knew of the debated NAACP letter and of Peter Fagan. She left little self-analysis of the period for historians. Presumably, she grieved the loss of Fagan. Perhaps her family, Anne Macy's departure, the color line of Alabama, and the way so many misunderstood her disability angered her.

Writing to Macy in Puerto Rico, Keller's concern about her own future is palpable. Her desire to start life anew in simpler terms is similar to her

Helen Keller, 1887.

Helen Keller, 1893.

Wright Humason School for the Deaf students, 1895, New York. Keller is in the front left, looking right.

John Hitz.

Helen Keller, Anne Sullivan, and Alexander Graham Bell at Bell's home
in Nova Scotia, 1901.

Helen Keller at her typewriter in her Cambridge, Massachusetts, home while a student at Radcliffe, 1900.

Helen Keller upon graduation from Radcliffe, 1904.

Helen Keller at Wrentham, Massachusetts, 1909.

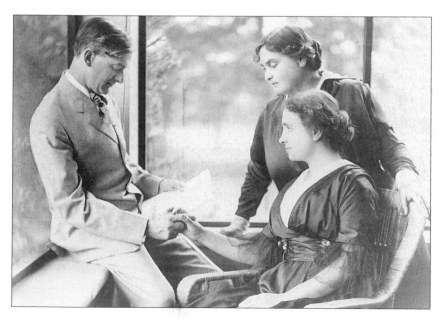

John Macy, Anne Sullivan Macy (top), and Helen Keller, 1914.

Phillips Keller (Keller's brother), Helen Keller, and Kate Keller, 1918.

Forest Hills, New York, party, circa 1919. This is most likely the party described in document 33. Keller is in the middle row, third from the right.

desire expressed in 1899 to John Hitz (document 6): "How I wish we could slip away, and live in the peaceful country for a year, at least, away from every one we know and just be happy, and free from care and anxiety!"

Dearest Teacher:

Your braille letter came just after I had received Polly's; but I didn't answer it, as I had to hurry off mine for the New York boat.

I hope you've had no trouble with those checks. Can you not suggest a way out of our present difficulty? Speaking of checks, it reminds me, I have one or two plain questions to ask you. If anything should happen to you suddenly, to whom would you wish me to turn for help in business matters? How could I best protect myself against any one who might not be honest or reliable? Mother loves me with a deep, silent love; but in all probability she will not be with me constantly.

Another thing, if you should be taken from me, or be unable to attend to our affairs, what should I do with all our papers? Whom could I trust to go over them with me? I hate to worry you with all these questions; but I know enough to realize my dependence upon others, and I try to think, plan and consult you so that I may find the right person or persons to depend upon. Oh, Teacher, how alone and unprepared I often feel, especially when I wake in the night! Please don't think, however, that I let this problem weight upon my mind more than I can help. The wonder is, Oh don't worry anymore. Look at Madame Galeron, the deaf blind poet. She has had her gifted father, her husband, her grown-up daughter, several able friends to help her in emergencies, and here you and I are with no thing settled! Won't you try to consider these problems calmly, while you listen to the wind rustling in the palms and breathe deeply the heavenly air you love, then write me what you think best. I need suggestions that you can make now while you are free and can think quietly.

How I long to be with you among the wild-flowers and the palms, in the bosom of the hills!

> I am sick of four walls and a ceiling,
> I have need of the sky,
> I have business with the grass.[12]

But hadn't we better wait and see how you feel before mother and I think of coming? You said it would be some time before you were good for much. I fear that if we came now, you would not have the rest and freedom you should have.

But I do think that when you are better, we must start our life over again, reducing it to the simplest terms possible. (Of course the simple life doesn't exclude a few modern conveniences, or machinery that turns drudgery into joyous activity.) We can travel more as we like without lecturing, and we can see some of our friends! We can bring about this change anywhere in Wrentham, or Porto [sic] Rico, or the Sandwich Islands. All we need is courage to do the sensible thing. Don't you dare tell me it's too late! You've just shown that you aren't yet old or fixed in your ways, you still have a heart to dare and to achieve. Only get well, let us try this scheme and work afresh, or have a life holiday, as the Fates may decree. I know it will work out right if we go at it right.

I'm keeping this letter until I see if yours comes tomorrow. With old love and new, pioneering thoughts, and with the vehement prayer that you may be getting better soon, I am

        Your affectionate,

        Helen

P.S. Polly's last note came this morning. I've just sent off the deed to Mr. Raymond with my signature and told him what you wished me to do about the coupons. We'll read the letters when we get a chance. We are busy preparing for a party this afternoon, Mildred has to entertain her card-club this Wednesday.

        H.K.

32 The Cruelty of Society Shakes Me so Violently

March 1, 1917, letter from Helen Keller to Anne Sullivan Macy, AFB.

While Macy remained in Puerto Rico and Keller in Montgomery, Alabama with her sister Mildred Tyson (whose daughter Katharine was called "Merry Sunshine"), Keller had few with whom to speak politics.

Despite the active social life of Montgomery, she missed Anne. Her letters provide evidence that she continued to read widely.

In this letter Keller repeats the opposition to World War I that she had expressed elsewhere. She had encouraged the purchase of war bonds once World War I began, but like the Industrial Workers of the World she continually criticized the war as a profit-making venture for military industrialists. The workers, she said, "suffer all the miseries [of war], while the rulers reap the rewards." In 1915, she had warned a crowd of 2,000 cheering socialists that the army had "already proved itself an enemy of liberty" by involvement in strike breaking and urged workingmen to "destroy the war of the trenches."[13] In 1916, she turned instead to the radical IWW because "the Socialist party was too slow. It is sinking in a political bog." It risked its "revolutionary character" by relying on electoral politics.[14]

Dear Teacher:

At last we are through with the repairs. The shades and pictures have gone up, and the rugs down. Some of the furniture had to be sent off to be cleaned; but Mildred's home looks bright and pretty again. We celebrated by having a nice luncheon Saturday for our friend from Florence, Miss Kate Jones, now Mrs. Moore. Among the guests were Marjorie, Mrs. Walker, Miss Mary Johnston and Mrs. Mapes. It was all gay chatter. The food was dainty—caviar sandwiches peppered with onion, olive and egg, bouillion flavored with lemon, birds, oysters cooked in celery sauce, baked apples with preserved cherries, grapefruit salad and pecans, fruit ice cream and two kinds of cake. I almost forgot the cocktails. Now am I not tempting you away from the simple life?

Mrs. Moore told me about her little girl three years old. Some one said to the baby, "Will you be good?" and she said, "Gosh, no!"

Have you read the report that, in the extremity, and after all peace efforts have failed, Henry Ford has offered his plant at Detroit for the Government to use in any way it sees fit? He has also offered his services and the loan to the Government, without interest, of a hundred million dollars, if it is necessary. There were several articles about him by John Reed reprinted in the Ziegler. They made me feel more than ever the greatness of my privilege in knowing the miracle worker of American Industry.

We are being blockaded according to the latest bulletins; but I can't get excited over it. I can't see the difference between a German and a British blockade, except that one is under the sea and the other on top. I feel that we shall not actually go to war for some time. President Wilson is playing for time.

Teacher, I am going to remain faithful unto the death, with God's help, in my social beliefs; but I am thoroughly angry with the American Socialist Party, and I am tempted to break with it. Its apostasy is grievous. It has turned traitor to the workers by saying that it opposes the class war. And the motion to call for a strike against war has been voted down! Shame upon those who wear the mask of Socialism! But I must be brave and loving in my public as well as my private life; so I shall stick by the workers, no matter what they do.

Doesn't it seem a travesty to read of our Treasury being filled with gold, while starving people march up and down Fifth Avenue with the terrible, unanswerable cry, "Bread, bread, bread!" I tell you, it was more tolerable for Sodom and Gomorrah than it will be for New York, that magnificent monument of the stupidity of man, when the whirlwinds of revolution sweep over it. They delay day after day to have a million dollars appropriated for supplies, while the children of Eastside are dying by hundreds. But enough of this, or you'll forget your fairy isle. Forgive this outburst, the cruelty of society shakes me so violently when I'm disposed to be quiet and asleep.

Merry Sunshine is perseveringly learning to write and read, although we don't think it necessary yet. Think of Dickens' delicious account of a child's clumsy, zigzagging, higgledy-piggledy handwriting, and you'll have a picture of Katharine's. Last night she asked mother to show her how to write "My heart is yours." I suppose she read these words on one of her Valentines.

Mildred and I have just come in from a long walk. We went out into the suburbs, and Mildred stopped to show me a curious house literally covered with sea-shells of all colors and shapes. There is a story that a sea captain from Mobile built that house, and had car-loads of shells brought to decorate it, and thus give him the happy illusion of nearness to his beloved ocean. Who he was, or why he came to Montgomery, no one seems to know.

Hoping you continue to improve,
    Every affectionately yours,
    Helen

33 Manifold Demands, Requests and Interruptions

July 8, 1919, letter from Helen Keller to Kate Keller, AFB.

In October 1917, Keller and Anne Sullivan Macy sold their beloved home at Wrentham and purchased a home in then-rural Forest Hills, New York. As this letter shows, however, they still had friends—even Thora, the dog—in Wrentham and visited on occasion. Friends in New York included Ned Holmes, an architect and inventor they had known from Cambridge days. Economic stresses continued to plague the household. Keller had hopes, however, that the future sale of her upcoming Hollywood film *Deliverance* would stave off the creditors.

Dearest Mother,

I have not written before because we have all been distracted by manifold demands, requests and interruptions. Finally we ran way for a few days' rest, and returned only last night.

I had a lovely birthday. It was a complete, overwhelming surprise. I had not had the slightest suspicion of the great preparations which were being made. I had begged Teacher to let us spend the day in a quiet, cosy [sic] way, and she had said "All right," and so we did. Friday morning Rebecca called, and brought me a present—dark blue beads that matched my new dress beautifully. Elizabeth Garrett (my blind friend) came to dinner with us, and we had a jolly time.

But the next day, when I went down-stairs, expecting only to find a caller, I was greeted with an avalanche of handshakes and good wishes from twenty-seven friends—deaf people who had come to spend the afternoon with me. Before I had recovered my breath, they hurried me out on the lawn, and lo, there stood a screened tent which Teacher had had fixed up for sleeping nights. We chatted, laughed, drank punch, ate, and ate again, and everybody seemed thoroughly happy. I received a shower of presents—handkerchiefs, candies, gloves, flowers and a very pretty chain of pink beads.

Mildred's and your remembrance came a day or two before the party. The night-gown is lovely, mother. We have all enjoyed the delicious peanut brittle. The fan came afterwards just when the weather was hottest, and made it a timely and welcome gift.

Poor Teacher and Polly were quite tired out with the picnic and the demands made upon them. So we decided to tell everybody we were going off for a three months' motor trip. As a matter of fact, we went to Boston to see John. He has been very ill, and we were much worried about him. He looked dreadfully, and seemed like a feeble old man. Something went wrong with his back, and that with the heat "knocked him out" as he expressed it. He said he would come back to New York as soon as he got back some strength.

We also went to Wrentham, and saw some of our old friends. Mr. Farrington had gone away on his vacation. We saw Miss Brastow, and she told us lots of news. Anna Walker has eloped with a handsome aviator. Dr. Vogel is married again. Walter Armsby has taken a house for his wife at Sharon. They say he isn't there much. I'm sorry if they are unhappy. Dr. Brastow has some trouble with his hip, and is very cross and troublesome. I pity Miss Brastow, she has had such a trying life looking after those men folk. Poor Miss Wilkinson is quite crazy now. She lives all alone, and the neighbors are afraid the house will fall down upon her, it is so dilapidated. Mr. Page is paralyzed, and Mrs. Page has had a severe operation for hernia. She was carrying out a basket of clothes, and she fell into a hole and tore herself badly. Oh dear, oh dear, so much ill luck in the world! I wonder why there is so much more pain than joy.

I thought I could visit the old Wrentham place again with some equanimity; but alas!—As we came away, I just sobbed aloud, greatly to my own mortification. The place is beautiful, mother. They keep up the flowers, the evergreens and everything else splendidly. They have six cows, and are building a two thousand dollar piggery. They have their own eggs, milk and butter. Thora looked fine, and knew us the minute she heard our voices. She insisted on getting into our car and coming away with us.

Ned Holmes drove the car. He is still here. His invention is finished, except for a touch or two, and he expects to see Commander Read shortly. (That is, the man who flew across the Atlantic.) Experts think Ned's "path-finder" will revolutionize flying. If Read thinks so, Ned's fortune will be made, and his name will be written across the sky.

We don't know what has become of Elsie. We sent "Pussy-Willow" a Good Fairy at Christmas-time; but neither she or Elsie has ever acknowledged it. When we saw them last summer, they were going to move. I suppose they have. Ned hears nothing from them. Oh, how sick and weary I am of those unhappy domestic upheavals! I shall be glad when we are left alone again in the peace of our little home.

I will write more later; but today I'm awfully tired after the trip. I do hope the poor babies are better, and will soon recover entirely. I can't be easy until I know they are all well. Mildred must be worn out with it all. I hope she can get away to the seashore or the mountains and rest a little. Please, please don't cut the grass again, mother! If you do, I shall have to come and bring you here to your other home and keep an Argus watch upon you.

With love from us all, I am,

    Your affectionate child,

    Helen Keller

P.S. We had very little definite information about the picture until two weeks ago when in desperation Ned called upon Mr. Schubert. You may not know that it is more difficult to see Mr. Schubert than the President of the United States—or even the Mikado of Japan. Ned was permitted to talk with Mr. S. only two minutes and a half. He learned that the picture had been sold, and that it would open in Schubert's Broadway theatre next October. That means we shall not receive our payment until then. We have been frightfully "hard up," mother. I don't remember a time since college days when we were so much "up against it." But we shall manage all right. Our credit is good, and people understand. Everyone believes in the success of the picture, and that keeps them quiet and contented because they know they will receive their money eventually.

    H.K.

34 Among the Hills in Los Angeles

September 13, 1918, letter from Helen Keller to Lenore Smith, AFB.

Life satisfied neither Keller nor Macy during the war and postwar period as each strained for personal, economic, and professional stability. Seeking money, both agreed to a Hollywood production of Keller's life, *Deliverance*, in 1919. While they were in Hollywood, stage hands and actors struck, forcing her to make her political and class stance less theoretical. The media swarmed when she threatened not to appear at the premiere unless the strikers' cause advanced. Studios strongly hawked the film along with publicity photos of Keller, Macy, and Hollywood stars Mary Pickford, Douglas Fairbanks, and Charlie Chaplin. The opening of *Deliverance* was to be a major event. Fortunately for the financial backers of the film, union and studio mediations began before the movie's premiere. That Keller influenced the strike outcome is unlikely. In chapter 12 of her 1929 biography *Midstream,* she wrote a lengthy description of the filming.

Dear Lenore,

Your letter found us way out here among the hills in Los Angeles. It did our hearts good to hear from you again, and to have such pleasant news too. Since I had written to you last, we had wondered what kept you silent so long, and only an unusual rush of events and tasks prevented me from sending you another letter before we left New York last July. How we should have loved to visit you and the children at the camp—It would have seemed much like the old days at the lake in Wrentham when we were all so gay and happy.

Well, well, the unexpected is always happening to us. We were living quietly in Forest Hills, trying to content ourselves with some pleasures and a few opportunities to help others when lo, the winds of destiny blew us out here. Some one came and said, "Why not make a motion picture of the story of Helen Keller's life? It may mean great help and encouragement to the brave boys blinded in this war." We looked into the matter, and the die was cast. A corporation called "The Helen Keller Film Company" was formed in June, (the president is Dr. Francis Miller, the historian and economist) and we all came here in July so as to have the best weather conditions for production. Can you imagine me in a "movie"? I thought I had worked hard enough writing my story, whose rather troubled genesis you witnessed at the house on Coolidge Avenue, and here we are trying to pull off a photographic story which doesn't look much like anything that ever befell any of us—Of course Teacher and I are no longer as young and fresh as we were, and there must be substitutes in the early part of the picture dream. Florence Roberts, a lovely child who has played in "The Bluebird," is acting my part as a little girl, and we are all charmed with her—but they say her picture doesn't look blind, though she keeps her eyes shut. There is a sweet girl from Virginia impersonating me when I was eighteen, and she is so graceful, I wish I had been born in her place. I can't say much about Teacher's substitute. I'm afraid she hasn't the imagination and force required to play the part of such a strong, original, helpful personality as Teacher's. But, knowing nothing about "movies," I can judge only from what the comments [sic] of others on the picture. Oh, how anxious I am to have the educational part of the picture "done proud," so that it may help carry further the message of right teaching, devotion, perseverance and love so nobly exemplified in her life—They say I'm to act the college scenes myself—so perhaps you may recognize me in them.

It is very funny the way the pictures are taken. You would laugh to see my "make-up"!! a golden tow wig and a face like a corpse. They say that it is necessary in order to get a nice effect on the screen. When the lights are turned on for the picture, they are hot enough to dissolve the "make-up," and the noise of the motor that produces them is villainous.

I don't think the picture is half done yet, and I don't know how much longer we shall stay here, perhaps until December. Then we may go to Washington, New York, and Boston to have some scenes made. We will surely see you if we are in Washington.

There is everything here to make our stay enjoyable!! a pleasant homelike hotel, the hills, the ocean a few miles away and the glorious odors of roses, oleanders, sage and eucalyptus! trees. Polly and I ride horseback every morning, starting at sunrise, and I can't give you any idea what a joy it is to me. I haven't had such a sense of freedom and buoyancy in a long time. We also walk a lot along the canyons, and our friends often take us motoring through the mountains or by the sea.

We are meeting interesting people here, among them a few "movie stars." I have already met the daughter of Godowsky, and I may be introduced to her father when he comes out here from Portland, Oregon. We may also meet Charlie Chaplin and see his new war! picture, which they tell us is most amusing.

One day we were asked to take part in a war service parade in Los Angeles to help the boys wounded and maimed in this inhuman war. I marched between two little children, and we kept time finely. Think of it, we led the procession, and it was a long one. A few evenings later I addressed an immense audience!! Several thousands of people!! on rehabilitation of the crippled and blinded soldiers. So you see, I am trying to justify my existence by doing what good I can here and there.

Who do you think is with me now? Oh, mother. We sent for her last month, and she arrived about four months ago. She seems happy to be back in California, she says she loves Los Angeles more than any other place. The trip is benefiting her. She hasn't been well this summer, nor have I. The old trouble with my stomach pursues me like a bad conscience, and lately it has been more obstinate than a donkey's tail. But now I feel much better, the riding is splendid for me in every way.

Teacher is trying to ride too, and has been out three times. Of course she gets very tired but if she is able to keep it up, we think she will feel quite "made over." She sends her love to you and Phil. Do write again and tell us how you all are. I hope you will keep well now, dear. Hug the children for me. I suppose Sidney is growing tall and learning fast.

If mother knew I was writing, she too would send you her love.

> Always affectionately your friend,
> Helen Keller

35 We Have Given Up Vaudeville Altogether

August 29, 1920, letter from Helen Keller to Kate Keller, AFB.

Keller and Macy decided to give up vaudeville in the fall of 1920, even though *Deliverance* did not bring the cash they had hoped for. In this letter Keller announces the change to her mother, hoping for her emotional support. Despite this, economic realities forced the two back on the vaudeville circuit for almost an additional two years.

Dearest Mother,

Not a word have I had from you since my birthday, except the little card Pat sent from Memphis. What can be the matter now? More sickness in the family? Or has the heat about killed you? Or is Mildred again without a cook or nurse?

Well, a lot of things have happened in the last three weeks. This is the chief news—Teacher and I have decided not to go on the long tour, in fact we have given up vaudeville altogether. We waited and waited, hoping we might look at things differently, but when Mr. Weber sent us a letter saying that the financial arrangements were "O.K." Teacher suddenly said, "I can't do it! I don't want to make all that money at such a sacrifice of our peace when I don't know what good it would do in the end!" The truth is, mother, she was not happy in that sort of work. I didn't mind so much, I rather enjoyed the excitement, and besides, as you know, I was trying to provide something for her against the day when she could work no more. But I did feel as she did that we were out of key with Vaudeville life. I'm afraid a great deal of money blinded us at first to some undesirable aspects of the matter. But finally we made up our minds that we would rather earn a little and live our lives according to our ideals than earn a great deal and lose our peace of mind. So there went another of our "big" changes, and—left us happy! Now, what will you do with us two? I'm sure Mildred will be down on us for "foolishness." But somehow I feel as if you would understand. I remember your saying when you first heard of the vaudeville proposition, "I know neither of you will like making all that money, there are so many things to spoil the good work that you would try to do. It isn't like the old lecture tours when you had audiences who were really interested and worth talking to." So perhaps you will be glad with us that our affairs have taken this turn.

Now I believe it is God's hand instead of man's that has been held out to us, and that's surely the only real Help. I wrote in answer to a letter from Mrs. Thaw how we had given up the tour, and why. Bless you, she wrote back saying, "you will consider coming to Cresson about the 30th and staying with me a while. The Coster cottage will be vacant, and we can drive about and discuss a number of things." Nothing will do but we must go, and she will give us a lovely time, as she always does. There is no telling what she may advise or plan that may prove helpful. But the happiness of being with her is all we care about. We shall leave Wednesday, I think, and stay as long as she tells us to, and see how things readjust themselves.

In the mean time we have been just like children, getting all the fun we could in a wholesome way. Two weeks ago we went off with Lord Marmon to Cape Cod. Ned got a little vacation so that he could drive the car. We camped out nights just as we did last year, only more comfortably. We took plenty of blankets and a bottle of citronella to keep off mosquitoes. The weather kept on its best behavior, except for an occasional shower, so our woodsy bed wasn't turned into a brook. It was amazing what a variety of beautiful spots we found to sleep—a dear old apple orchard, part of an abandoned farm in R.I., a bed of hay, a thick pine wood, a grove of firs or a shelter of tremulous birch and maple. Always a warm, sweet wind smote the trees and our hearts like a harp, and just to be alive, free, roaming about seemed the joy of joys. We drove around Brewster, passing Mrs. Hopkins's house and other places we once knew. They all seemed shut up, and all was quiet along the beach. The little place seemed asleep, desolate, haunted forever by the sense of wasted effort, grim, hard lives and loneliness that runs throughout its past. In parts the Cape appears to be dying slowly. But Province Town is intensely alive, picturesque, amazing. We spent a wonderful day there, and had a delicious, old-fashioned shore dinner at an old-fashioned restaurant. Think of one long, narrow street with small cottages, queer little shops, a street winding in and out, in and out until it reaches the very end, where the sands shift endlessly—green, gold and purple, and a fine simple monument to the Pilgrims rises way up into an ever changing sky, and you have Province Town. Polly and I climbed the monument, and she described the various inscriptions on the tablets arranged from the foot to the very summit, giving the names of the New England towns and villages where the first settlers made their home. The people are now preparing to celebrate the tercentenary of the landing of the Pilgrims next November, and some of the villages along the Cape are already gay with bunting. Afterwards we motored to Plymouth, and Polly and Ned visited Pilgrim Hall.

When we came back Friday night, we were rather bewildered, so startling was the contrast between the free, scented woods and this limited, humdrum suburb of an overcrowded, sun-heated metropolis. The house smelt so strongly of dampness, I could hardly breathe. It is hard to get the upholstery or the curtains or our clothes dried out. There still seems to be something eerie over all, I've felt the magic and the primal soul-withdrawing power of nature so deeply.

I almost forgot to tell you that on our way home we went up to Mark Twain's home at Redding and camped under his lovely shrubs. The place was as beautiful as ever, but seemed quite deserted. Moss, lichens and weeds had come upon the stone walks, and we saw only two men tidying up a bit. We learned that they heard the place had been sold, but they didn't know to whom or anything else. Could there be a more pathetic story of a great, lovable, life-wearied man than this—the one home he really was happy in left to emptiness and neglect?

I'll write again from Cresson. Polly has just told me of her letter from Mildred. I hope my five letters since the last of June have reached you. Do take a rest, mother, and get away for a week or so. A change of scene would surely do you more good than you seem to think. With a heartful of love to you all, I am,

Affectionately your child,
Helen Keller

36 Memories of Mother's Journeyings with Us

November 20, 1921, letter from Helen Keller to Mildred Keller Tyson, AFB.

Two hours before Keller and Macy were to appear on a Los Angeles vaudeville stage in November 1921, she received a telegram notifying her of the death of her mother Kate. In previous years her mother had purchased a braille typewriter, and being able to receive letters from her mother without an intermediary only strengthened Keller's appreciation for her mother. As she characterized the relationship in 1929, "fine ligaments of love and sympathy had knit us together."[15] The letter below is the first one Keller wrote to her sister Mildred after their mother's death.

Kate Keller had apparently considered her coming death. In March 1920, she had written to Helen of her love, promising that if she died first she would try to contact her daughter from the dead. "How many times since you went away I have waked suddenly with the feeling that your step across the hall had waked me! Who knows? Perhaps, as one grows older, the curtain which separates one from those one loves grows thinner. Be very sure that if I go first, if it is possible, I shall let you know how, and where I am. Yes, I shall remember."[16] Helen missed her mother. In 1929, she wrote, "I had absolute faith that we should meet again in the Land of Eternal Beauty; but oh, the dreary blank her going left in my life!"[17]

Dearest Sister,

This is the first chance I have had to sit down quietly for a few minutes, and even now my heart aches so that I can hardly write. But I want you to feel my arms around you and the wee ones while I am waiting to hear from you. It is so hard for me to be far away at this time! And this is a road full of memories of mother's journeyings with us in days gone by. As we go from city to city, I shall long and long for the touch of her hand, and I do not know how I shall bear the loneliness, or when I can get to you. We have signed all our contracts up to April, and that means we cannot leave our work now. But if Teacher's strength gives out by then, she will take a rest, and I will come to you. Be sure that I shall come when I can.

How strange it all is! It seems as if we were dreaming, and I should wake any minute to find a letter from mother, saying she was in Texas. Only last summer she was with us, and she told me how much she enjoyed the rest, the sunshine and the lovely country when she felt well enough to go motoring. I begged her to stay longer, but she simply would not. She insisted that she was better, and Teacher must rest a bit. As soon as she was able to use the braille machine after her illness, she wrote a lovely letter about her visit in Hendersonville, and how cheerful she was! What a joy it was to have her own dear words in braille! You know she never felt that she was writing to me as she wished to when she used a pen. Her last letter made me happy too because she said it was such a relief to her to know that everything was well with us, and I was enjoying the tour. She told of Katherine's birthday, and spoke of going to Texas soon. I was full of bright anticipations of seeing her there this winter, and of having another visit with her next summer. And now—but no, dear, for her sake let us not think about it more than we can help. I know she would want us to feel her near, and look forward to seeing her again in a more beautiful world. Just as she was leaving me at the station in New York, she said suddenly, "Helen, you will not see me again, but whatever happens, I shall wait for you." Afterwards she wrote, "Do not let your feelings or nerves spoil your work, always do the best you can, and think of mother watching until you come."

I am sure, sister, she is much closer to us now than ever, and her dear spirit will give us comfort as time passes. So let us try to brace up by thinking how very happy she must be, freed from weariness and the anguish of unsatisfied longing. Let us remember how she "desired good every day" and prayed to find again the loved ones she had lost, and now her wishes are fulfilled. We can make her even happier by feeling her joy as our own, and you know how our griefs and delights were reduplicated in her heart while she lived with us.

When you write, be sure and tell me about the flowers we telegraphed for mother. I do hope they were pretty. The florist here said he could not tell if they would have what we wanted in Montgomery. Teacher sent sweetpeas and carnations, Polly heliotropes and lilies, and I ordered a pillow of roses and lilies with the letters "Mother."

Do you know if she wrote me more than two letters? She said she thought I missed several. Did she pass away without suffering? Did Phillips get there in time to see her? Was there anything she wished me to do? Tell me everything, and try to write often. I shall write to you every week now, and my thoughts will hover about you most tenderly until you feel my embrace.

We are all keeping well. We have had colds, but this wonderful air has driven them away, and I hope Teacher can manage all right until the rest of the tour. She and Polly send their warm love and sympathy.

Hug the little ones for me, and try to be comforted for her sake and mine.

> Your affectionate sister,
> Helen Keller

37 Our Expenses Are of Necessity Greater than for People in Ordinary Circumstances

September 9, 1922, letter from Helen Keller to Henry Ford, AFB.

By 1922, Macy's ill health and dislike for the vaudeville circuit had made that income source an impossibility. This letter to Henry Ford illustrates Keller's anxious efforts to seek economic support. The impetus for her letter, she insists, is her desire to aid Macy. Note that she never directly asks for money.

Dear Mr. Ford,

All that I have ever heard of you makes me think you will read what I am going to write with patience and sympathy. I wonder if you remember my visiting your plant in Detroit several years ago, when you were kind enough to talk with me and show me the great master dynamo. I hope you do, for then I shall not seem a perfect stranger to you.

I have just finished reading an article by you, "My Life and Work" which has been re-printed for the blind. I was very much interested in it. It made me realize more than ever what a great power for good you are in the world. Without doubt you have solved many complicated problems, and helped other people to accomplish important tasks. That is why I feel sure you will appreciate the work and service of one who is very dear to me. I refer to my teacher, Mrs. Macy, who was with me when I met you, and interpreted for me what you said.

She has been my teacher and inseparable companion for thirty-five years. When she came to Alabama to teach me, she was a young girl. She had been blind herself, but an operation had partially restored her sight. She had been educated at the Institution for the

Blind in Massachusetts, and when my father wrote to that school for a teacher, the director selected Miss Anne Sullivan. Ever since she took my hand on the door-step of my home, she has been not only my eyes and ears, but also a light in all dark places, a bond between me and the life of the world. To you, Mr. Ford, with all your faculties, this statement may mean little. I do not think any one in the world can fully realize what my life would have been without my teacher.

Now this is my problem. For years it has been the desire of my heart to make life easier for the woman to whom I owe my education and happiness. It distresses me to see my friend growing old beside me, weighted down with work and anxieties. But handicapped as I am, it has been up-hill work for me to make anything like an adequate provision for her. In fact, if I die before her, she will be left destitute in her old age. It seems unfair some how that one who has done so much should have received so little in return. Her achievement as a teacher has been recognized the world over, but that has not brought her financial independence.

Together we have toured the country lecturing, and I have written some books, but our earnings have not enabled us to save much. Indeed, we could not have managed at all but for an annuity of five thousand dollars which Mr. Carnegie gave me many years ago, and six hundred a year which Mr. H. H. Rogers left me at his death. For a long time we managed to get along on that fairly well. But now it is very hard. My teacher's sight has failed so that she cannot read to me any longer. That means, I have to have a secretary, which adds very considerably to our expenses. I do not know in a letter how to tell you that, situated as we are, our expenses are of necessity greater than for people in ordinary circumstances. Because people see my name in the newspapers, they imagine I must be wealthy, and I receive many heart-breaking letters asking for help, and to the utmost of my ability I have helped. Three years ago it became absolutely necessary for us to increase our income, and we went into Vaudeville. No one can ever know what a terrible trial that was to my teacher at her age (she is now fifty-six years old) to have to go before a Vaudeville audience two or three times a day. But it had to be done, and she did it with splendid courage. We managed to save about thirteen thousand dollars out of our earnings which I have invested for her. For in case I die first, the Carnegie and Rogers annuities will cease, and she will have nothing.

We three women (Mrs. Macy, Miss Polly Thomson (my secretary) and myself) live here in Forest Hills in a small house which represents about twenty thousand dollars, and there is a mortgage of seven thousand on that. We live as economically as we can. We keep no servants. Now we are waiting to hear from the Vaudeville management with regard to engagements for the coming year, wanting and dreading them at the same time.

You have the whole story now—not interesting, not important, except as it sets forth human effort and struggle under peculiarly difficult circumstances. As I read your article, something in your big, friendly attitude towards "the ninety-five percent" gave me courage to write you about my problem. I know what a very busy man you are. I realize that you are concerned with tremendous affairs. But just because you have found a way to put heart and understanding into the great social machine of life, perhaps you may find a way to bring peace of mind and happiness to two individuals who, in their small way, have tried to keep the light of hope and courage burning in men's hearts.

But, whether this letter interests you or not, I want you to know I feel the warmest esteem and gratitude to you for your noble service to humanity, and I wish you continued and ever increasing success.

With cordial greetings, I am,
        Sincerely yours,
        Helen Keller

A Major Works

38 My Religion

New York: Doubleday, 1928, chapter 2.

My Religion is designed to explain and draw others to the Swedenborgian Christian faith tradition. It introduces the reader to Emanuel Swedenborg, a Swedish Christian mystic, attempts to explain the basic tenets of his teachings, and describes her conversion. *My Religion's* rambling and confusing nature perhaps reflects the toil and difficulty required for the trio to develop an intellectual and practical editing process that worked. It was not a widely popular book, but Keller treasured the opportunity to explain her faith.

The book is the first published without the editorial assistance of John Macy. Doubleday sent Nella Braddy Henney to assist with *Midstream*, a continuation of Keller's 1903 autobiography, but Keller insisted on *My Religion*. Apparently neither Henney nor Macy warmly supported the effort, but Helen insisted and Doubleday cooperated. The relationship with Henney was at first bumpy. Henney originally didn't know finger-spelling. Helen and John Macy had developed an editing process that worked for them. The method she and Henney first adopted prompted her to insist on changes. As a result, the two adopted a new method, meaning that Henney spent ten to seventeen hours a day in the Forest Hills, New York household. To a Swedenborgian leader, Keller wrote, "it would be such a joy to me if I might be the instrument of bringing Swedenborg to a world that is spiritually deaf and blind."[1]

Chapter 2 describes Keller's queries about God and her eventual embrace of the teachings of Swedenborg. The Swedenborgian belief in "the separateness between soul and body" thrilled her. Swedenborg taught that there was a "spiritual body within the material one with perfect senses" that mattered more than the material body. Thus, her deaf-blindness mattered little. In fact, because Swedenborg believed that the "matter-clogged, mirage-filled senses"[2] sometimes kept the faithful from the spiritual senses that enabled them to know God, Helen believed her disability may have made possible a *deeper* sense of spirituality that would open to her "a world infinitely more wonderful, complete, and satisfying than this one." Everyone had the potential to access that world, according to Swedenborg, both before and after death.[3] While others interpreted her disability as debilitating, Keller's faith tradition interpreted her disability as a possible spiritual bonus. Today many people with disabilities embrace theologies that similarly reject the importance of a physical body and emphasize the importance of a spiritual body.

My impressions of my first contact with the writings of the great Swedish seer of the Eighteenth Century, which came about thirty years ago, will seem without meaning unless I go back to my first questionings about God. As a little child I naturally wanted to know who made everything in the world and I was told that Nature (they called it Mother Nature) had made Earth and sky and water and all living creatures. This satisfied me for a time, and I was happy among the rose-trees of my mother's garden, or on the banks of a river, or out in the daisy pranked fields, where my teacher told me true "Arabian Nights" tales about seeds and flowers, birds and insects and the fishes in the river. Like other children, I believed that every object I touched was alive and self-conscious, and I supposed we were all Mother Nature's children. But as I grew older, I began to reason about the parts of Nature I could touch. Obviously, I am using mature words and the ideas of later years to make intelligible the groping, half-formed, ever-shifting impressions of childhood. I noticed a difference between the way human beings did their work and the way the wonders of Nature were wrought. I saw that puppies, flowers, stones, babies, and thunderstorms were not just put together as my mother mixed her hot cakes. There was an order and sequence of things in field and wood that puzzled me, and at the same time there was a confusion in the elements which at times terrified me. The wanton destruction of the beautiful and the ugly, the useful and the obnoxious, the righteous and the wicked by earthquake or flood or tornado I could not understand. How could such a blind mass of irresponsible forces create and keep alive, always renewing what was destroyed, and keep up an unfailing succession of spring, summer, autumn, and winter, seedtime and harvest, day and night, tides and generations of men? Somehow I sensed that Nature was no more concerned with me or those I loved than with a twig or a fly, and this awoke in me something akin to resentment—"the fine innuendo by which the Soul makes its enormous claim," and declares that it has a prerogative of control over the course of events and things.

Turning away from Nature, I inquired about God, and again I was baffled. Friends tried to tell me He was the Creator, and that He was everywhere, that He knew all the needs, joys, and sorrows of every human life, and nothing happened without His foreknowledge and providence. Some with a generous disposition said He was merciful to all, and caused His sun to shine on the just and unjust alike. I was drawn irresistibly to such a glorious, lovable Being, and I longed really to understand something about Him. Then I met Phillips Brooks, and he helped me, with his simple soul-stirring words, to grasp the central truth that God is Love, and that His Love is the "Light of all men."

But I could not form any clear idea of the relation between this Divine Love and the material world. I lost myself many times in shadows and uncertainties, wandering back and forth between the Light which was so ineffably reassuring and the chaos and darkness of nature that seemed so real as not to be gainsaid. One day I was made radiantly happy and brought nearer to a sense of God when "I watched" an exquisite butterfly, just out of its cocoon, drying its wings in the sun, and afterward felt it fluttering over a bunch of trailing arbutus. Someone told me how the ancient Egyptians had looked upon the butterfly as a symbol of immortality. I was delighted. It seemed to me as it should be, that such beautiful forms of life should have in them a lesson about things still more lovely. Nevertheless, the same buzz-saw continued to worry me until one day a sudden flash of intuition revealed an infinite wonder to me.

I had been sitting quietly in the library for half an hour. I turned to my teacher and said, "Such a strange thing has happened! I have been far away all this time, and I haven't left the room." "What do you mean, Helen?" she asked, surprised. "Why," I cried, "I have been in

Athens." Scarcely were the words out of my mouth when a bright, amazing realization seemed to catch my mind and set it ablaze. I perceived the realness of my soul and its sheer independence of all conditions of place and body. It was clear to me that it was because I was a spirit that I had so vividly "seen" and felt a place thousands of miles away. Space was nothing to spirit! In that new consciousness shone the Presence of God, Himself a Spirit everywhere at once, the Creator dwelling in all the universe simultaneously. The fact that my little soul could reach out over continents and seas to Greece, despite a blind, deaf, and stumbling body, sent another exulting emotion rushing over me. I had broken through my limitations and found in touch an eye. I could read the thoughts of wise men—thoughts which had for ages survived their mortal life, and could possess them as part of myself. If this were true, how much more could God, the uncircumscribed Spirit, cancel the harms of nature—accident, pain, destruction, and reach out to his children. Deafness and blindness, then, were of no real account. They were to be relegated to the outer circle of my life. Of course I did not sense any such process with my child-mind; but I could know that I, the real I, could leave the library and visit any place I wanted to, mentally, and I was happy. That was the little seed from which grew my interest in spiritual subjects.

I was not at that time especially enthusiastic about the Bible stories, except the story of the gentle Nazarene. The accounts of creation and the driving out of Adam and Eve from Eden for eating a particular fruit, the Flood and all the wrath and vengeance of the Lord seemed to me very similar to the Greek and Roman myths I had read—and there were very few gods and goddesses I could admire.

I was disappointed not to find in the Bible that my good aunt held up to me as a Divine Book, a likeness of the Being whose face shone so benign, beautiful and radiant in my heart. She told me tales out of the Apocalypse, and still I felt a void I could not explain. What could I see in a war between God and dragons and horned beasts? How could I associate the eternal torture of those cast into the lake of fire with the God whom Christ declared to be love? Why, I wondered, should one particular City of God be described with pavements of gold and walls and precious stones when heaven must be full of everything else just as magnificent—mountains, fields, oceans, and the sweet, fruitful earth, restful to the feet? The touching story of Christ, comforting the sorrowful, healing the sick, giving new light to the blind and speech to mute lips stirred me to the depths; but how could I worship three persons—the Father, the Son, and the Holy Ghost? Was that not the sort of false worship so terribly punished in Old Testament days?

Such were the bewildered, dissatisfied thoughts on the Bible which possessed my mind when there came into my life one of the friends I loved most, Mr. John Hitz, who had for a long period held the position at Washington of Consul-General for Switzerland in this country. Afterward he was superintendent of the Volta Bureau in Washington, which Dr. Bell founded with the Volta Prize money he received for inventing the telephone. This bureau was established for the purpose of collecting and distributing information about the deaf, and publishing a magazine in their behalf, which is now called *The Volta Review.*

I met Mr. Hitz first in 1893, when I was about thirteen years old, and that was the beginning of an affectionate and beautiful friendship which I cherish among the dearest memories of my life. He was always deeply interested in all I did—my studies, my girlish joys and dreams, my struggle through college and my work for the blind. He was one of the few who fully appreciated my teacher and the peculiar significance of her work not only to me, but to all the world. His letters bore testimony to his affection for her and his understanding of what she was to me—a light in all dark places. He visited us often in Boston and Cambridge, and every time my teacher and I stopped over in Washington on our way to or from my southern home, we had delightful trips with him.

After my teacher and I settled down in Wrentham, Mass., he spent six weeks with us every summer until the year he died. He loved to take me out walking early in the morning while the dew lay upon grass and tree and the air was joyous with birdsongs. We wandered through still woods, fragrant meadows, past the picturesque stone walls of Wrentham, and always he brought me closer to the beauty and the deep meaning of Nature. As he talked, the great world shone for me in the glory of immortality. He stimulated in me the love of Nature that is so precious a part of the music in my silence and the light in my darkness. It is sweet as I write to recall the flowers and the laughing brooks and the shining, balmy moments of stillness in which we had joy together. Each day I beheld through his eyes a new and charming landscape, "wrapped in exquisite showers" of fancy and spiritual beauty. We would often pause that I might feel the swaying of the trees, the bending of the flowers, and the waving of the corn, and he would say, "the wind that puts all this life into Nature is a marvelous symbol of the spirit of God."

On my fourteenth birthday he presented me with a gold watch he had worn for more than thirty years, and I have never been separated from it since, except one time when it was sent to Switzerland for some parts that were worn out. Curiously enough, it was not made for the blind in the first place. It once belonged to a German ambassador who had it fixed so that he could keep important appointments exactly. He was obliged to call upon a high dignitary of the Kaiser, and it was not etiquette to look at the watch, nor was it etiquette to stay too long. So the Ambassador went to a jeweler and gave him instructions about making the watch so that he could slip his hands into his pocket and "feel" the time. It has a crystal face, and a gold hand on the back, which is connected with the minute hand, and goes with it and stops with it. There are also gold points around the rim of the watch which indicate the hours. I wear it always against my heart, and it ticks for me as faithfully as my friend himself worked for me and loved me. He whose love it keeps ever before me has been gone nearly twenty years, but I have the sweet consciousness that each tick is bringing me nearer and nearer to him. Truly a treasure above price, linking time and eternity!

Mr. Hitz and I corresponded for many years. He learned the Braille system so that I could read myself his long and frequent letters. These letters are a record of spiritual kinship which it comforts me to read over when I long for the touch of his hand and the wise, inspiring words with which he encouraged me in my tasks. His first and last thought was how to lessen the obstacles I encountered. He quickly perceived my hunger for books I could read on subjects that particularly interested me, and how limited were the embossed books within my reach. For eight years he devoted a part of each day to copying whatever he thought would give me pleasure—stories, biographies of great men, poetry, and studies of Nature. When, after reading

"Heaven and Hell," I expressed a wish to know more of Swedenborg's writings, he laboriously compiled books of explanations and extracts to facilitate my reading. All this he accomplished in addition to his duties as superintendent of the Volta Bureau and his extensive correspondence! In his letters he often referred to "the quiet morning hours before breakfast" he spent transcribing for me, and his "joy of being in daily touch with his *innigst geliebte Tochter Helena*." Many friends have done wonderful things for me, but nothing like Mr. Hitz's untiring effort to share with me the inner sunshine and peace which filled his silent years. Each year I was drawn closer to him, and he wrote to me more constantly as the days passed. Then came a great sorrow—separation from the friend I loved best next to my teacher. I had been visiting my mother, and was on my way back to Wrentham. As usual, I stopped in Washington, and Mr. Hitz came to the train to meet me. He was full of joy as he embraced me, saying how impatiently he had awaited my coming. Then, as he was leading me from the train, he had a sudden attack of heart trouble, and passed away. Just before the end he took my hand, and I still feel his pressure when I think of that dark time. I could not have borne the loss of such an intimate and tender friend if I had thought he was indeed dead. But his noble philosophy and certainty of the life to come braced me with an unwavering faith that we should meet again in a world happier and more beautiful than anything of my dreaming. With me remains always the helpful memory of his rare personality.

He was a man of lofty character, a man of rich spiritual gifts. His heart was pure and warm, full of childlike faith in the best he saw in his fellow-creatures, and he was always doing for other people something lovely and dear. In all his ways he kept the Commandment, "Love thy neighbour as thyself." At eighty years of age he had the heart of an evergreen, and his inexhaustible power of enjoyment lifted him far above the average of humanity. He remained young with the young. He was never old to me, and I was never deaf and blind to him. He spelled with difficulty on his fingers, and he was so hard of hearing I had often to repeat a sentence six times with my imperfect speech before he could understand me. But our love covered a multitude of difficulties, and our intercourse was always worth every effort it cost us.

As we talked thus, Mr. Hitz came to realize fully my hunger for literature I could read on subjects that especially interested me. He himself had grown deaf, and that enabled him to see the distorted angle of my thoughts with regard to the world of the senses. He told me that if I would only try to put myself in the place of those with sight and hearing and divine their impressions of things, they could unite their senses with mine more and more and thus wonderfully increase my enjoyment of the outer world. He showed me how I could find a key to their life, and give them a chance to explore my own with understanding. He put into my hands a copy of Swedenborg's "Heaven and Hell" in raised letters. He said he knew I would not understand much of it at first, but it was fine exercise for my mind, and would satisfy me with a likeness of a God as lovable as the one in my heart. He told me always to remember that it is easier to see what is good than what is true in a difficult book. For, as Swedenborg put it, "Good is like a little flame which gives light, and causes man to see, perceive, and believe."

When I began "Heaven and Hell" I was as little aware of the new joy coming into my life as I had been years before when I stood on the piazza steps awaiting my teacher. Impelled only by the curiosity of a young girl who loves to read, I opened that big book, and lo, my fingers lighted upon a paragraph in the preface about a blind woman whose darkness was illumined with beautiful truths from Swedenborg's writings. She believed that they imparted a light to her mind which more than compensated her for the loss of earthly light. She never doubted that there was a spiritual body within the material one with perfect senses, and that after a few dark years the eyes within her eyes would open to a world infinitely more wonderful, complete, and satisfying than this. My heart gave a joyous bound. Here was a faith that emphasized what I felt so keenly—the separateness between soul and body, between a realm I could picture as a whole and the chaos of fragmentary things and irrational contingencies which my limited physical senses met at every turn. I let myself go, as healthy, happy youth will, and tried to puzzle out the long words and the weighty thoughts of the Swedish sage. Somehow I sensed the likeness of Him whom I loved as the One and Only, and I wanted to understand more. The words Love and Wisdom seemed to caress my fingers from paragraph to paragraph, and these two words released in me new forces to stimulate my somewhat indolent nature and urge me forward evermore. I came back to the book from time to time, picking up a line here and a line there, "precept upon precept," one glimpse then another of the Divine Word hidden under the clouds of literal statement. As I realized the meaning of what I read, my soul seemed to expand and gain confidence amid the difficulties which beset me. The descriptions of the other world bore me far, far over measureless regions bathed in superhuman beauty and strangeness, where angels' robes flash, where great lives and creative minds cast a splendour upon darkest circumstances, where events and mighty combats sweep by endlessly, where the night is lit to eternal day by the Smile of God. I glowed through and through as I sat in that atmosphere of the soul and watched men and women of nobler mould pass in majestic procession. For the first time immortality put on intelligibility for me, and earth wore new curves of loveliness and significance. I was glad to discover that the City of God was not a stupid affair of glass streets and sapphire walls, but a systematic treasury of wise, helpful thoughts and noble influences. Gradually I came to see that I could use the bible, which had so baffled me, as an instrument of digging out precious truths, just as I could use my hindered, halting body for the high behests of my spirit.

I had been told by narrow people that all who were not Christians would be punished, and naturally my soul revolted, since I knew of wonderful men who had lived and died for truth as they saw it in the pagan lands. But in "Heaven and Hell" I found that "Jesus" stands for divine Good, Good wrought into deeds, and "Christ" Divine Truth, sending forth new thought, new life and joy into the minds of men; therefore no one who believes in God and lives right is ever condemned. So I grew to womanhood, and as unaccountable as Conrad found in English the language of his choice, I took more and more to the New Church doctrines as my religion. No one encouraged me in this choice, and I cannot explain it any more than anyone else. I can only say that the Word of God freed from the blots and stains of barbarous creeds has been at once the joy and good of my life, wonderfully linked with my growing appreciation of my teacher's work and my own responsibilities of service, hours of struggle and solitude, hours of deepest joy, harsh truths faced squarely and high dreams held dearer than the pleasant baits of ease and complaisance. Those truths have been to my faculties what light, colour, and music are to the eye and ear. They have lifted my consciousness of the complete being within me. Each day comes to me with both hands full of possibilities, and in its brief course I discern all the verities and realities of my existence, the bliss of growth, the glory of action, the spirit of beauty.

39 Midstream: My Later Life

New York: Doubleday, 1929.

The production of *Midstream* agonized the household. Neither Keller nor Anne Macy completely trusted Nella Braddy Henney yet, and thus Macy insisted on reviewing material before letting Nella see it. Helen typed drafts on the manual typewriter that accompanied her virtually everywhere. Nella read these drafts to Anne, whose eyesight remained weak. Nella and Anne then literally cut and pasted editorial changes. Nella read them to Anne while Anne finger-spelled the drafts to Helen, and the process would start again. Anne insisted that some material on herself be excluded, hoping not only to write her own book but also to keep some material from becoming public. Helen struggled with what to say about her politics and her romance with Peter Fagan.[4]

Finally, in 1929, Doubleday published *Midstream*. The book received some attention, but the reading public cared less about her adult life than her dramatic childhood acquisition of language. Helen missed John Macy's editorial advice and personal friendship. In *Midstream,* she wrote fondly of John, "if this book is not what it should be, it is because I feel lonely and bewildered without his supporting hand." She sent him a copy of the book, one wonders if Anne knew, and he responded with praise. She wrote him again with thanks: "always you were in my mind, and how I longed for your reassuring approval!"[5]

These selections describe Keller's private and public life. Chapter 3 describes the life at Wrentham with Anne and John Macy as beautifully pastoral. Chapter 11 deals with Keller's antiwar Chautauqua tours, carefully discusses politics, and gives the story of her relationship with Peter Fagan. To this she says, "I cannot account for my behaviour."

Chapter 3: My First Years in Wrentham

The French article from which I have quoted says that I was given a home in Wrentham by the public, who wished to honour me as the ancients did when they bestowed upon a victorious general an estate where he could live and enjoy his laurels:

> Boston, la ville la plus intellectuelle l'Athenes des Etats Unis, a, au lendemain de ses examens offert cette maison en hommage à la jeune fille qui a remporte une victoire sans pareille de l'esprit sur la matière, de l'âme immortelle sur les sens.

Others who have tried to describe the house without knowing it have added an extensive park and a wonderful garden. No such pomp and circumstance marked my triumphal entrance into the village of Wrentham. Miss Sullivan and I had already bought a small, old farm-house, long and narrow, decidedly Puritanical in appearance, with a neglected field of seven acres. Miss Sullivan converted a dairy room and two pantries into a study for me. The French article describes it as follows:

> Helen Keller passe la plupart de ses journées dans son elegant cabine de travail, orné de bronzes et d'objets d'art offerts pars ses adorateurs, et dont les murs disparaissent du haut en bas sous des centaines et des centaines de gros volumes au pages blanches couvertes de points en relief—ses chers livres en Braille.

As a matter of fact, the study was very simple. The only "works of art" were a plaster Venus di Milo which my foster-father, Mr. John Hitz, had given me, a bas-relief medallion of Homer, a gift from Dr. Jastrow of the University of Wisconsin, and some curios sent to me by friends from foreign countries. Only one wall "disappeared" behind large volumes of braille, and that did not mean hundreds of books. In most cases there were three, four, or five big volumes to a book. They were few enough in comparison with what I wanted, but to any-one as hungry for ideas as I was any bit of honest thinking was a treasure trove. The chief attractions of the study were sunshine, the big eastern window full of plants I tended, and a glass door through which I could step out into a cluster of pines and sit alone with my thoughts and my dreams.

Miss Sullivan had a balcony built for me which opened out of my bedroom so that I could walk whenever I wanted to. The evergreens came so close to the railing I could lean over and feel their rustling music. It was on this balcony that I once "heard" the love song of a whippoorwill. I had been walking up and down for an hour or more, pausing every now and then to breathe the scented air of May. At the south end I could reach out and touch a wisteria vine which clung to the rail with long, tenacious fingers. At the opposite end I faced the garden and the apple trees, which were in full bloom, and oh, so heavenly sweet! I was standing under the wisteria vine with my thoughts far away when suddenly the rail began to vibrate unfamiliarly under my hands. The pulsations were rhythmical, and repeated over and over, exactly as I have felt a note repeated when I have placed my fingers on a singer's throat. All at once they ceased, and I felt the wisteria blossom ticking against my cheek like the pendulum of a fairy clock. I guessed that a breeze or a bird was rocking the vine. Then the rail began vibrating again. A queer beat came always before the rhythmical beats, like nothing I had ever felt before. I did not dare move or call, but Miss Sullivan had heard the sound and put out her hand through the window and touched me very quietly. I knew I must not speak.

She spelled, "That's a whippoorwill. He is standing on the corner post so close to you I believe you could touch him; but you must not—he would fly away and never come back."

Now that I knew he was saying "Whip-poor-will! Whip-poor-will" over and over I could follow the intonations exactly. The singing seemed joyous to my touch, and I could feel the notes grow louder and louder, faster and faster.

Miss Sullivan touched me again and spelled, "His lady-love is answering him from the apple trees. Apparently, she has been there all the time, hiding. Now they are singing a duet."

When the rail stopped vibrating she spelled, "They are both in the apple tree now singing under billows of pink and white blossoms."

We paid for this house in Wrentham and the alterations by selling some shares of sugar stock which Mr. J. P. Spaulding of Boston had given us about ten years before. I feel moved to say something here about one who took the most generous interest in us both at a time when we needed a strong friend.

I was nine years old, I think, when Elsie Leslie Lyde, the beautiful child actress who played "Little Lord Fauntleroy," introduced us to Mr. Spaulding. He was so tender and understanding, he won me at once, and from that day he was eager to do anything for our comfort or pleasure. He liked to come to the Perkins Institution when we stayed there, and join in our midday meal. He always brought a big box of roses, or fruits or candies. He took us for long drives, and Elsie accompanied us when she was not appearing at the theatre. She was a lovely, vivacious child, and Mr. Spaulding beamed with delight to see "his two darlings together." I was just learning to speak, and it distressed him very much because he could not understand what I said. I practised saying "Elsie Leslie Lyde" one day, and kept on until I cried; but I wanted Mr. Spaulding to hear me say it intelligibly, and I shall never forget his joy when I succeeded. Whenever I failed to articulate well, or there was too much noise for him to hear me, he would hug me and say, "If I can't understand you, I can always love you," and I know he did with a deep affection. Indeed, he was beloved by many people in every walk of life. Elsie called him "King John," and he was a king in spirit, royal and noble of heart.

Mr. Spaulding assisted my teacher and me financially for a number of years. He told us many times that he would provide for our future. But he died without making any provision for us in his will, and his heirs refused to continue the help he had given us. Indeed, one of his nephews said that we had taken advantage of his uncle when he was not in a condition to know his own mind!

I see I have again wandered far afield; but I could not pass over in silence a rare and beautiful generosity which imposed no obligations up nor asked anything in return, except the satisfaction of having us happy.

Somehow Mr. Spaulding seemed very near indeed when we threw open the doors and windows of our home—the first home of our own —to the June sunshine and started our new life full of bright hopes for the future.

On May 2, 1905, the year after my graduation, my teacher married John Macy. She had devoted the best years of her womanhood to me, and I had often longed to see her blessed with a good man's love; I felt the tenderest joy in their union. Dr. Edward Everett Hale, one of our oldest and closest friends, performed the ceremony in the sunny, flower-filled sitting room of our white farmhouse, and I stood beside my teacher. Lenore spelled the ceremony into my hand. My mother and a few close friends were present. Then Mr. and Mrs. Macy left for their wedding trip to New Orleans, and I went south with my mother for a visit. A few days later we were delightfully surprised to see Mr. and Mrs. Macy walking into the house! My cup ran over! It seemed like a dream, having them with me, revelling in the beauty of early summer in the Southland. The air was laden with the odour of magnolias, and they kept saying how heavenly the song of the mocking birds was—they called it their wedding music. When we were all back in Wrentham, I heard that several people thought I was jealous and unhappy, and one letter of condolence was actually inflicted upon me!

I wish I could engrave upon these pages the picture in my fingers that I cherish of those two friends—my teacher with her queenly mind and heart, strong and true, going direct to the core of the subject under discussion, her delight in beauty, her enthusiasm for large service and heroic qualities; her husband with his brotherly tenderness, his fine sensibilities, his keen sense of humour, and his curious combination of judicial severity and smiling tolerance. Since I was out of active life, they both strove to keep my narrow round pleasant and interesting. Both had a magical way of breaking up the monotony for me with bright comments and rapid, frequent reports of what I could not see or hear. And such a difference as there was in the way each talked! My teacher's comments on scenes and news and people were like nuggets of gold, lavishly spilled into my hands, while her husband put his words together carefully, almost as if he were writing a novel. He often said he wanted to write a novel, and certainly there was material for one in his brilliant conversation. His hands were seldom still, and even when he was not spelling to me I could tell by his gestures whether he was arguing or joking or simply carrying on an ordinary conversation.

I cannot enumerate the helpful kindnesses with which he smoothed my rugged paths of endeavour. Once, when my typewriter was out of order, and I was tired with the manual labour of copying, he sat up all night, and typed forty pages of my manuscript, so that they might reach the press in time.

Next to my teacher, he was the friend who discovered most ways to give me pleasure and gratify my intellectual curiosity. He kept me faithfully in touch with the chief happenings of the day, the discoveries of science, and the new trends in literature. If he was particularly pleased with a book, he would have Mr. John Hitz put it into braille for me, or he would read it to me himself when he had time.

Not long after we moved to Wrentham Mr. Gilder asked me to write a series of essays for the *Century* about my ideas of the world around me. The essays appeared in the magazine under the title, "Sense and Sensibility," but as Jane Austen had used that title for one of her books, I called them *The World I Live In* when they came out in book form. I poured into it everything that interested me at one of the happiest periods of my life—my newly discovered wealth of philosophy and the feeling of the New England beauty which surrounded me. I had always revelled in the wonders of nature; but I had not dreamed what abundance of physical enjoyment I possessed until I sat down and tried to express in words the lacy shadows of little leaves, the filmy wings of insects, the murmur of breezes, the tremulous flutter of flowers, the soft-breathing breast of a dove, filaments of sound in the waving grass, and gossamer threads intertwining and unreeling themselves endlessly.

The next book I wrote was *The Song of the Stone Wall*. The idea of writing it came to me with the joy of spring while we were building up the old walls in our green field. In it I tried to image the men who had built the walls long ago. I dedicated the book to Dr. Edward Everett Hale because he, too, loved the old walls and the traditions that cling about them. Moreover, the zeal of the men who built them was upon his lips and their courage in his heart.

While I was writing these books Mr. Macy was always near by to help me. He criticized me severely when my work did not please him, and his praise was sweet when I wrote something he liked. We read the pages over and over, weeding out the chaff, until he thought I had done my best. "When one's best is not satisfactory," he would say, "there is nothing to do about it."

He had the art of pulling me out of a solemn or discouraged mood with laughter that leaves the heart light and soothes the ruffled mind. I used to love to ramble or drive with him along the winding roads of Wrentham. With a gesture of delight he would point out a pond smiling like a babe on earth's breast, or a gorgeous bird on the wing, or a field full of sunshine and ripening corn, or we would sit together under the Great Oak on the edge of Lake Wollomonapoag while he read to me from one of Thoreau's books. There are no words to tell how dear he was to me or how much I loved him. Little incidents hardly noticed at the time but poignantly remembered afterwards crowd upon me as I write. On a still summer evening or by a winter fire, my thoughts still wander back to those days and dwell with sweet longing on the affection of those two friends sitting beside me in the library, their hands in mine, dreaming of a bright future of mutual helpfulness. I can never quite accustom myself to the bewildering vicissitudes of life, but, despite the shadows upon it, both my teacher and I feel that all that was loveliest in the Wrentham days is ours forever.

When we went to Wrentham to live I had in mind a vision of a real farm, like my father's in Tuscumbia, Alabama, where I could live in the midst of the strong, abiding simplicity of homely things among trees and animals.

The only animal we owned was Phiz, whom we carried with us from Cambridge. He died a year after we moved to Wrentham. We buried him at the end of the field under a beautiful white pine tree. I grieved for him a long time, and resolved never to have another dog. But everybody knows how, in the course of time, the proverbial other dog arrives. Kaiser was his name. He was a sturdy French bull terrier. A friend of Mr. Macy's presented him to the family. Having lived all the days of his three years with a man, Kaiser was at first inclined to assume a supercilious attitude towards women folk. He pondered over what we said to him, and usually decided that it might be ignored. We undertook to teach him he must obey in order to eat. But he found out quickly that apples could be used as a substitute for meat and bread. He learned to hold an apple between his paws and eat it with a good deal of gusto. But when he fully made up his mind that he could not maintain the fallacy of masculine superiority in an establishment where the feminine forces outnumbered the males three to one, he surrendered all the major points, also his pretence that he had a special fondness for apples, though to the end he retained a certain masculine swagger which was not unbecoming.

There is not much to tell about Kaiser. His fate confirms the story of modern civilization. He found food abundant and obtainable without exertion; therefore he took advantage of every opportunity to gourmandize. Both dogs and human beings find this a pleasant pastime, but they must make up their minds that sooner or later they die of it.

A similar fate overtook some Rhode Island Reds, which we bought from Mr. Dilley, our next door neighbour, who was a bird fancier. I fed them myself, and they soon became very tame. It was fun to watch them, but after a while I noticed that they sat down to their meals, and it was very hard to get them to move about. Our neighbour was called to give advice. He declared that I had overfed them to such an extent that he doubted if Mr. Pierce, our marketman, would take them. I was so disappointed with the little gourmands I gave up the idea of trying to raise chickens again.

But it seemed a shame to waste the enclosure we had put up with so much trouble and expense. So we bought Thora, a beautiful brindle Dane. I knew it would be easier to raise puppies; and anyway I loved dogs better than chickens. In due time Thora's eleven puppies arrived. Of course I had not dreamed that there would be so many, or that they would be so mischievous.

I have not space to give a detailed account of the upbringing of that family of Dane puppies. They were as temperamental as poets and musicians are supposed to be. There was one everybody singled out as the gem of the clan. We called her Sieglinde and lavished special care and affection upon her. Her colour was red gold, and her head was moulded on noble lines. Of all the dogs we have ever owned she was the most beautiful and intelligent, and I am not belittling my splendid Danish baron, Hans, nor my fascinating, perverse Scotch lassie, Darky, who are clamouring at the door of my study as I write.

In the meantime there was the barn—a fine, large barn with no living creature in it. It did not seem right that there should be no livestock to enjoy it. We began to read the advertisements in the Boston *Transcript*. We were surprised to find how many fine animals were without a comfortable home. The tears actually came to my eyes when I heard of a lady who was going abroad, and must leave her noble Great Dane to the mercy of strangers. She said that if some one who loved animals would only give Nimrod a home, she would part with him for seventy-five dollars, which was like giving him away. We wrote the lady that we should be glad to take Nimrod. It was arranged that Mr. Macy should meet her and Nimrod at the North Station in Boston. Mrs. Macy and I waited at home.

I have never seen such a huge dog. He was more like a young elephant than a dog. Mr. Macy insisted that he should be left out on the porch until we found out what his upbringing had been, but we could not think of such inhospitality to a stranger within our gates. The door was flung open, and Nimrod was invited to enter. There was a small table with a lamp on it near the door. In passing it, he knocked it over. Fortunately the lamp was not lighted—in those days we used kerosene—or I suppose the house would have been burned. As it was, the crash frightened the poor dog, so that he charged into the dining room, knocking Mr. Macy's supper off and the dishes all over the room. With great difficulty Mr. Macy succeeded in getting the terrified creature out to the barn. Family relations were somewhat strained that evening, and I did not learn much of what happened, except that the conductor on two trains had refused to let Nimrod on, and that he had caused a stampede in the waiting room of the station.

Thora would have nothing to do with him. She even growled at him when he tried to make friends with the puppies. Out in the field Nimrod seemed contented to be by himself; but somebody noticed that he was eating stones. There were too many stones in the field. Our distress was not caused by any regret over their disappearance, but we were concerned about Nimrod's digestion. We sent for our neighbour, Dr. Brastow, the state veterinarian. He controlled his feelings wonderfully when he gave us the report of his diagnosis.

"The dog," he said, "is about fourteen years old. He has no teeth, and very little sight. Probably he thinks the stones are bones. His former owner was, no doubt, too tender-hearted to have him put to sleep." However, we thought our friend rather heartless when he proposed to do forthwith that which had been left undone. Still it seemed best.

It was some time before we began to read the advertisements in the *Transcript* again. But inevitably history repeats itself. We had a marvellous, versatile gift of forgetting previous unfortunate ventures and joyously entering upon new ones. There is nothing to be said in favour of this gift, except that it lends spice to life. The day came when we felt that we must have a horse, and that very day we read a column of advertisements of wonderful horses which could be purchased for half or a third of what they would naturally sell for; but their owners were in various difficulties, and wanted to part with them for stated amounts. The horse we decided to buy was described as a spirited dark bay; weight, 1150 pounds; age, six years; gentle, fearless, broken to saddle, suitable for a lady to drive or ride.

We three innocents went to Boston to see the horse. The stable man said the owner was out of town, but he showed us the horse, and certainly the animal was a beauty. His coat was as smooth as satin and he held his head so high I could scarcely reach his ears. One of his feet was white, and there and then, with several endearing pats and caresses, I christened him Whitefoot. We paid for him on the spot, and it was arranged that a boy should ride him out to Wrentham. We learned afterwards that Whitefoot had thrown the boy three times on the way; but he never said a word to us. The next morning Mr. Macy hitched the horse to a light Democrat wagon we had, and started for the village. He had not got out of the driveway when Whitefoot began to give trouble. Mr. Macy jumped out to see if there was anything wrong with the harness. At that moment the Foxboro car passed the gate. The horse reared, and dashed across the lawn and out through the neighbour's gate. The wagon caught on a stone post and was smashed to kindling. Two days later a country man brought the horse home. He had found him in a wood road with scraps of harness still hanging to him.

We finally sold Whitefoot to a man in Attleboro who claimed to be a horse tamer. We learned a year or so later that Whitefoot had been the cause of the death of a cabman, and was pronounced crazy by the state veterinarian and shot.

It was a long time before we summoned up courage to try our luck with horses again. But we finally succeeded in getting what we wanted. King was an English-bred cob, a rich bay in colour. We used to say that he stepped as Queen Elizabeth danced, "high and disposedly." He was a horse tempered like finest steel—strong, patient, good-natured with common sense—the kind of horse erratic drivers should prize above pearls and rubies. Our various enterprises with livestock having not only failed, but plunged us into deeper financial tribulations, we were advised to plant an apple orchard. This seemed just the thing. We bought a hundred choice three year nurslings and planted them according to the rules sent out by the United States Department of Agriculture. They prospered. The fifth year we were delighted to find a few apples on them. I knew how many apples each tree had, and almost daily I made a note of their size. The apple orchard was such a comfort to us that we were annoyed with ourselves for not having thought of it in the beginning.

All went well until one fateful summer afternoon when Ian Bittman, our Russian man of all work, came rushing up to my study where Mrs. Macy and I were reading. "Look! look! Look, Madam! See, the wild cow have come," he cried.

We ran to the window, and in great excitement Ian pointed out five wonderful creatures disporting themselves through the orchard. Mrs. Macy could scarcely believe her eyes—they were wild deer—a great antlered buck, a doe, and three half-grown fawn! They were beautiful in the afternoon sunlight, skipping from tree to tree and stripping the bark with their teeth. Indeed, they were so graceful and lovely, it did not occur to one of us to chase them out of the orchard. We stood there fascinated until they had destroyed nearly every tree before we realized what had happened. That year Massachusetts paid thousands of dollars to farmers for the losses they had sustained from marauding deer. It never occurred to us to send the state a bill for our apple trees. The last time I visited the old place, I saw perhaps half a dozen of the trees we had planted, and which had escaped the sharp teeth of the invaders, grown to a goodly size, and bearing fruit each year.

I used to stay out of doors as much as possible and watch that most delightful form of progress—the preparation of the old garden for young plants, and the new vegetation which spread over it more and more. I found paths I could follow in my daily walk through the field, and explored the wood at the end of it which was to be the retreat of my happiest hours. All this was most pleasant to live through, but not much to write about. However, it indicates the sort of material I have for an autobiography. I have no great adventures to record, no thrilling romances, extraordinary successes. This book contains simply the impressions and feelings which have passed through my mind. But perhaps, after all, our emotions and sensations are what are most worth relating, since they are our real selves.

As the seasons came round, I would run out to gather armfuls of flowers, or watch trees being pruned, or help bring in wood. There were some big elms and apple trees which Mr. Macy used to look after with pride, and they responded beautifully to his care. Every autumn I would put up a ladder against one of the ancient apple trees, climb as high as I could, hold to a branch, and shake down the rosy, fragrant fruit. Then I would descend, pick up the apples, and fill barrels with them for the winter. Those were delicious hours when my soul seemed to cast aside its earthly vesture, glide into the boughs and sing like the birds about me. I also walked a great deal. By following the wire which Mr. Macy had stretched along the field, I easily found my way to a pine wood, where I could sit and dream, or wander from tree to tree. In summer there were tall, bright grasses, timothy, and wonderful goldenrod and Queen Anne's lace. Altogether, it was the longest and most free walk—about a quarter of a mile—that I ever had by myself. These details may seem trivial, but without this bit of freedom and sunny solitude I could not have endured the exacting nature of my daily work. Occasionally some one took me for a "spin" on my tandem bicycle. There long, delightful rides on the trolley cars through the New England woods. I remember with pleasure that no odour of gasoline marred the purity of the air.

As I look back, everything seems to have moved with the slowness of a woodland stream—no automobiles or aeroplanes or radios, no revolutions, no wars. Such was our life in Wrentham, or something like it, between 1905 and 1911. For it so far away, I sometimes feel as if it were a sort of preexistence—a dream of days when I wore another body and had a different consciousness. Yet I clear enough, all the more vivid because it was free from the external distractions which keep one's thoughts occupied with trivial things and leave no leisure for the soul to develop. Where gayety was infrequent, the simplest amusements had the perfume of heavenly joy. Where the surroundings were rural, and life monotonous, any beam that shone upon them precious. Any flower discovered among the rocks and crannies or beside the brook had the rareness of a star. Small events were full of poetry, and the glory of the spirit lay over all.

Chapter II: In The Whirlpool

On our second trip across the continent Miss Polly Thomson, who became my secretary in October, 1914, accompanied us in place of my mother. Her position was, and has been ever since, nominally that of secretary, but as the years passed she has taken upon herself the burden of house management as well. She has never known the luxury of the usual secretary's hours or well-defined duties. A new day for her frequently begins an hour or two after the previous day ends. She has to account for all our engagements, lightning changes and caprices, our sins, commissions, and omissions. Yes, Polly Thomson manages it all. She is our friend, kind and true, full of good nature, often tired, but always with time to do something more. Had it not been for her devotion, adaptability, and willingness to give up every individual pleasure we should long ago have found it necessary to withdraw into complete isolation. For in spite of our income from Mr. Carnegie and the money we made ourselves our expenses were always a ravenous wolf devouring our finances.

After the outbreak of the World War it was impossible for me to enjoy the lecture tours as I had before. Not a cheerful message could I give without a sense of tragic contradiction. Not a thought could I sing in the joy of old days! Even the deepest slumber could not render me quite unconscious of the rising world calamity. I used to wake suddenly from a frightful dream of sweat and blood and multitude, shot, killed, and crazed, and go to sleep only to dream of it again. I was often asked why I did not write something new. How could I write with the thunder of machine guns and the clamour of hate-filled armies deafening my soul, and the conflagration of cities blinding my thoughts? The world seemed one vast Gethsemane, and day unto day and night unto night brought bitter knowledge which must needs become a part of myself. I was in a state of spiritual destitution such as I had not before experienced. Works are the breath and life of happiness, and what works could I show when cry upon cry of destruction floated to me over sea and land? Nothing was sadder to me during those years of disaster than the thousands of letters I received from Europe imploring me for help which I could not give while my teacher and I were with difficulty working our way back and forth across the continent to earn our daily bread. If I did not reply to them it was because I was utterly helpless.

It was extremely hard for me to keep my faith as I read how the mass of patriotic hatred swelled with ever wider and more barbaric violence. Explanations without end filled the pages under my scornful fingers, and they all amounted to the same frightful admission—the collapse of civilization and the betrayal of the most beautiful religion ever preached upon earth.

I clung to the hope that my country would prove itself a generous, friendly power amid the welter of hostility and misery. I believed that President Wilson possessed the nobility and steadfastness required to maintain his policy of neutrality and "Christian gentleness." I determined to do and say my utmost to protest against militarism in the United States. My teacher and I were both worn out; but we felt that we must at least try to carry a message of good will to a stricken world.

Accordingly, during the summer of 1916 we undertook an antipreparedness Chautauqua tour. We were booked for many towns in Nebraska and Kansas a few in Michigan. This tour was far from successful. Most of our audiences were indifferent to the question of peace and war. Fortunately, the weather was unusually cool, and we took advantage of the early morning hours to motor to the next place where we had an engagement. It was a restful experience to ride past hamlets and towns buried in fields of corn and wheat, or over immense prairies bright with sunflowers which were as large as little trees, with big, rough leaves and heavy-headed blossoms. When one saw them at a distance they must have seemed like yellow necklaces winding in and out the bright grass of the prairies. I loved the odour of great harvests which followed us mile after mile through the stillness. But it was not always sunshine and clam. I remember terrific storms with metallic peals of thunder, warm splashes of rain and seas of mud through which our little Ford carried us triumphantly to our destination.

We spoke sometimes in halls or in big, noisy tents full of country folk, or at a camp on the edge of a lake. Occasionally our audience evinced genuine enthusiasm; but I felt more than ever that I was not fitted to address large crowds on subjects which called for a quick cross-play of questions, answers, debate, and repartee.

The attitude of the press was maddening. It seems to me difficult to imagine anything more fatuous and stupid than their comments on anything I say touching public affairs. So long as I confine my activities to social service and the blind, they compliment me extravagantly, calling me the "archpriestess of the sightless," "wonder woman," and "modern miracle," but when it comes to a discussion of a burning social or political issue, especially if I happen to be as I so often am, on the unpopular side, the tone changes completely. They are grieving because they imagine I am in the hands of unscrupulous persons who take advantage of my afflictions to make me a mouthpiece for their own ideas. It has always been natural for me to speak my mind, and the pent-up feelings which kept beating against my heart at that time demanded an outlet. I like frank debate, and I do not object to harsh criticism so long as I am treated like a human being with a mind of her own.

The group of which I was part was doing all it could to keep America out of the war.[6] At the same time another group, equally earnest, was doing all it could to precipitate America into the war. In this group, the one who at the time seemed most important, was ex-President Roosevelt.

I had met President Roosevelt in 1903 during a visit to my foster father, Mr. Hitz. He sent me a great basket of flowers and expressed the wish that I might find it agreeable to call upon him at the White House. The President was very cordial. He asked Miss Sullivan many questions about my education. Then he turned to me and asked me if there was any way in which he could talk to me himself. I told him he could learn the manual alphabet in a few minutes, and at his request showed him the letters. He made a few of them with his own hand. "F" bothered him, and he said impatiently, "I'm too clumsy." Then

Miss Sullivan showed him how he could communicate with me by lip-reading.

He asked me if I thought he should let young Theodore play football. I was embarrassed because I could not tell whether he was joking or seriously asking my opinion. I told him, with straight face, that at Radcliffe we did not play football, but that I had heard that learned Harvard professors were objecting to it because it took so much of the boys' time away from their studies. Then he asked me if I had heard of Pliny and when I told him I had he asked if I had read his letter to Trajan in which he says that if the Greeks are permitted to keep up their athletics their minds will be so occupied with them that they will not be dangerous to Rome. We talked about Miss Holt's work for the blind in New York and what I had been doing in Massachusetts and he urged me to keep on prodding people about their responsibilities to the blind. "There's nothing better we can do in the world than to serve a good purpose."

My impression of him then was of an alert man, poised as if to spring, and besides alertness there was a kind of eagerness to act first. During those years preceding America's entrance into the war it seemed to me, as it has seemed ever since, that he was more precipitate than wise. It was the speed at which he moved that gave us the impression that he was accomplishing mighty things. Only in aggressiveness was he strong.

What the group I represented desired was fair discussion and open debate. I wanted to have the whole matter put before the people so they could decide whether they wanted to go into the conflict or stay out. As it was, they had no choice in the matter.

I do not pretend that I know the whole solution of the world's problems, but I am burdened with a Puritanical sense of obligation to set the world to rights. I feel responsible for many enterprises that are not really my business at all, but many times I have kept silence on issues that interested me deeply through the fear that others would be blamed for my opinions. I have never been willing to believe that human nature cannot be changed; but even if it cannot, I am sure it can be curbed and led into channels of usefulness. I believe that life, not wealth, is the aim of existence—life including all its attributes of love, happiness, and joyful labour. I believe war is the inevitable fruit of our economic system, but even if I am wrong I believe that truth can lose nothing by agitation but may gain all.

I tried to make my audiences see what I saw, but the people who crowded the great tents were disappointed or indifferent. They had come to hear me talk about happiness, and perhaps recite, "Nearer, My God, to Thee, Nearer to Thee," or "My Country, 'Tis of Thee, Sweet Land of Liberty," and they did not care to have their peace of mind disturbed by talk about war, especially as the majority of them believed then that we would not be drawn into the European maelstrom.

No words can express the frustration of those days. And, indeed, what are words but "painted fire" before realities that lift the spirit or cast it down? No real communication of profound experiences can ever pass from one to another by words. Only those who are sensitive to spiritual vibrations can hear in them the fluttering of the soul, as a disturbed bird flutters in the depths of a thicket. One's life-story cannot be told with complete veracity. A true autobiography would have to be written in states of mind, emotions, heartbeats, smiles, and tears, not in months and years, or physical events. Life is marked off on the soul-chart by feelings, not by dates. Mere facts cannot present to the reader an experience of the heart in all its evanescent hues and fluctuations.

I am now going to dig an episode out of my memory which has contradictory aspects. For that reason I would rather keep it locked up in my own heart. But when one writes an autobiography, one seems, tacitly at least, to promise the reader that one will not conceal anything just because it is unpleasant, and awakens regrets of the past. I would not have anyone think that I have told in this book only such things as seemed to me likely to win the approbation of the reader. I want whoever is interested to know that I am a mere mortal, with a human being's frailties and inconsistencies.

On the second Chautauqua tour I was accompanied by Mrs. Macy and a young man who interpreted for me. Miss Thomson was on a vacation at her home in Scotland. The young man was very much in earnest, and eager to have the people get my message. He returned to Wrentham with us in the autumn of 1916 after our disappointing and exhausting summer. Our homecoming was far from happy. Mr.

Macy was not there to greet us. Dear Ian had done everything he could to make the house attractive and the garden beautiful with flowers; but there was no cheerfulness in our hearts, and the flowers seemed to add to the gloom. I telegraphed my mother to come to Wrentham, and in a few days her presence sweetened our loneliness.

But we were scarcely settled when Mrs. Macy fell ill. She had succumbed to fatigue and anxiety. She developed pleurisy and a tenacious cough, and her physician advised her to go to Lake Placid for the winter. That meant that our home would be broken up. We should have to let Ian go, since we could no longer afford to keep him. This hurt us more than anything. For we all loved Ian. Mrs. Macy had taken him from the fields—a Lithuanian peasant who could not speak three words of English—and trained him to be a cook and butler and houseman. He was devoted to us, and we felt when he went that the heart of the Wrentham place would stop beating.

I could not work, I could not think calmly. For the first time in my life it seemed folly to be alive. I had often been asked what I should do if anything happened to my teacher. I was now asking myself the same question. I saw more clearly than ever before how inseparably our lives were bound together. How lonely and bleak the world would be without her. What could I do? I could not imagine myself going on with my work alone. To do anything in my situation, it was essential to have about me friends who cared deeply for the things I did. My experience of the summer had brought home to me the fact that few people were interested in my aims and aspirations. Once more I was overwhelmed by a sense of my isolation.

Such was the background of the adventure I shall relate. I was sitting alone in my study one evening, utterly despondent. The young man who was still acting as my secretary in the absence of Miss Thomson, came in and sat down beside me. For a long time he held my hand in silence, then he began talking to me tenderly. I was surprised that he cared so much about me. There was sweet comfort in his loving words. I listened all a-tremble. He was full of plans for my happiness. He said if I would marry him, he would always be near to help me in the difficulties of life. He would be there to read to me, look up material for my books and do as much as he could of the work my teacher had done for me.

His love was a bright sun that shone upon my helplessness and isolation. The sweetness of being loved enchanted me, and I yielded to an imperious longing to be a part of a man's life. For a brief space I danced in and out of the gates of Heaven, wrapped up in a web of bright imaginings. Naturally, I wanted to tell my mother and my teacher about the wonderful thing that had happened to me; but the young man said, "Better wait a bit, we must tell them together. We must try to realize what their feelings will be. Certainly, they will disapprove at first. Your mother does not like me, but I shall win her approval by my devotion to you. Let us keep our love secret a little while. Your teacher is too ill to be excited just now, and we must tell her first." I had happy hours with him. We walked in the autumn splendour of the woods, and he read to me a great deal. But the secrecy which circumstances appeared to impose upon us made me suffer. The thought of not sharing my happiness with my mother and her who had been all things to me for thirty years seemed abject, and little by little it destroyed the joy of being loved. As we parted one night, I told him I had made up my mind definitely to tell my teacher everything the next morning. But the next morning Fate took matters into her own hands and tangled the web, as is her wont. I was dressing, full of the excitement of what I was going to communicate to my loved ones, when my mother entered my room in great distress. With a shaking hand she demanded, "What have you been doing with that creature? The papers are full of a dreadful story about you and him. What does it mean? Tell me!" I sensed such hostility towards my lover in her manner and words that in a panic I pretended not to know what she was talking about. "Are you engaged to him? Did you apply for a marriage license?" Terribly frightened, and not knowing just what had happened, but anxious to shield my lover, I denied everything. I even lied to Mrs. Macy, fearing the consequences that would result from the revelation coming to her in this shocking way. My mother ordered the young man out of the house that very day. She would not even let him speak to me, but he wrote me a note in braille, telling where he would be, and begging me to keep him informed. I kept on denying that I knew anything about the story in the papers until Mrs. Macy went to Lake Placid with Miss Thomson, who had returned from Scotland, and my mother took me home to Montgomery.

In time she found out how I had deceived her and everyone else. The memory of her sorrow burns me to the soul. She begged me not to write Mrs. Macy anything about it until we knew that she was stronger. "The shock would kill her, I am sure," she said. It was months later when my teacher learned the truth.

I cannot account for my behaviour. As I look back and try to understand, I am completely bewildered. I seem to have acted exactly opposite to my nature. It can be explained only in the old way—that love makes us blind and leaves the mind confused and deprives it of the use of judgment. I corresponded with the young man for several months; but my love-dream was shattered. It had flowered under an inauspicious star. The unhappiness I had caused my dear ones produced a state of mind unfavourable to the continuance of my relations with the young man. The love which had come unseen and unexpected departed with tempest on its wings.

As time went on, the young man and I became involved in a net of falsehood and misunderstanding. I am sure that if Mrs. Macy had been there, she would have understood, and sympathized with us both. The most cruel sorrows in life are not its losses and misfortunes, but its frustrations and betrayals.

The brief love will remain in my life, a little island of joy surrounded by dark waters. I am glad that I have had the experience of being loved and desired. The fault was not in the loving, but in the circumstances. A lovely thing tried to express itself; but conditions were not right or adequate, and it never blossomed. Yet the failure, perhaps, only serves to set off the beauty of the intention. I see it all now with a heart that has grown sad in growing wiser.

All that winter was a time of anxiety and suffering. My teacher's health did not improve and she was very unhappy in the bleak climate of Lake Placid. Finally, about the beginning of December, she sailed for Porto [sic] Rico, accompanied by Polly Thomson. She remained there until the following April, and almost every week brought me a letter with her own hand in braille, full of delight over the wonderful climate of Porto Rico. She described "the loveliest sky in the world," the palms and cocoanuts, tree-like ferns, lilies, poinsettias, and many beautiful flowers she had never seen before. She declared that if she got well anywhere, it would be on that enchanted island. But she did not really recover until the fall after she returned to Wrentham; she could not lecture again for more than a year.

I had often been urged to write a book about the blind, and I was eager to do it now, not only because I thought it might help their cause but because I wanted something to take my mind away from war questions. I might have done it that winter, but I could not collect material for such a book without my teacher's help and I could not afford expert assistance. I dwell so much on the inadequacy of my income, not because I see in it a reason for complaint, but because many people have criticized my teacher and me for the things we have left undone. If they only knew how many of our years have been sacrificed to practical and impractical ways of earning a living!

In various ways our small fortune had become so depleted that we were obliged to sell our home in Wrentham. We had been one with the house, one with the sweetness of the town. Our joys and affections had peopled the rooms and many objects had woven themselves by long companionship into my daily life there. There was a friendly sense about the long, handsome oak table where I wrote and spread out my papers with comfort, the spacious bookcases, the big study windows where my plants had welcomed me with blossoms and the sofa where I had sat by a cheery fire. How many of those fires had shone upon faces I loved, had warmed hands whose clasp I shall feel no more, and gladdened hearts that are now still! The very sorrows we had endured there had endeared that home all the more to us.

The house seemed to have a personality, and to mourn our going away. Each room spoke to us in unheard but tender accents. I do not think of a house merely as wood, stone, and cement, but as a spirit which shelters or casts out, blesses or condemns. It was a sweet old farmhouse that had enfolded me, and which had stored away in its soul the laughter of children and the singing of birds. It was a home where rural peace had smiled upon my work. There I watched the ploughing and harrowing of the fields, and the sowing of seed, waited for new flowers and vegetables in the garden. When we left the sun was shining, and the magic of June was everywhere, except in our hearts. My feet almost refused to move as we stepped out of a house where I had thrilled to the beauty of so many golden seasons! Oh, those Mays with dainty marsh-marigolds and a sea of violets, pink and white drifts of apple blossoms! Oh, the Junes with the riot of ramblers up the walls, the red clover and white Queen Anne's lace, purple iron-weed, and all about the divine aroma of pine needles! Oh, the breezes with the coolness of deep woods and rippling streams! All my tree-friends were there, too—the slender white pines by my study, the big, hospitable apple trees, one with a seat where I had sat wrapped in bright dreams, the noble elms casting shadows far over the fields and the spruces nodding to me. Nowhere was there a suggestion of world wars, falling empires, and bitter disillusionment, but a sense of per-manence and charm which I have not experienced so fully since. Thirteen years we had lived there. It was not a long period measured by years and much of the time we had perforce been away, yet it was a lifetime measured in seasons of the heart.

The one thought which cheered us as we drove away that sad morn-ing was that the house we had loved so well would be good to others. It is now a rest home for the girls working at Jordan Marsh department store, Boston; but it is so endeared to me by all intimate joys and sor-rows that no matter who lives in it and no matter where I go I shall al-ways think of it as home.

40 Helen Keller's Journal

London: Michael Joseph, 1938.

Only two weeks after Anne Macy's October 1936 death, Keller began a journal that chronicled the next six months—her escape to Scot-land, the return to a home without Anne, the preparations for Japan, and time aboard the ship *Asama-Maru*. This very honest chronicle of the period includes her profound mourning as well as reflections on King Edward's abdication, Christmas in Scotland, and *Gone With the Wind*. These selec-tions from the *Journal* provide glimpses of the chronicle that ends on April 14, 1937, Anne's birthday. She had been dead almost six months.

Aboard the S.S. Deutschland, en route for England.
Midnight of November 4, 1936.

The deepest sorrow knows no time—it seems an eternal night. Truly did Emerson say that when we travel we do not escape from ourselves, we carry with us the sadness which blurs all places and all days.

This is the first voyage Polly and I have had without Teacher, who was the life and the center of our journeyings by land and sea. Not until now have I realized that I shall not see her on earth. Our friends who came to bid us good-bye brought flowers and fruits only for Polly and me. We have just one room for two beds and coffee served mornings for only two. Dear, brave Polly, who used to read aloud to Teacher constantly now reads to me with her fingers when I can pay attention. The anguish which makes me feel cut in two prevents me from writing another word about these life-wrecking changes.

Most of the time I appear to myself to be a somnambulist, impelled only by an intense faith. It is sweet because it helps me to cross half-way with Teacher into her new and infinitely richer life. It is terrible because it drives me relentlessly to think of others' sorrow before my own, to hold up the torch of hope for the blind when tears blot out all the stars for me, to perform one task after another when the joy of work is fled.

November 5th

A day dreadful beyond words. I am beginning to come out of the stupor of grief, and every nerve is acquiver. It does not seem possible that the pain flooding through my heart can ever be stilled, but I know it is a sign of returning spiritual health.

Sometimes as Polly and I walk up and down the deck, she describes to me the gulls dipping and circling about the ship and the tiny white sea-swallows that fly incredible distances—from three to four thousand miles.

Are those sea-swallows wise or foolish to go so far out to sea, defenceless [sic], small, beyond rescue? At first I was inclined to think it was contrary to the laws of nature for them to risk such long flights, especially as great numbers perish from cold or fall a prey to large fish as they sleep on the water.

On the other hand, many reach safely "lands that keep the sun," and return triumphantly north with the spring!

November 8th

What earthly consolation is there for one like me whom fate has denied a husband and the joy of motherhood? At the moment my loneliness seems a void that will always be immense. Fortunately I have much work to do—more than ever before in fact—and while doing it I shall have confidence as always that my unfulfilled longings will be gloriously satisfied in a world where eyes never grow dim nor ears dull.

This evening, after a brilliant day, Polly kept telling me how marvelous the sunset was. She said sky and sea were suffused with a rose tinge defying the power of the brush or the pen to capture. Often I had felt petals showered upon me by a passing breeze; so I could imagine the sunset as a vast rose-garden from which the petals had been shaken, and were drifting through the sky before sinking into the grey November night.

November 11th

Armistice Day. Sorrow has borne me far from earth, and as yet I sense happenings in the world only with the surface of my mind, but dimly I realize that this is Armistice Day. What a glorious homage we shall pay to the dead of the Great War when we call November 11th World Peace Day. To-night Polly saw the Lizard Lighthouse, and we were homesick remembering how when Teacher first saw Cornwall she was captivated by its beauty and its wealth of legends and ballads.

Old Neptune is true to form as we approach the rocky, dangerous Cornish coast.

The ship is listing; our trunks are falling all over the room. The table is almost on top of me as I lie upon my bed, and my hands can scarcely keep their balance on the keys of the sliding typewriter.

November 18th

In the Shakespearean phrase my eyes are still "seeled up" by drowsiness, but a cup of hot coffee has waked me sufficiently to write.

English bacon and eggs for breakfast—the first I have had since arriving in London, and how good they tasted! I have just said to Polly that I rather enjoy this hard work, and the English way of life that enables me to do it in peace of mind and body. Yesterday the weather treated us to its worst usage, and I exclaimed: "Men may come and men may go, but the rain goes on forever." However, the air feels lighter to-day, and I think we shall have a pleasant journey.

En route to Scotland, November 18th

An autumn day sweet with sunshine and the odour of fields still green and falling leaves that I smelt through the open window. The cattle grazing peacefully; the countryside changing from pastures to smoke-blackened towns; and then to grassy hills "attune with the wind," and streams playing hide and seek with the sunbeams among the trees and great moors.

Polly and I were alone in the compartment until lunch-time, and I could hardly believe it. Teacher had always journeyed with us through Britain, doubling with her passionate love of beauty our delight in what we saw and touched. She must be asleep, I thought, or she would be spelling into my hand the charm of light or colour or flying cloud.

The yearning for her companionship almost unnerved me; but despite her skepticism, she has not challenged for nothing my faith that our spiritual nearness would outlast death, and I braced myself thinking of her blessedness in seeing without effort or pain and the joyous, unfettered use of her powers.

I pictured her, brilliant, animated, spreading charm and gaiety among her friends rediscovered. A sweet awareness came over me that the loveliness which she had cherished on earth was shining about her as an aura. Though beyond my reach, I knew she had not forgotten our sojourn together amid the shadows, and that she wanted to share with me the infinitely higher knowledge and happiness of her unhandicapped life. For every thorn of poverty, every disappointment endured, every ache of loneliness and misunderstanding, and the sight she vainly strove to keep to the end, there was without doubt a splendid recompense.

No; perhaps I should not say recompense, but rather the unfolding of her own inner personality with undreamed power to quicken the eye and make the ear sensitive to loftier harmonies. Since teaching had been her work and her glory, I imagined her tenderly receiving the sensorially-crippled from this world to the next, and so instructing them that they need not grope nor be buried in silence nor stumble along desolate ways. Who knows, this may have been real news she whispered into my listening mind. Certainly my soul was so conscious of her presence, I could not—I would not—say she was dead, and I do not know.

I still perceived, as it were, a lameness in my spirit. The wrench of separation from a beloved, unique, life-long companion seemed to have torn away an essential part of me. Deaf-blind a second time, I find any effort to speak cheerfully, to resume interest in a changed world, to work along through substituted guides and minders different from Teacher's—all these I found as hampering as sharp pain-throbs. Nevertheless, as the hours glided by, fresh life pulsed through me; and my hold on present duties and opportunities grew stronger.

I turned to a book I had bought, André Maurois's *Life of Disraeli*. It appeals to me as an internationalist, written in French by a Frenchman about one of Britain's most eminent political leaders. It is vivid, instructive, generous as far as may be to all the actors in a fateful empire drama, balanced by a just regard for spiritual values and the large perspective of history.

I do not remember a more impressive word-picture than Maurois's portrayal of Gladstone and Disraeli. Gladstone, robustly self-confident, exalted with rectitude, a dragon breathing fire against the arch-enemy of mankind in public, and at home felling mighty trees with the conviction that he was the divinely appointed woodsman who should clear away the dense, unhealthy vegetation of corrupt politics from the British Empire. Disraeli, always ill, old, struggling for breath, unable to walk, yet steering Britain with indomitable will out of a disastrous European conflict and planning the change of an empire based on force into a federation of self-governing peoples with an imperial parliament. Sixty years have elapsed, and only now this statesmanlike policy won an advocate here and there! While recognizing the equal sincerity of the two titans, I prefer Disraeli because of his long views, his gentleness and tolerance to all races, his imagination and revealing humour. Never did he forget a moment his motto: "Life is too short to be little." Democracy that means freedom for all the people from oppression by one or many, is the rock upon which I rest my hope for a saner, more finely organized society; but Gladstone's fierce partisanship blinded him to the ultimate good both of his own people and the nations at large.

Closing the book, I leaned back and marveled for the millionth time at the wealth and freedom literature has made mine.

Later—The Manse, Bothwell

To-day at lunch on the Scots express I was agreeably surprised to be recognized by a waiter who had seen me three years before on my last trip to Scotland. He said I gave him some flowers which he took home to his mother. I could not recall the flowers, but it warmed my heart to know he had never forgotten me.

Tea was especially enjoyable this afternoon, because there was a cheery Scotswoman sitting by to share it with us. Polly liked her wholesome face, and I was glad of the sweet home talk that strikes a common chord in the souls of all travelers. I noticed she was knitting stockings, and I said I envied her that skill in handicrafts. It had always been a joy for me to create a useful or attractive article, and I had rarely squeezed in time enough to gratify this instinct.

Suddenly Polly spelled: "Helen, here we are in Glasgow!"

Her brother the Minister and his wife were waiting for us, and the warmth with which they embraced us both made me feel that I too had come home. As we walked along the platform, a porter from the Central Hotel (where Teacher, Polly and I had often stayed) greeted me most kindly. It makes me proud to receive such cordial salutations from those who do the work of the world.

At The Manse, the door was opened long before the Minister turned the car into the driveway and everybody crowded on the steps to welcome us—his oldest son, David, who is studying at the University of Glasgow; Effie, the only daughter; and the two younger boys, Robert and John; Jean, the soul of loyalty in household service; even the dog Skye. There was a general rush to bring in our luggage, the children guiding me with adorable solicitude upstairs to my room.

I have been here several hours, and the boys cannot yet realize that I can find my way about; they are so afraid I may fall or bump into something. I am happy to have two such dear little knights on the lookout for my safety and comfort.

Like the foolish city folk we have become, Polly and I were thinly dressed, and despite our fur coats we got chilled motoring through a heavy fog, but the fire in the Minister's study and Jean's delicious Scotch broth warmed us up quickly. After supper we gathered round the fire to hear and tell the thousand and one little things which only a look, the tone of voice, or a gesture, can truly interpret. It was good to feel Polly's fingers less weighed by grief than they had been for months. Skye lay at my feet, his big paws on the fender, his nose almost in the fire, and did not seem to mind being roasted. He is quite as affectionate to me now as when he was a two-month-old puppy; I saw him first in August, 1932, when the Thomsons, Teacher, Polly and I went on a fascinating trip to the Island of Skye, and on our way back to the mainland stopped at a hotel at Lochalsh. Two puppies belonging to the hotel frisked about us while we sat in the sunshine, and Effie played with them. We bought one for her as a living souvenir of one of our happiest outings, and that is how he came to be called Skye. He was one with the heather-breathing hills, the sparkling loch and the rocks and moors. Heavier grown, he is still lovable—a fat, comical cross between a fox-terrier and an Airedale or a spaniel— long ears and feet big enough for a Newfoundland.

November 23rd

Up at half-past seven. From nine until one I wrote letters which did not soothe me. Weary and restless, I was glad when the children entered the room like sunshine. . . . Sometimes I am uneasy about my hands; I use them too constantly, writing, reading, listening to conversation and reading people's lips; but work is the only sure bulwark against despair.

December 22nd

If Santa Claus were to descend the chimney, reindeer, pack and all, there could not be more running to and fro here this morning. Round me are flowing two streams of Christmas cablegrams, letters and packages, one out to the post-office, the other in the holly-wreathed front door.

Six of us have been stirring the plum pudding, and now it is boiling, bubbling, sending a jolly odour through the house. . . .

The Central Hotel, Glasgow, December 23rd

This morning I awoke positively sure I had seen Teacher, and I have been happier all day. I dreamed she was driving with Polly and me through a countryside resembling South Arcan with heather-plumed hills and hawthorn-bloom waves rolling from hedge to hedge.

She glowed with health and the joy of finding me so close to her; she looked and looked as if she could not have enough of the loveliness about us. She gave me an exquisite violin-like instrument, saying: "*Listen, Helen, and this will be an ear for you. It will rain sounds upon your hand—song-birds, passing footsteps from afar, murmuring water you cannot reach. Another of your fetters shall be broken.*"

A caress—and she was gone; yet I was not troubled. Somehow I knew her presence had been a blessed presence, and I awoke with peace that had not nested in my heart for long months. As to the sound-bringer, I still have to learn whether it was only a dream or a prophecy. . . .

It is a real pleasure to walk through the streets of Glasgow to-day while doing our Christmas shopping. The crowds were dense, but good-humoured. Almost everyone was carrying parcels and holly, and I felt that the Christmas spirit truly reigned in the city as well as out in the quiet countryside. The assistants, too, though working early and late in packed shops, found time to be pleasant and full of good wishes for "a Merry Christmas." Happily I anticipate to-mor-row, with the children free from desk work and the heartache it often brings.

December 28th

How pleasant the room I write in is! Drinah visits me every morn-ing and puts her golden paws up on my knee to attract my attention. Evidently she understands by now that I cannot see or hear her.

While I am here I give the dogs their daily tidbit of roll. After lunch or dinner they are allowed in the dining-room. They always take ex-actly the same position, Hamel, the mother, between her two daugh-ters and Drinah at the end of the row. As I pass the tidbit from one to another, I feel the ruffle in Carrie's neck, in fact a little golden mane, which I believe is rare among Labradors.

To-day my head is buzzing with a letter that seems the call of des-tiny. Two years ago a blind man who champions the cause of the blind in Japan, Mr. Iwahashi, called on me in New York. We quickly be-came friends, he was so understanding, full of the delicate Japanese imagination that blossoms in faith, art and philosophy. He commu-nicated with me by writing in Braille what he wished to say; and my odd, halting speech did not seem to puzzle him after the first few sen-tences.

When I said I hoped I might visit Japan, his answer took away my breath:

"Will you come to Japan, please, Miss Keller, in the Spring and open doors of help for our brothers and sisters shut out in a great darkness, if I arrange with the Japanese Government to sponsor the trip?"

Hardly believing my fingers' report of his Braille invitation, I thanked him and explained that I could not leave Teacher who was ill and rapidly becoming blind. In quaint English he replied: "God's miracles never stop. Perhaps by a way higher than earth's ways He will help your teacher to see, then she can come to Japan with you."

I thought the matter would rest there.

Several months later Mr. Iwahashi sent a formal invitation, leaving the date open for my convenience either in the spring or autumn of

1936. Plans had been made by the Japanese Government to provide hospitality for the three of us during the whole trip. He also informed me that all my books had been translated into Japanese, and he said it would mean much to the cause if I would be present at the dedication of the new Lighthouse for the Blind at Osaka during October, 1936. Such a magnificent opportunity to kindle new hope for the handicapped, not only in Japan but throughout the Orient, dazzled my imagination. Nevertheless, I declined. Teacher's sight had not improved despite two operations, and her health was completely broken.

My Japanese friends' attitude towards this refusal did honour to their hearts. They invited us a second time last spring, not knowing that Teacher was growing worse. She was unhappy that I should let go another unique opportunity, and almost overrode my objections. Still I said, "No," and felt sure that would be the end.

Early this month, to my amazement, I had a cable begging me to visit Japan in the spring. Polly and I said, "Yes" to ourselves, but prudence dictated that we should consult Mr. Migel. I wrote him at once expressing a strong wish to obey the third summons, which I looked upon as a miracle. Mr. Migel sent a letter warmly approving the plan; and now here I am with a long Braille letter from Mr. Iwahashi entreating Polly and me to accept, and declaring that everything is ready for us. He wishes us to be there the middle of April, travel though Japan, Korea and Manchukuo and finish our tour towards the end of June. While awaiting further developments, my thoughts crowd and obliterate each other like fogs that hide landmarks. So swiftly are things happening, we must keep planning ahead every day now if we are to be prepared for any turn our affairs may take.

Later. The Manse, Bothwell

This afternoon we motored to Edinburgh to do a little shopping and visit some friends. Going back to Bothwell in the evening, Polly gave a jump of delight: "Helen! There is Edinburgh Castle floodlighted—it looks like Fairyland." From all accounts it must be a glorious sight, suspended in space, casting an enchanting spell of unreality upon the grey city.

Scarcely inside the Manse, we find another army of letters tumbling about our ears; but I am marching Polly and myself off to bed, foreseeing that we shall need all possible sleep to face the barrage tomorrow.

January 6th

A sun-burst touched my face early this morning and actually coaxed me out of bed. I opened the window and exuberant greetings floated up to me from the box hedges, just as in April. Polly said the crows were cawing lustily, the thrushes and tits twittering all around. Out in the garden I saw the yellow jasmine blooming, and they tell me snow drops and other spring flowers will appear soon. How different Scotland, with its frost and snow melting at noonday and a happy imminence of spring throughout the winter, is from the northern United States with the sod frozen hard and not a sign of greenness or fragrance during four or five months!

Six long notes and two short written this morning, and there are still a dozen in the offing, but my hands demanded a rest. . . . Curiously enough, a presentiment keeps knocking away at my mind's door that I shall not much longer be able to keep at the typewriter as steadily as I have. Often my hands feel cramped or limp, which does not surprise me, as they have never been still, except in sleep, since I was two years old. They mean the world I live in—they are eyes, ears, channels of thought and goodwill. Sooner would I lose my health or even the ability to walk (and walking is among the few cherished bits of personal liberty I possess) than the use of these two hands. However, if I take proper care of them now and use other muscles not already overtasked, I shall still have the joy of working in different ways. What these ways will be I am not certain, but I shall know when I begin experimenting.

Later. The Manse, Bothwell

Happy to be back with the children, whose lives are so far from the maddening cares and griefs of the world. Caught in a downpour hurrying from the cinema at Hamilton, and came home by starlight. The picture we saw was "Fury," a powerful impeachment of lynching and of the citizens who perpetrate it in some parts of the United States. In my opinion their mob inhumanity is without excuse. Wendell Phillips, one of America's great anti-slavery champions, had wide experience with mobs, and said they were usually "respectable," well dressed, with some education. Since childhood, my heart has been hot against lynching, whether the victim is white or black. However horrible the crime, I would insist that no human being be denied a fair trial; and if the trial is delayed, a mob—insanity let loose—is unthinkable for dealing justice. Revenge is given as the motive. Revenge indeed! Do not those who stoop to it place themselves on a level with the evil-doers they execute?

It is curious how thoughts behave. They elude me in a crowd. Like spirits, they must be spoken to in solitude before they will explain themselves.

February 23rd

This has been one of the rare days on which Polly is left undisturbed long enough to read me the large batch of mail always waiting for us. Then followed a long sitting for my answering letters, autographing books and pictures which Polly wrapped and addressed. After seventeen hours we are just beginning to relax.

A gust of irritability is blowing through me just now because there has been a recurrence of a tendency in some people to try to run my affairs. This seems all the stranger to me because since I was seventeen I have managed my own life. At the age of twenty-two I began working very hard for whatever money I have earned during the past thirty-four years. Of my own accord I have undertaken public responsibilities in America and other lands. After Teacher's health broke down I worked very much alone with Polly's hand to furnish information and her voice to reinforce my halting speech. Yet there are still those who appear to think it is incumbent upon them to alter my life course according to their own ideas! There was some excuse when I was young and bewildered in search of something worth doing. But Mother and Teacher knew me better than anybody else ever did, and they never dictated the course of action I should follow. There have always been other friends with power to advance the work for the blind, and they respect my desire as a human being to be free. It is beautiful to consider how their co-operation has increased my happiness and rendered possible whatever I have accomplished. However, unless I keep on my guard against uncalled-for though well-meant interference, they cannot help me any more than they can help any other person who weakly surrenders his will to another.

March 3rd

Herbert was still suffering terribly this morning. He did not want to leave us in the midst of everything, but I knew he must go, and Polly took him to the hospital.

Heartsick and discouraged, I went down to see Wendy and her darling puppies. It was a comfort to stroke their lovely forms and notice how they grow. By their uncertain movements I know they have not got their eyes open yet.

No sooner had Polly returned than we hurried away to take out her naturalization papers. Judge Richards had done all he could to expedite matters, but we were kept an hour and a half. Polly was asked innumerable questions. Then I was called in as a witness. Barney, who had come with us, took me to the desk. I was required to hold up my hand and swear that I am a citizen supporting the Government of the United States. Then the judge placed my fingers on his lips and asked my name and where I live. I answered, and turning to Barney he told her to repeat his words while I read them from her lips: "Do you recognize Miss Thomson as a citizen of the United States"? Dr. Saybolt also served as a witness.

Polly did not get her papers after all, because there are some details about which the immigration authorities are not quite satisfied, and she must appear before them again in the autumn. Those aliens laws are most exasperating and confusing.

It was nearly three o'clock when we lunched at the Pomonoc Country Club. It was Judge Richards's birthday, and Polly and I arranged a luncheon in honour of the occasion. I would have given much to be in a festive mood: he has such a big, warm heart, and never misses a chance to do us a kindness.

Stopped at the hospital a few minutes to see Herbert; then I wrote until and after dinner. This is the strangest, saddest 3rd of March I ever spent, and Teacher has not seemed so far away as to-night.[7]

March 19th

Dr. Berens was pleased with my eyes which are improving rapidly. From his office we rushed to the dentist's, and afterwards lunched at the St. Regis Hotel with Edith Cooper. She had interesting things to tell us about her recent trip to Mexico—the incredible ignorance of the peons; the 160 million pesos they send annually to Rome, Aztec gods worshipped as well as Christian saints, and how beautiful Mexican babies are. . . .

At Bendel's an hour, then on to Bonnie MacLeary's studio. She made a cast of Teacher's hand thinking it might comfort me. It was a touching tribute to Teacher wrought by a true artist. I summoned what composure I could to touch the grateful outline of the hand and the thumb and index finger from the letter L suggesting Love. I traced each line in the palm, startling distinct and true—a likeness snatched as it were from death's relentless waves. In spite of myself I succumbed to the old heartbreak; my tears fell; and I could not speak. It troubles me that I could not more fittingly thank the artist who had earnestly striven to express a lovely thought for my consolation.

I was cheered to-night to find Herbert much better—looking quite like himself, Polly said.

Aboard the *Asama-Maru,* April 1st

Why, oh, why did I start this diary, knowing how crowded my life had been for many years? When it is almost impossible to write letters, it seems the height of absurdity to attempt self-recording of any sort. As it is, I can only snatch moments to jot down fragmentary paragraphs or ideas which I have no time to develop, as a hungry man seizes mouthfuls of food. But, having gone so far as I have, I cannot now surrender the raw material I have retrieved from oblivion; it will brighten my dull moments in retrospect.

A hectic morning. A good-bye interview with reporters who asked for my impressions of the San Francisco bridge precisely at the moment when I felt most idealess. . . .

Kate Foley called. She knows the hand alphabet, and as we have long been comrades in the struggle towards a happier world for the blind, we spent a cosy hour together. Now there is another close bond between us. Her sister, whose discerning sympathy and rich helpfulness carried her through innumerable difficulties, passed away last year, and Kate is quite as much alone as I am on the dark trail. More than ever I admire the cheerful courage with which she raises the newly blinded out of despair and pushes forward the campaign for the prevention of blindness. With modest simplicity she startled me by saying she would travel all by herself to the convention for the blind in Toronto, she, Kate Foley, who is both crippled and without sight!

Finished my packing in breathless haste, and Polly and I found ourselves in Elsie's car, skidding through a pouring rain and congested streets. The *Asama-Maru* was due to sail at noon, and I felt the last warning whistle as we arrived. A large throng—Americans and Japanese, including the deaf and the blind—greeted us, and I almost disappeared beneath a mound of hothouse and garden flowers. Elsie and "Pussy-Willow" parked the car, but evidently the crowd swept them aside, for they were nowhere to be seen when Polly and I came on deck to wave good-bye. With imperative fingers Polly spelled "Helen! a picture," and though the rain came down in torrents we swung into a pose for the camera. Already I know the Japanese will want to photograph us constantly on our way to the Orient and back.

When we sailed through the Golden Gate a god plucked me by the ear, as the Romans would say, and winged memory bore me back twenty-two years to Mount Tamalpais where Teacher, Polly and I sat one heavenly day with San Francisco Bay gleaming, green-gold-blue, and the giant sequoia forest below us. Ned Holmes held us spellbound with romantic tales of the ships that entered the harbour, laden with jade, ivory, mahogany, myrrh and frankincense from the Far East. As we listened, Polly and I resolved (I did not then know our wish was simultaneous) that some time we would go the way of those ships from the Golden Gate to the Orient. Wonder-smitten, I felt the *Asama-Maru* bearing us like a mighty genie at the command of Aladdin's lamp through that world gateway. In a midst of rain we moved slowly under the great Golden Gate Bridge, which is almost completed, and past the cliffs that rise sheer out of the sea. Then I had a sensation as if we dropped out of a life into another—into unknown vastitudes of experience.

Yet I did not feel lost; rather I exulted in the thought of new horizons opening before my mind. Perhaps that was the beginning of my release from the torturing sense that a world had been burnt out with Teacher's passing. Certainly she seemed nearer than she had since she last kissed me. My purpose was revitalized, as if she had spoken from her celestial home encouraging me to go forth into the darknesses and silences yet untouched by hope. With her earthly presence is gone the dear familiar home atmosphere, and it may be that the task now required of me is to grow a new self out of the emotions and impressions I shall no doubt bring back to America. My heart is still like a house where friends come and go, but no one else can ever be Teacher or mother or father to me, and that means that one intimate chamber remains closed until I, too, depart. Since I have no husband or child, I do not know if other rooms will be opened for satisfying human relationships, but "before me, as behind me, is God, and all is well."[8]

Our stateroom resembled a conservatory. One unusual basket of flowers was sent by the Japanese women of San Francisco. In this most touching gesture, sixteen groups—Buddhists, Shintoists, Christians— were represented. There was a delectable basket of fruit from Mr. Pfeiffer with a warm-hearted letter of good wishes and a cheque for Polly and me which he hoped we would use to pick out a souvenir we especially liked in Japan.[9]

I find it more blessed to give than to receive—and here I am receiving far more than I shall ever be able to give. But this multitude of kind thoughts and prayers is gratifying, since it springs from the very generosity that has enabled me all these years to raise funds for the blind of America. . . .

Captain Kaneko called soon after the ship left the harbour. From his handshake I know that we shall like his friendly personality. The second Japanese we met on the voyage was Mr. Ishi, a wealthy tea merchant of Yokohama.

We were almost crowded out of our room by the flowers, and had them taken to the dining-room so that they might be enjoyed by all the other passengers. Overcome by drowsiness natural on the first day at sea and long excitement, I sank down on the bed and never moved until Polly woke me for dinner.

April 8th

At half-past five Polly and I pulled ourselves out of bed. We had told each other solemnly that we needed exercise, and the speeches must be practiced while few people were around. We paced the upper deck an hour. It was cool and pleasant. The sea was a soft grey, and I felt a light spray as the ship ploughed along. Some gulls circled overhead, and my spirit rose with a hymn to the fresh, still morning. There is no blessedness for one task-driven like "being aware of the morning hour upon sublunary things."[10] We met a Japanese in his kimono chanting, and I thought he must be a priest. I began practicing, and then had a heart-sinking emotion because three of the speeches I had prepared did not please me. During the harum-scarum rush of the seven weeks we had been in Forest Hills I had not had a sufficiently calm mind to examine them critically.

After breakfast I wrote and rewrote the speeches until I felt mentally black and blue. They must be as short as possible if I am not to overtax my listeners' patience with my halting delivery, and I am anxious to put over as many worth-while ideas as I can in my pleas for the Japanese blind.

Again we had lunch sitting on deck so as to be by ourselves. I became absorbed in the part of *Gone With the Wind,* describing Scarlett's frantic ministrations to Melanie in her childbirth agony, her flight from Atlanta and how she killed the thief. No light reading—far from it! But I am glad to see Scarlett being transformed from a spoilt belle into a courageous, responsible worker. Rhett Butler is out of the picture at present, much to my relief. He is one of the sensible people without heart whom I shun as heartily as any fool—he is supremely selfish, sarcastic and bitter. I hate his truths conveyed with a sneer no less than falsehood. . . .

More work on the speeches. Then there were pictures and autographs. There seems to be no escape, I sign them and sign another bunch and another until I feel like the man in the tale who was bound hand and foot when ants attacked him, and died a slow death.

To-night we had a pleasant time dining with Captain Kaneko up in his cabin. In the middle of the table was a small stove on which he cooked a delicious Japanese dish, sukiyahi. First he put oil into the saucepan then all kinds of vegetables, rice and bamboo and juicy meat on top. He kept putting nice morsels hot from the stove on my plate; and was as kind as he could be cutting them up for me. He said we would often have a sukiyahi dinner while in Japan. Polly and I were glad to hear that; we knew we should be sure to like it. We were served a cocktail and some delicate *saki,* tasting like sherry. At first I was a bit perturbed finding chopsticks beside the plate, I had visions of dropping every morsel and making myself ridiculous, but I managed better than I expected; and the captain was so courteous, I felt quite at my ease during the meal. With simple dignity he dwelt most on the quiet kind of work he enjoys doing in his leisure moments—writing up sporting events for the papers and tending plants.

This evening we were at the cinema. The picture that interested me especially was "The Island of Mahi." It showed the great sugar plantations, how the sugarcane is cut, crushed in the mills and sent down the railway to the sea. I do not care for the cheap love-making pictures shown on this ship.

April 9th

Up soon after 5 a.m., so that Polly and I could rehearse more of the speeches on deck. The decks and windows were being washed, and we had to move about gingerly. But these are days when we cannot afford to let inconveniences put us out, and it was interesting to watch the sailors at work in the sweet, grey calm of a Pacific dawn.

Oh, those speeches! Every time I go over them I feel as if I were sitting on a volcano. I know there is going to be an eruption of unexpected circumstances associated with the lectures, and I have no idea how much time I shall be given to speak or how I shall arrange the material to suit the purpose of the meeting. Owing to the difficulty of communicating with the workers for the blind of Japan over eight thousand miles, it is impossible to plan our work or to anticipate any plans they may have made. Nor can I be sure what the attitude of the audiences in some parts of Japan is towards the handicapped. Alas! with all the advantages of the telephone, telegraph, cable and aeroplane, distance can still be a terrible obstacle to quick, effective action.

The captain came in before lunch and gave me an autobiographical sketch which I know I shall enjoy if Polly and I ever get a chance to read it. His cheerful serenity despite ill-health and heavy duties and his pleasant talk helped me forget my nerve-trying uncertainties, and I started work again refreshed.

Gone with the Wind is still delightful, though repetitious at times. It stirs in me a nostalgia for the drowsy, sweet spring and early summer days in Tuscumbia, the red earth, the huge old magnolia-trees and live oaks. Again I smell mother's royal wealth of roses of all kinds and fragrances, the masses of tangled honeysuckle and paulonia blossoms heavy in the afternoon heat. Again the air about me vibrates with excitement as the men fulminate against some political group or refight the Civil War. Or perhaps it is the big spring to which my retrospective thoughts drift. There the negroes come, young and old, with buckets to fetch water. Picturesque in bright-coloured bandanas, barefooted, always singing or dancing or performing a cake-walk, they warm my heart, and I long for the joyous piccaninnies who so good-naturedly played with the insatiate tomboy I was. But time's disillusioning searchlight has years ago fallen upon those days which seemed to me a glorious playtime forever. Sadly I recall the degrading poverty, the ignorance and superstition into which the little ones were born and the bitterness of the Negro problem through which many of them are still living.

April 14th

A mist was floating round the ship like incense out of a burner when Polly and I took our last walk on deck at 6 a.m. We were silent, but each knew what the other was thinking—"This is Teacher's birthday." That thought has continued uppermost the whole day, however busily I might attend to pressing tasks with the surface of my mind.

When I awoke this morning, I started to find Teacher and tell her somehow my joy that the world had been blessed in her birth. Then I remembered and was transfixed with pain. There was no language for my yearning to See her—to keep not merely reaching out through aching heartbeats, but to Be With her and a part of her other home where joy is in its fullness. I felt like the monk of de Machlinia's tale who was walking with his beloved patron, Saint Nicholas, in a vision. They came to "a full glorious wall of crystal whose height no man might see, and length no man might consider and a shining gate with a cross in the middle." The cross was lifted up to give free entrance to those who were admitted, but let down to prevent others from coming in. St. Nicholas entered, holding the monk's hand, with a prayer that they might be received together, but was forced to let him go as the cross descended between them. Heartbroken, the monk stood before the shut gate thinking he was the one who had died, just as I think in such forlorn moments. . . . But those moments are only shadows on life's dial; and by tracing them back to the Divine Sun, I again find the brightness of Teacher's spirit living with me, no matter what barrier may hide one from the other. . . .

Ever since I started reading about the religious beliefs of Nippon, I have had a very warm sympathy with the Buddhist in his attitude towards immortality. It is a religion of affection which regards the departed not as dead, but as a part of the home life of those who love them. Unseen they guard the house and watch over everyone in it; every night they hover in the glow of the shrine-lamp, and the stirring of its flame is said to be their motion. Dwelling most within their memorial tablets, they observe and hear everything that happens to the family; they delight in the voices and the warmth about them. Sometimes, it is said, they can animate a tablet, change it into a human body and thus return to aid and comfort the living.

While the ancestor-worship and the animist element in this creed do not appeal to me, the Buddhist's confidence that the invisible world sustains and nourishes the visible is refreshing in the midst of present-day vagueness and agnosticism.

Thankfully I gather courage also from the innumerable details in Swedenborg's writings concerning the other world. For they help me to share by imagination Teacher's limitlessly varied, colourful, many-worlded experience. "Plucking the flower of life," the Chinese say of death, and how magnificently that flower spreads out before me in Swedenborg's word-pictures! I can think of nothing to suggest its richness even slightly except the emblem of perfection—odorous lotus opening in the morning sunshine with curving petals and leaves whose shiny surfaces reflect every mood of the sky and constantly change colours as the day passes over them. As I contemplate it, the curtain between Teacher and me becomes no longer the devouring silence of death or the desert, but a silence interpreted by the music of nature and "scanned by the prosody of humanity."

What is so tragic to me on this anniversary is that I lived too long with Teacher's scintillating, unique, stimulating personality to be content among ordinary folk. Always I shall look about, despite myself, for the sparkle with which she charmed the dullest person into a new appreciation of beauty or justice or human rights. My fingers will cry out for her descriptive touches which were nuggets of gold, her exquisite tendernesses, her bright summaries of conversation or books not in raised print. Then, too, the trust I had in her from my childhood was a support not easily to be replaced. Anyone who knows how sentiments shrivel "in the gradual furnace of the world"[11] will understand the enthusiasm such memories awaken and the loneliness after such a parting. . . .

However, I am certain that Teacher is exceedingly with me on this voyage. Both Polly and I notice that strength flows into us for tasks to which we never dreamed we should be equal. Surely it is towards this supreme undertaking that Teacher strove with such an urge in her heart. It was for this that she worked so painstakingly, making the most of the circumscribed life with which I was equipped.

In a book on China I read that a man had a small rock garden with a pool, a pavilion and bamboos. His wife was a poet, and he wished her to have a quiet spot for meditation. He separated this retreat from the rest of the garden with a hedge of dwarf pines. It was contained within a few yards, but he so carved the flat land that he produced a perspective seemingly of many miles. The winding path went by a waterfall, climbed through mountain foliage, passed a flower-sweet dell, entered a forest, came out by a lake where tall lilies bloomed, followed a slow river through a sunny green field and terminated at the door of the rustic cottage. Even so did Teacher gather into the small compass within my reach knowledge, beauty, chances of usefulness—and lo! the path we followed during fifty years has wound magnificently around the world to Nippon! Having come thus far, she will reinforce my labours with an inner power given only to those who have loved deeply and believed unwaveringly. . . . And as I stood on deck this morning in the mist of the dawn, looking westward to the land where a Great Adventure awaits me, I thought I could feel her by my side.

B Politics

41 How Important the Foundation Is

June 7, 1924, letter from Helen Keller to Mildred Keller Tyson, AFB.

Keller entered the 1920s seeking a meaningful public life and adequate financial support for personal stability. She had found it impossible to have the political and publishing life she desired. Macy's earning potential was very limited and her health in flux. The newly created American Foundation for the Blind supplied support and stability, becoming the center of her and Anne Macy's lives. Founded in 1921, the AFB united a coalition of the American Association for the Instruction of the Blind and the American Association of Workers for the Blind. By 1924, it provided the bulk of their income and cemented Keller's public identification with the cause of blindness. It also became the dominant organization pertaining to blindness in the United States. She remained affiliated with the AFB for the rest of her life and blindness became her primary public focus. This letter to Keller's sister Mildred Tyson explains the decision and its consequences for their daily life.

Dear Mildred,

I've just finished a long stretch of voice work which I need badly, as my speech has fallen off since I left Mr. White, and now I'm going to write to you between jobs. I feel like sending cries of penitence all over the house when I think how terribly I've neglected you the past two months. I think I wrote you in April that I should be separated from my typewriter during our Vaudeville tour, as we were traveling about so fast, going to a new place every three days. We have been back from New England since the middle of May; but we have been taken up with Foundation work and speech practice and duty letters to "perfect strangers" who want us to do something, say something or go somewhere. Now I'm preparing to speak over the radio next Tuesday in Newark, and try to interest more people in the Foundation's work. I'll tell you about it when the ordeal is over. I confess, I feel a bit funny when I think of speaking to an invisible audience. But I keep myself calm by imagining that I shall address just one or two persons in the same room with me.

Well, there were pleasant spots in our tour. Some of the towns where we appeared were in the Berkshires, and we managed to get in several lovely motor runs, and once Polly and I had a real walk in the hills, with the early morning light upon everything. We also had some beautiful audiences, especially in Brockton, which you may remember is about twenty miles from Wrentham.

Several of our dates were right near Boston, and we found a nice old hotel, the Canterbury, looking out on the Fenway. There we stayed for ten days. We saw Mr. Raymond twice, and he invited us out to tea at his country home. We saw Polly's uncle too, and had dinner with him one evening in Boston. We appeared in Cambridge three days, and Bridget—dear, sweet Bridget, came to see us. The following Sunday we spent with her, and oh, what a good time she gave us in her cosy [sic], pretty home! She is not strong, she suffers from what the doctors call nervous exhaustion. But she seems to be improving. We begged her to visit us this summer, and I hope she will, I know a change would do her a world of good. While we were working around Boston, she sent us such delicious food—nut-bread, stuffed eggs, ham, cheese and cookies. That helped us a lot, as we had three shows a day, and were obliged to stay in the theatre from eight to nine hours. You see, the shows were close together, and it took so long to make up and unmake, it wasn't any use for us to go out. Alas! There were three shows a day most of the time, and we were all tired out. So it was a joy to come home and enjoy our garden. It was gorgeous with tulips, and bridal wreaths drifted over the hedge like snow. I've just been out, and oh, how gaily the blue-flags are waving their banners! The wigelia is running riot with blossoms. The ramblers are climbing up the wall towards the roof where my study is. The birds built their nest in the ramblers this spring, and the male would sit on the pine-tree singing all day, while his mate kept the eggs warm.

To come back to the news: we have now attended twelve meetings of the Foundation, some last March, and five since our return. Most of them were in the northern part of New Jersey, and we never got home until one or two o'clock a.m. The worst of it was, we couldn't even sleep in the morning, but had to rise betimes and "be at it" again. The meetings have been fairly successful. It is difficult to give the people an idea of what we are trying to do. It would be easier if we were raising money for a single object. But the Foundation is a big thing, its aims are many, and the needs of the blind widely varied.

I haven't given you any details about this work, have I? For instance, there is the question of embossing more and better literature for the sightless. There has been little progress in printing for the blind since the beginning because it is not commercially important enough to interest experts and inventors. Of course they give their attention where the reward is greatest. As you know, the braille writers we must use are clumsy, and liable to get out of order. It is believed that all the apparatus for the blind could be greatly improved if only enough time and money were spent on it. Then it is desirable to increase opportunities of usefulness for the blind as far as possible, and enlist the interest of their fellow-citizens, so that they will give them a chance to become self-supporting. Again, no proper provision has been made for the care and education of the deaf-blind. Neither the schools for the deaf nor the schools for the sightless want them because they require such constant attention, and should have special teachers. One of the Foundation's objects is to seek out deaf-blind children, and see that the state where they live gives them opportunity to receive special instruction. The chief part of the enterprise is prevention of blindness. You will be delighted to hear that ophthalmia of the new-born has been practically wiped out in Massachusetts. It can be eradicated everywhere. All these matters appeal to our commonsense when we understand them. But naturally, the general public can't grasp them so readily. A nation-wide campaign of publicity, legislation and money-raising must be carried on for some time to come.

I'm writing all this, dear, so that you can see how important the Foundation is to the happiness of all the blind, and why we are working as hard for it as we have. Wouldn't it be wonderful if you or Warren should come across a person with plenty of money or ability who would join hands with us in this great cause! Beside Teacher, I tell you, we need another genius like what Sir Arthur Pearson was to the blind of Great Britain.

There! Elizabeth Garrett, who is to spend the week-end with us, has arrived, and I must stop. I haven't seen her since New Year's. I believe she is making her way nicely, singing at concerts and teaching.

My goodness, I don't know what will become of this letter! And I don't know what I was saying last any more than I know where Halley's comet is at this moment! I think when I stopped, I was starting off to speak over the radio in Newark. They said I did very well, and I have had letters from quite a number of "radio fans" who said they understood me and liked my speech. That made me especially happy because I had such a struggle getting my voice to be possible for the occasion. I tell you, the household almost flew out of the window hearing me repeat the speech so frequently. It was a curious sensation to find myself addressing an invisible audience with just a disk held up near my lips, in fact, I felt lost—out of touch with the listeners. I don't like the idea of doing it again.

After the radio experiment I went over to Hackensack, N.J. to spend a few days with one of my deaf friends. Teacher, Polly and Harry motored to Boston to visit her uncle. They said they had a nice time, and I think the change did them all good. They went out to Wrentham and saw several of our old friends. I got a delightful rest, and came back to New York ready for a luncheon given by the "Lions Club." They are interested in raising money to give radio sets to the young blind of New York, and I was asked to speak that day. I talked about happiness, and told them what joy the radio would bring to many blind people who cannot in any other way hear music or the interesting news of the day.

Since then we have been taken up with propositions from Mr. Migel, the president of the Foundation, for next year. They want us to start our campaign for large funds next October. But the arrangements they propose are not quite to our liking, and it will be some time before we can agree upon a practical programme. I know of nothing more fatiguing than this business of threshing out plans, objecting, suggesting, negotiating and explaining matters to strangers.

We don't know the personnel of the Foundation well yet, and so we are feeling our way all along most cautiously. They don't seem to realize that Teacher isn't equal to all they would like us to do. They talk about our attending five meetings a week! Now, Mildred, we have all we could manage going to three meetings a week, and each meeting has consumed many hours of activity, beside depriving us of a good night's sleep. In Vaudeville it isn't so bad, although we have so many appearances a week. We are on the stage less than an hour, and are always back in our room before eleven o'clock. But I am sure that if we stick to our terms, everything will come out nicely.

Your letters have been a joy to me, and I think you are a darling to keep on writing. What a lovely time Katharine must be having with Ravia, Phillips and baby! How I should love to be with them, and with you other dears too! Has Pat written any more verse? It would be perfectly lovely to have a real poet in our family, wouldn't it? I suppose school has closed by this time, and Pat and little Mildred are running wild out in the Cloverdale fields. I don't think they ever know when they are tired of games, red birds, butterflies, berries and chatter. I should think you'd be worn out with all the costumes you have been making for their dances, masquerades, picnics, parties and whatnot! You keep at it, while we just grin and bear one or two terrible days in the city buying the new dresses we need. I wish you could see mine, they are so light and cool, and wear so well. One is a lovely blue, another pink, and another fawn, I think. I've got a pretty new coat too; so I feel pretty well prepared for any hurry-up calls like those of the Foundation or a ride in somebody else's "Rolls-Royce." We were really taken in one to the "Lions" luncheon.

Ned has been here twice, once four days, and now a whole week.[1] Here's great news for you. Last May he sailed with his compass for Baton Rouge on the "Hoxbar"—a trip of sixteen days. The compass worked splendidly, despite the fact that on the way back the "Hoxbar" collided with another ship in a heavy fog, and there was a terrible hole made way down in her bottom. The excitement on board was beyond description. The ship caught fire, and she was loaded with oil—an equivalent of fifteen thousand barrels—which had to be pumped and thrown overboard in mad haste. They managed to get the ship to port, and the compass was safe. Ned wanted us to see it; but when we went over to the Brooklyn docks, we found that the "Hoxbar" had been pushed out into the water for repairs, and we couldn't reach her without climbing over another steamer. We didn't dare try; so we just sat and watched the workmen on the ship. Before they could repair the damaged parts, they had to take out innumerable rivets, applying intense heat to them. As they worked, an incessant shower of sparks flew in every direction. I know the children would have enjoyed that magnificent sight immensely.

Polly is to sail for Scotland with her uncle on the 20th of July. He is failing fast, and I fear he will be a great care to her. But once "on her native heath," I know she will have a real rest, which she needs badly.

I hope to catch up with my letters this summer and lay in a new stock of energy for next year's strenuous work. I must stop now, or this letter will never start Montgomerywards. We all send our love to you all.

Affectionately your sister,
Helen Keller

42 Who Better Than the State Can Be That Friend?

Undated 1927 speech before the Iowa State Legislature, as they considered creating a state Commission for the Blind. Legislation: State, General, AFB.

Once employed by the AFB, Keller was an unparalleled lobbyist. As Migel noted, "Only a heart of stone could fail to respond to an appeal from Helen Keller." Legislators were "spellbound," wept, and reportedly "adjourned temporarily to greet her."[2] In the late 1920s through the 1940s, she either visited or wrote targeted letters to at least eighteen weepy state legislatures, most often encouraging funding for or creation of state commissions for the blind. Other causes included funding for educational institutions for blind people, bills to allow blind persons to travel with a guide on public transportation for one fare, and funds for braille books. Sometimes the AFB initiated the visits, sometimes local organizations wrote to the AFB seeking her assistance, sometimes local organizations wrote her directly. Visited states include but are likely not limited to Arkansas (1945),

Colorado (1925), Delaware (1931 or 1932), Florida (1929, 1941), Hawaii (1937), Illinois (1931, 1946), Iowa (1924), Maine (1939), Mississippi (1929, 1941, 1942), Nebraska (1947), New Jersey (1934), New Mexico (1925, 1941), North Carolina (1935), North Dakota (1933), Tennessee (1943), Texas (1941), Utah (1941), Vermont (1929), Virginia (1924).

Gentlemen,

I am very glad of this opportunity to speak before the Legislature of Iowa in a cause which is so near to my heart. I rejoice that you are taking such an intelligent interest in the welfare of the blind.

I understand that you are about to consider a bill to create a commission for the blind. I have read the bill. It is very similar to the act which has been in operation in Massachusetts for twenty-five years with conspicuous success.

I think it would be a great mistake to include the work for the blind in a general welfare organization, since the problems of the sightless are different from those of other handicapped people, and their work is highly specialized.

I understand also that you are asked to appropriate twenty-five thousand dollars to carry on this work for two years. That means about twelve thousand a year. Gentlemen, that is not enough. You should double it. Please remember, there are two thousand blind people in this state, the majority of whom can, through training and special aid, become self-supporting citizens. Surely, gentlemen, it is worth while to grant a generous appropriation when the subject is to enable dependent people to help themselves and relieve the state of the burden of caring for them.

It seems to me, the civilization of a state should be measured by the amount of suffering it prevents and the degree of happiness it makes possible for its citizens. It must be good for the strong to help the weak—otherwise there would be no excuse for our having the unfortunate always with us. It is good statesmanship to meet halfway those who are fighting the battle of life under a handicap. No matter how intelligent and brave the blind are, they will always need your assistance and encouragement. They will always need a friend, and who better than the state can be that friend?

Helen Keller

43 Giving the Blind Worthwhile Books

March 27, 1930, testimony before the Committee on the Library,
House of Representatives.

In *The Story of My Life* Keller wrote, "literature is my Utopia. Here I am not disfranchised. No barrier of the senses shuts me out from the sweet, gracious discourse of my book-friends."[3] As a lobbyist, she frequently supported efforts to expand federal financial support for braille books. In this example she melodramatically appeals to the legislators to imagine what it would be like to be blind.

Mr. Chairman, Ladies and Gentlemen:

The Bill (H.R. 9042) which you have under consideration today, asks for an appropriation to supply braille books to a class of persons who, through no fault of their own, are unable to read regular print. I hope the Bill passes. Giving the blind worthwhile books is a practical way of helping them to overcome their handicap. Indeed, it is far more than a practical measure, it partakes of the nature of a boon.

Books are the eyes of the blind. They reveal to us the glories of the light-filled world, they keep us in touch with what people are thinking and doing, they help us to forget our limitations. With our hands plunged into an interesting book we feel independent and happy.

Have you ever tried to imagine what it would be like not to see? Close your eyes for a moment. This room, the faces you have been looking at—where are they? Go to the window keeping your eyes shut. Everything out there is a blank—the street, the sky, the sun itself! Try to find your way back to your seat. Can you picture who is sitting in that chair, day in and day out, always in the dark, and only the dark gazing back at you. What you would not give to be able to read again! Wouldn't you give everything in the world for something to make you forget your misfortune for one hour? This Bill affords you an opportunity to bestow this consolation upon thousands of blind men and women in the United States.

When you closed your eyes just now you were assuming the sable livery of the blind, knowing all the time how quickly you could fling it aside. You felt no heavier burden than a grateful sight that your blindness was a mummery. We who face the reality know we cannot escape the shadow while life lasts. I ask you to show your gratitude to God for your sight by voting for this Bill.

44 To Earn Their Livelihood

May 19, 1933, letter from Helen Keller to President Franklin Roosevelt. Legislation: federal file, AFB.

At the request of the president of the American Foundation for the Blind, M. C. Migel, Helen Keller lobbied President Roosevelt about employing blind people at federal building news-stands. As she did repeatedly, she emphasized the personal and social benefits wage employment made possible for people with disabilities.

Dear President Roosevelt,

Mr. Migel, President of the American Foundation for the Blind, has told me of bringing to your attention the question of permitting blind people, under proper regulations, to run news-stands in federal buildings. I think you are wonderfully kind to give thought to this problem at a time when the demands upon your mind and heart must be overwhelming. The warmth of your active good-will is all the more touching because it is rare to find a man with world responsibilities who has room in his consideration for small groups of handicapped human beings.

It will be truly splendid if through your influence, it is made possible for more people without sight to earn their livelihood and enjoy some measure of independence and self-respect. I do not forget, as I write this, that there are other groups of hindered persons equally eager for a chance in life. But, all things considered, they have sight, and it is easier for one with eyes to earn his bread than for one who is blind.

Work is the only way for the blind to forget the dark and the obstacles in their path. Where there is interesting work, there is no morbidity or fear. I know that if it is at all possible, you will help the AFB to negotiate this precious boon for the sightless of this country.

Still, I shrink from intruding such a matter upon you at this crisis in world affairs. My only excuse is that I have written this letter in the spirit of service. I am exceedingly with you in your heroic efforts for world peace and the reorganization of our national life. You are living greatly in a world that cries aloud for brave men and women with ideas in their heads and faith in mankind.

With the proud sense of having you as a friend, I am,

Cordially and admiringly yours,

Helen Keller

45   The Talking Book to Every Corner of Dark-Land

April 20, 1935, letter from Helen Keller to Eleanor Roosevelt; Folder: Helen Keller; Series 100; Papers of Eleanor Roosevelt, Franklin D. Roosevelt Library, Hyde Park, New York.

As a lobbyist Keller was both effective and creative. In this example, she directly asks the First Lady to host a White House tea in order to aid Keller's promotion of talking-books.

Dear Mrs. Roosevelt,

Your kindness to everybody encourages me to come to you with a request the granting of which would help me immensely in my work for the blind.

The AFB has developed a machine called the talking-book for the blind. It is an adaptation of the phonograph to the recording of books. A book of ninety thousand words can be recorded on a dozen discs. This enables the blind to listen by ear instead of the slow process of finger reading, and avoid the tedium of waiting until others have time to read aloud to them. Thus they gain a measure of independence as well as entertainment, which is very precious to those who meet with restraints at every turn in life. The talking book is especially a godsend to people who lose their sight in adult years when it is extremely difficult to impossible for them to learn to read by touch.

The Library of Congress supplies the records free as fast as the sightless are provided with the machines. Unfortunately the majority of the blind cannot afford the machines, and the Foundation is endeavoring to raise funds to purchase them.

The President is Honorary President of our organization, and he has graciously given his approval to the talking-book. I am wondering if you would give a tea at the White House to help me send the talking-book to every corner of Dark-land. As you are the First Lady of the land, such a tea would awaken national interest in this new blessing to the blind. The Foundation would do everything possible to make it easy for you and your staff. A talking-book would be sent to the White House for the occasion, and your guests would see for themselves what a wonderful thing it is. If you feel that you can do this beautiful deed for the blind of America and for me, I know you will give us this great joy.

I should very much like to call on you anyway. I am to be in Baltimore April 30th, speaking on prevention of blindness. Would you permit me to come to see you with my secretary, Miss Thomson, and our friend Miss Bain of Stirling, Scotland? It would make me happy to clasp again the hand of one whom the whole nation loves.

I dare not hope for the pleasure of meeting the President, his days are so terribly crowded with important matters. I am reading with intense interest of his tremendous efforts to bring the American people renewed confidence out of a desperate situation, and I admire his magnificent faith in a higher destiny for the nation.

With kindest Easter Greetings, I am,

> Cordially yours,
> Helen Keller

46 An Amendment of Great Importance to the Blind

June 21, 1935, letter from Helen Keller to Mr. Thomas H. Cullen (legislator). Legislation: federal, Social Security Act, AFB.

Keller and the AFB enthusiastically supported the Social Security Act. When it first passed in 1935, as the Wagner Economic Security Act, she allowed her name to be put on the amendment proposed by Senator

Robert Wagner (NY, Democrat) to expand vocational training for blind people. In this lobbying example, she emphasizes the amendment's economic as well as human benefits.

Dear Mr. Cullen,

I understand that you are one of the Committee who will consider the Wagner Economic Security Bill containing Title X, an amendment of great importance to the blind of America. As no doubt you know it was sponsored by Senator Wagner and Senator Harrison. Its object is to render constructive service to the blind.

It is true that schools are provided for blind youth, and some of the aged and infirm are sheltered in homes, but nothing adequate has ever been done in this country for the adult blind who desire work and a measure of independence. Probably you have met them moving along crowded streets with faltering feet, holding out their petty wares for sale or a cap for your pennies—and in their hearts throb the same ambitions and feelings you have!

Any blind person who is mentally and physically sound may with proper training become at least partially self-supporting. That is why I plead with you in the name of economic commonsense as well as humanity to sanction Title X as it came [*sic*] through the Senate.

Hoping that you will be our champion in a struggle which lasts as long as life itself, I am, with kindest regards,

Sincerely yours,
Helen Keller

47 The Double Shadow of Blindness and Deafness

June 11, 1941, letter from Helen Keller to Walter Holmes, AFB.

Sporadically, throughout her life, Keller tried to focus additional attention and resources on deaf-blind people. Her most sympathetic ally in this effort appears to have been Walter Holmes, a long-time friend and the editor of *Matilda Ziegler Magazine,* a well-established monthly braille publication unaffiliated with the AFB. In 1938, the two had lamented the lack of support for deaf-blind people in the United States. In 1941, they repeatedly discussed the issue in person as well as by correspondence. Holmes pursued organizational and "practical methods of assisting the doubly handicapped" and sought her assistance. She responded with enthusiasm, but warned him that the AFB was unlikely "ever to find room among its many interests" for the deaf-blind. There, she wrote, "'hangs a tale' which it will be easier for me to speak than write." The lack of organizational support infuriated her. "Why cannot means be found to appoint a national council composed of workers for the blind and workers for the deaf who would meet annually and give special consideration to the problems of the deaf-blind?"[4]

Dear Uncle Walter,

Your visit to Arcan Ridge seems like a vision, it passed so quickly, but it left a deep trace of happiness. How like you it was to bring those exquisite roses, the wren's nest and sugar tubes for humming-birds. Herbert is putting up the tubes today. It will be a joy indeed if a lot of humming-birds come to flash and buzz around our windows. No wonder writers despair every time they try to describe those tiny creatures' fairylike beauty. You can now have a cheerful sense of my life in New England's rural quietude, and as always after seeing you I sense delicate ligaments of sympathy between us which give renewed fighting power to my elbow.

It was a tender sorrow that you should visit Polly and me without seeing Teacher. Yet I felt her presence in the room overpoweringly, and you two braced me with a knowledge of more good still to be wrought before I depart from earth's dear but imprisoning habitation. Whatever may be the cause of the slowness in assisting the deaf-blind of America, friends whose hearts beat as yours does big with good-will towards them give me assurance that the doubly handicapped will come into their own at last.

Time and again I have thought a champion was raised up for the large number who still live unbefriended in the double shadow of blindness and deafness, and I have been cruelly disappointed. The bitter drop must [undecipherable] remain in my cup of blessedness until a concerted effort under responsible management is made to rescue them. Naturally the blind who are also deaf appeal to me most poignantly. Fully I realize the complications and difficulties involved. Our deaf-blind are so widely scattered over an immense continent that it is hard for normal people to know how many of them there are, but when one comes to think of it, I was taught fifty-five years ago when there was not a single fact to warrant such an attempt except Laura Bridgman's education, an account of which had reached my mother by the merest chance in a small out-of-the-way town. Why cannot many others beside myself be aided now in a general atmosphere of good-will and intelligent research intensified by the radio, the multiplying town-meeting, physicians and district nurses? Why cannot means be found to appoint a national council composed of workers for the blind and workers for the deaf who would meet annually and give special consideration to the problems of the deaf-blind? Surely representatives of the A.A.W.S. could be found willing to confer with members of the American Society for the Hard of Hearing and the American Association for the Teaching of Speech to the Deaf in a cause which potently tests their sincerity towards the handicapped. Such a step would hasten the day when all the needy deaf-blind would be wisely cared for, and those with capabilities assisted to their place as useful and reasonably contented human beings. Perhaps you will make suggestions as to how that kind of council may be formed.

In the meantime, there is a matter I wish to communicate to you. Many urgent reasons have led me to withdraw my name from the American League for the Deaf-Blind. Will you kindly put this statement in the "Ziegler" and request all other magazines for the blind to print it? That will help me tremendously in clearing the way for whatever course may be adopted later to rehabilitate the deaf-blind.

Please tell Virginia how glad Polly and I were to meet her. It is a blessing that you have a friend who helps in the war against darkness and shares your interests with enthusiasm and a mind open to progressive ideas.

With our love and wishes for a restful summer, I am,

      Affectionately your friend,
      Helen Keller

48 The Hardest Pressed
and Least Cared-for

October 3, 1944, testimony before the House Subcommittee of Labor Investigating Aid to Physically Handicapped. Legislation: Social Security Title X file, AFB.

Keller had supported the Social Security Act in 1935 and urged its expansion in this 1944 testimony. Here she emphasizes the particular needs of "the colored blind" and "the deaf-blind." Throughout the 1940s and 1950s, she continued to draw connections between racism, the discrimination faced by people with disabilities, and the additive discrimination confronted by African Americans with disabilities.

Members of the House Committee of Labor,

Nothing could please me more than to speak here this morning as it gives me an opportunity to direct your attention once more to the consideration of a handicap allowance for the blind. Fully I endorse it as expressing the best thought of our day concerning the needs and difficulties of those who cannot see. You will, I am sure, be favorably disposed towards this constructive effort.

As Mr. Irwin has clearly shown in his testimony before your Committee at its hearings in Washington, the Social Security Act has not provided sufficiently for the particular needs of the poorer blind, or taken into account their severe curtailments in bread-winning opportunities and personal liberty. As a result they must incur unaided peculiar expenses which lack of sight entails. For instance they must pay a guide or a reader at the sacrifice of other precious necessaries. Most of them cannot afford Braille writers or typewriters. Can you imagine yourself in the dark, unable to send a written message to a son or brother overseas or to a friend at home?

There are two groups of the blind who should have an adequate handicap allowance and for whom I especially plead. One is the colored blind. In my travels up and down the continent I have visited their shabby school buildings and witnessed their pathetic struggle against want. I have been shocked by the meagerness of their education, lack of proper medical care and the discrimination which limits their employment chances. I feel it a disgrace that in this great wealthy land such injustice should exist to men and women of a different race —and blind at that! It is imperative that colored people without sight be granted financial aid worthy of their human dignity and courage in the face of fearful obstacles.

The other group, the deaf-blind, is small but heartbreaking to contemplate. They are tragically isolated, and it is difficult to arouse enough interest to soften their fate. They are so scattered that it is hard to find out how many of them there are. Even if the deaf-blind are taught, how seldom anyone offers to entertain them or gladden them with pleasant companionship! In every State there is an agency trained and willing to help the blind in their economic problems and diversions, but not one has been organized to rehabilitate the loneliest people on earth, those without sight or hearing. They have no funds to buy little advantages or enjoyments that would bring sunshine into their double dungeon—darkness and silence. If we are not to be haunted by remorse and shame at all our blessings while they have nothing, a definite effort must be started to raise them from ultimate disaster to life's goodness and friendship's consolation.

What I ask of you is to use your influence to revise the Social Security Act so that it may minister generously to the hardest pressed and the least cared-for among my blind fellows. If you do, the sight and liberty you enjoy will be all the sweeter to you.

Helen Keller

49 Multitudes of Injured Servicemen

February 8, 1945, letter from Helen Keller to Clare Heineman,
Clare and Oscar Heineman file, AFB.

Though deeply saddened by World War II, Keller tried to aid the war effort. She participated in the development of protective measures for blind and deaf people during air raids. She then explored service as a "Gray Lady," a wartime hospital volunteer, but that never proved viable. Finally, though for most of her life she tended to avoid other people with disabilities, she and Polly spent significant time with veterans disabled by the battles of World War II.

This letter to her friend Clare Heineman describes the visits she made to newly disabled military veterans. The media loved her veterans' hospital tours, as did the AFB, the army and navy. The AFB publicized each of her tours of several months and numerous states as coast-to-coast tours to cheer the soldiers. These visits, however, were not made as a friend and equal. The always unstated inference was that she served as an inspirational model to the depressed young men because of who she was *despite* her disability. In this effort, she presented two solutions to the problems posed by disability: work-oriented rehabilitation and a good attitude. Her ceaseless praise of the work-oriented rehabilitation efforts corresponded with her constant emphasis on work as an overwhelming need of people with disabilities. She argued that for all people with disabilities, but especially for veterans, work would provide economic and social usefulness. She then praised good attitudes, the aspect most highlighted by the media.[5]

Dearest Clare,

Now that I have got a bit ahead of the nagging tasks I found on the very threshold of Arcan Ridge when we came home, I am writing you our love and thanks.

You and Mr. Heineman were just the friends we needed to rest with—and what lazybones Polly and I were during our last visit in your home! But it was a godsend, as events have shown. Between work for the American Foundation for the Blind, the Christmas flood which swept through the house and is only now subsiding, and a mass of unopened mail we haven't had a proper day's respite yet.

As I write, I feel your loving thought enveloping me in the delectable cosiness of the dressing-gown you gave me. It is a priceless defense against this continued severe weather with icicles hanging everywhere and snow-banks piled higher than our heads. And in addition to gasoline fuel shortage we have had no hot water since we returned because the heater exploded and nearly blinded Herbert as he was trying to put it in working condition.

Your letter is a sweet temptation to us to break away from everything and drop in upon you on the 20th. But I received word from Mr. Crabtree that the meeting of the National Education Association in Chicago had been cancelled owing to travel difficulties. Since then we have been asked to appear before the Arkansas Legislature in behalf of the blind around the 20th of February, and that means we shall not be within coming distance of Chicago. However, arrangements for us to visit other Government hospitals, this time in the South, later in the middle West and then the North, are now under way, and we may get to you sometime in the spring when the birds sing again, and the joy of a creation new each year is upon the blossoming earth.

As I look back upon the recent tour, I am awed that such a magnificent, soul-expanding event should have befallen me. It is an epic beside which all Iliads and Aeneids seem pale and insular. As Polly and I journeyed through Arkansas, Oklahoma, Texas, New Mexico, Colorado, Utah, California, Oregon and Washington we were kept highstrung by the miracles of rehabilitation we saw. Hospitals which would once have been places of heartbreak are today bright with a dynamic faith and the purpose it inspires. Wounded soldiers who a few years ago were thought doomed are regaining health, interest in living and self-confidence to reshape their future. Surgeons, physicians, educators and scientists are striving towards an unprecedented goal—restoring multitudes of injured servicemen to normal society and usefulness in a measure that has never been done in the history of the world.

There was a thrilling climax to our trip when we attended the President's 4th Inauguration, to which I had been especially invited. Judging from all I have read and heard, that occasion resembled Lincoln's inaugural ceremonies. There was the same grim simplicity, the same atmosphere electric with historical and political significance. There I sensed the widening horizon of the people's desire to push forward all good faith, fair play and everything that is fine and constructive in our time.

As Franklin Delano Roosevelt stood addressing the silent but tensely attentive throng, he reminded me forcibly of Cape Cod which I used to visit frequently. He too impressed me with his harsh yet noble austerity. There was about him the same generous endeavor to work fruitfulness and verdure out of bleak winds and bitter sands. Fearfully battered by a sea of difficulties, he stirred me with a titan resolve to wrest from it "a better life for ourselves and all our fellowmen" and the achievement of God's Will to peace on earth.

We are having yet another heavy snowfall today, and I am thankful that we aren't starting out on the road just now. I hope you aren't feeling the winter too much. It was good to hear that you and Mr. Heineman were keeping well.

Polly will write herself when she has a free moment. With an embrace to you two from us both, I am,

Affectionately your friend,
Helen Keller

C Travel

50 The Japanese Nation Has Watched Over Us Both

July 14, 1937, letter from Helen Keller to John H. Finley, AFB.

During Anne Macy's last months in 1936, Keller's friend Takeo Iwahashi thrilled her by urging that she visit Japan. Her memoirs frame this interest in Japan as the result of the 1936 death-bed promise exacted by Macy, never as a personal desire to travel or to involve herself in international politics. The 1937 trip certainly met her profound personal needs, grief-stricken by Anne's death and unsure of the rest of her life. Travel also kept her in the public realm and kept the public closely within her realm.

The 1937 trip to Japan, Korea, and Manchuria constituted almost pure pleasure, despite the forthcoming war brought on by Japan's invasion of China. In Japan, where people had known of her since at least 1897, she drew huge crowds while visiting 39 cities and giving 97 lectures. Buddhists at the ancient city of Nara honored her and Polly Thompson by allowing them to become the first women to touch the city's famed bronze Buddha. In a further rare privilege, the emperor and empress received her in a formal reception. In Japan, Keller also felt her public presence to be effective. For one who had constantly questioned the effectiveness and worth of her public work in the United States, this was a heady experience. Japan also provided an entirely new sensory experience. As she describes below to her Westport, Connecticut neighbor and newly appointed *New York Times* editor-in-chief John H. Finley, "Never had I had so many ecstasies crowded into my touch."

Dear Dr. Finley,

Greetings from the ancient Capital of Chosen [Korea]—the beginning of the real Orient, a world as unlike Nippon [Japan] as the dusk is unlike the dawn! It is only lately that the tyranny of love which has kept me tied to the new venture for the handicapped in Nippon, and absorbing adventures have given me an occasional chance to write to my friends.

First I must send you my proud, though sadly belated congratulations, in which Miss Thomson joins, on your new editorial kingship. You have ever written and spoken only from the noble motive to promote constructive service and international friendship. With happy confidence I look upon the scepter which you are wielding through America's mightiest newspaper, not with "the dread power of earthly kings," but with the gentle authority of your wide human sympathy.

It is delightful to have an understanding friend like you to whom I may write freely about the indescribable charm Nippon has had for me and my at-homeness in its spiritual atmosphere. The respect the people everywhere have shown for my teacher's memory, their flowers and other gifts offered to her spirit, their perceptiveness in helping me to feel her nearness will always fill my heart with sweet comfort like sacred music.

Our work has been tremendously interesting. I am full of admiration for the courage with which the blind and the deaf throughout the Empire are striving to rise from ignorance and prejudice to the rank of acceptable, useful human beings. Of course their social status is still far from what it should be. Many of their schools are primitive and unsanitary, their directors incompetent, their training in handicrafts inadequate, and it will take a long time to remedy these defects, but the will to go forward is there, and the Government is already beginning to take an active interest in their rehabilitation. You will be glad to hear that now a followup campaign is starting in Osaka to expand the work of the Lighthouse for the Blind which Mrs. Mather opened there last year, and that a new lighthouse will be established in Tokyo in the near future. Miss Thomson and I feel encouraged and thankful that we have had this opportunity to share in Nippon's humane endeavor to bring light and hope to the unprivileged and the unbefriended.

It is touching to recall what beautiful audiences we have had ever since we came to this country, and how royally I have been welcomed as a representative of the handicapped. Vainly I try to think of a fitting return for the protective affection and care with which the Japanese nation has watched over us both. I can but do my best to strengthen the bonds of amity between Nippon and the United States, and I should indeed be gratified if sometime you should help me with one of your precious paragraphs of good-will towards other countries.

This trip has outrun our brightest anticipation in sustained interest and variety. There is no putting through language the natural splendors of which we have caught many intimate glimpses.—The foam-like seas of cherry blossoms last spring, the bowers of azaleas and wisteria everywhere, the neat rice fields tended with infinite patience the length and breadth of Nippon, the placid streams reflecting temples, rustic bridges and the colorful kimonos of the graceful girls crossing them.

The grandeur of Nippon's volcanoes with sulphur-mantled, rumbling Mount Aso as monarch, its pine forests, Nikko with its cryptomeria avenue twenty-two miles long, the Inland Sea with its jade waters and its kaleidoscopic display of uncounted islands and fantastic mountain crests, Hokkaido in the far north with its spacious fields and great herds of cattle—all these have overpowered us with wonder and the sense of a mighty epic forever in the making.

I have been spoiled, I fear, for the mechanical civilization of America by Nippon's artistry which seems as inexhaustible as fancy ideals. Never have I had so many ecstasies crowded into my touch—the arrangement of garden and shrubbery that perpetually changes like magic, the pines and other trees trimmed through centuries to the strangest shapes, the surprises of originality I discover even in small objects—the cups out of which I drink green tea, the fruit dishes, vases and screens.

Vibrations, too, flow about me in surprising abundance. Sleeping on the tatami in Japanese hotels I have felt through the matting a myriad soft little echoes from sliding door and window, the maids passing back and forth like a zephyr, the rustle of kimonos and the hum of voices and even the noises in the street outside. Truly Nippon has a glory for those who cannot see and a voice for those who cannot hear.

But now these experiences are in the past, and Chosen is bewildering me with a mass of unformulated impressions. As excavations show, Korea was once the center of a mighty empire. Its arts and industries were highly developed, and its forests were as imposing as its mountains. Since then the country has been laid low by misrule, neglect and the greed of war lords. The joy of a creative artist soul that shines over Nippon seems absent. The Koreans are struggling against poverty that benumbs the facilities. Life conditions are still primitive, ignorance and disease are distressingly prevalent.

But the last thirty years the Japanese and Koreans have been working together, and what they have already done is encouraging to us who believe we should never despair of humanity. The land is gradually being reforested, banks are being constructed for the rivers to prevent floods, and schools are increasing. After agelong disaster Chosen is renewing its strength much like the eagle and, I believe, progressing towards new knowledge and achievement. Miss Thomson and I marvel at the wide streets of Keijo, the handsome government building of Korean marble and other modern edifices. The river flowing through the city and the motor traffic are strangely in contrast with the ox-carts which are still the means of transportation in the Korean countryside.

Just now, however, the grim specter of war is stalking almost on our very racks. Since hostilities recommenced between China and Nippon a week ago we have been travelling with soldiers by boat from Shimonoseki to Fuzan, by train to Taikyu and here. Wherever we go we hear crowds shouting "Banzai! Banzai!" as the troops march northward. Every little while a special bulletin is given of how the barracks are filling up with the Chinese and Japanese near Pekin, and the atmosphere has grown electric. It is impossible to guess what may happen the next moment. As we go to Mukden and Dairen we shall get closer to the Great Horror. My heart bleeds for the men who may be blinded, deafened and maimed on both sides. I can only hope war may be averted.

In the mean time we try to forget by watching the beautiful lotus lilies in the pond under our windows, the people in the street—the men with queer black steeple hats and pipes a yard long in their mouths, the women all in white costumes.

Miss Thomson and I are very well, tired of course but not overworking. This is the rainy season, and we manage to keep cool much of the time. At the place where we have spoken twice there are huge blocks of ice both on the platform and in the hall that are a great comfort to the audience and ourselves.

We sail back to America August 10th on the S.S. Chichibu Maru, and we intend to rest before our campaign for the Foundation for the Blind begins in October.

We hope you escaped the dreadful heat we read of in New York. It grieves me to think of all the suffering and deaths it has caused.

Miss Thomson sends her greetings with mine. How good it will be to feel your big hand-clasp again!

Cordially yours,
Helen Keller

51 The Impressions I Have Had of Japan, Korea, Manchuria, and the Pacific

September 14, 1937, letter from Helen Keller
to M. C. Migel, Migel file, AFB.

Before Keller left Asia in late summer 1937, she toured Korea and Manchuria. Fearing war, AFB president M. C. Migel had attempted to stop her, but she sought travel for continued comfort. Macy's death continued to weigh upon her. Japan, however, invaded China. During her last month, she traveled in darkened trains and spoke in darkened auditoriums as a precaution against air raids. In August, the AFB announced that the trip to China was cancelled. She felt both relief and sorrow to leave Asia. She regretted leaving her dear friends Takeo Iwahashi and his wife Keo in what would likely become a war zone. She lamented leaving Asia without visiting China, but recognized what war meant and felt her visit to be fruitful. She may have felt her deathbed promise to Macy partially unfinished. She also simply appreciated being home, and all the benefits—such as the Mayo clinic—that the United States offered her.

While abbreviated, Keller's 1937 trip to Japan was pivotal. It centered her global travel, her global vision, and hopes for global harmony. Most important, the trip demonstrated to her, the AFB, and the federal government that she had international impact no one else could duplicate. In his public speech at Helen's departure, U.S. Ambassador Joseph C. Grew called her, in what was presumably intended as a compliment, "a second Admiral Perry": "Never before has an American created so great an atmosphere of friendship in Japan. . . . She is a second Admiral Perry, but whereas he opened the door with fear and suspicion, she has done it with love and affection."[1]

Dear Mr. Migel,

It was a happy moment for Polly and me when we received a letter from Elizabeth Bain expressing her delight in meeting you and having you visit the family at The Whins. It will be still nicer to hear your news when we see you.

I am especially glad that you had an opportunity to see Scotland in another of its "pretty bits o' ways"—its home life. For its heart-warm, garden-bright homes are as precious as its hills and burns running through a fairyland of golden broom. Much as you may enjoy the heather in August, I am sure you would experience a greater thrill of adventure if you would look in upon Scotland during the spring with its massed wild flowers and a myriad different trees blooming as radiantly, and more fragrantly than the cherry-trees of Nippon.

It is good to be back in America! I find that each time I roam through the tradition-fettered Old World I return loving America better than ever because, despite its many tragic blunders, there glows at its heart a noble democratic spirit which I pray may not pass away altogether. But, like Niagara that "falls without speed," the impressions I have had of Japan, Korea, Manchuria and the Pacific Ocean still pour upon my mind in retrospect so abundantly, I do not yet seem to have finished the voyage.

Polly and I held our last meeting for the blind at Dairen, Manchuria, July 24th. By that time we were tired, and taking the hot consequences of mid-summer in an excessively humid climate. But Manchuria fascinated me as a land being reclaimed from the desert, the agelong terror of brigands and ignorance. No, I do not forget that Japan demeaned itself as a world bandit seizing that country, but, while I hate imperialism, I can see that Manchuria must somehow be developed and disciplined if it is to become a vigorous, self-governing nation.

One of the cities which interested me most was Mukden with its colorful Chinese quarter, or Castletown as it is called because it is a walled town with a city. We visited the castle where a Chinese war lord (still living) dwelt with his harem and two enormous Manchurian tigers—I touched them. (Don't be alarmed, they were stuffed.) We also went through the mediaeval palace of the Manchu Dynasty with the sweet old garden and amazing lacquered doors leading from one court into another. Dairen also impressed me. To think that from a tiny country-place it has grown since the 1830's into a world seaport with spacious streets and handsome modern buildings!

The last month of our campaign we lived under a strict war regime. We traveled in trains darkened as a precaution against air raids. The last seven or eight cities where we lectured were in darkness nights, and we were obliged to speak in the daytime and endure the heat as best we could. We passed camouflaged troop trains, and everywhere immense crowds waved to the soldiers shouting "Banzai!"

As there were ten days to wait before our ship sailed, we stayed in a Japanese mountain village surrounded by pines between Osaka and Kobe. We took early morning walks among the hills and wrestled mightily with the correspondence which had been held up by our campaign through the Empire. A beautiful, touching send-off was accorded us at Kobe and Yokohama. Great crowds, including the blind and deaf, came to wish us well. Flowers, gifts, telegrams of gratitude and bon voyage literally deluged our state room. There were exquisite orchids on a daintily carved sampan with crickets to sing good wishes from Prince and Princess Takamatsu. Polly and I each received a beautiful picture of a Buddhist temple from Countess Otani, the Empress's sister, also her books and a record of her popular song, "Fellowship." (We had met Countess Otani and her husband, the High Priest at Kyoto, during a sail on the Inland Sea.)

It was hard to part from Takeo Iwahashi and his wife, Keo, who had been so wonderfully kind and thoughtful of our comfort during five months. The two little maids who had served us lovingly sobbed aloud when saying goodbye. It cost me hours of heartache to bid farewell to a people whose affection I had really felt and reciprocated, but as we sped farther away, and the news bulletins grew more sinister, I was relieved to escape the horrible war atmosphere. I do not know whom I feel more sorry for—the long-enduring, shamefully insulted Chinese dying by the thousands for freedom they are beginning to understand, or the Japanese millions staggering under the heaviest taxation in their history. But I must not run on and on in a gloomy mood, or this letter will become a jeremiad.

We stopped at Honololu August 19th and spent a delightful, quiet day with Mrs. Hamman who is at the head of the work for the blind in Hawaii. You can imagine how gratified I was when she said I had been of service in her effort to establish a bureau of welfare for the blind and obtain an appropriation to carry on the work. We lunched with Mrs. Hamman and two other friends at the Royal Hawaiian Hotel, then drove up to the Pali and visited the grass hut where Stevenson found such peace. I had a chance to see how the leis are strung together blossom by blossom. It must be delicate, colorful work, but I should not care to keep at it from dawn until dusk as the Hawaiian flower-pickers do. Before leaving the island we dined with Mr. and Mrs. Hamman in their sweet home. It was a joy to me to find friends with such an alert interest in the vital problems of our time as well as in ordinary daily happenings.

On arriving in San Francisco we found Mrs. Quinan at the dock. She was kindness itself helping us at the customs through her influence. Before going to Dallas to visit my brother we went to the San Francisco Blindcraft Shop which interested and pleased me greatly. Polly, whose eye for beauty cannot be questioned, was delighted with all the kinds of furniture the employees had produced and the handsome new building where two hundred blind persons will soon know the joy of excellent workmanship and self-support.

From Dallas we came to the Mayo Clinic to be thoroughly examined, so that we may take effective measure to be fit for next year's work. I have just heard my report, and it shows that I have a diseased gall-bladder which has caused me severe pain off and on for years. The doctors advise me to have it removed, and I am determined to do it while I am strong. I feel I owe it to others as well as to myself to get rid of this obstacle to continued health and usefulness. You can rest assured that I am happy at the prospect of being delivered from nerve-racking uncertainty as to my future work.

The only shadow is my distress at the thought that I shall not be at my post in October. At least I am sure the doctors will not permit me to do any kind of work for some time. However, I know you, Mr. Irwin and the associates with whom I have labored all these years will push forward valiantly the enterprise upon which depends the happiness, yes, the lives of a hundred and twenty thousand stricken human beings.

In the meantime I count it a rare good fortune that we should be here in a sweet, quiet, tree-shaded town—an ideal place to recreate ourselves. Every one at the Clinic is so kind, and the atmosphere is so cheerful and wholesome, it heals and strengthens us.

It made me proud the other day when we met Dr. Charles Mayo. His noble presence and modest simplicity reminded me of Einstein. Each day I realize more fully what a world-wide beneficence the Mayos are spreading through the Clinic. Not only are they improving the health of the American people, they and all the doctors under them work together in a genuine spirit of brotherliness. They practice true Christianity, giving the same attention to every patient regardless of caste, color or race, and treating free one-fourth who are not able to pay. Indeed, I am almost glad of the ailment that has brought me an opportunity to grasp the meaning and splendor of their endeavors.

Tuesday the 14th. Last night I was too weary to finish my letter, and yours of the 9th has just arrived. I thank you for sending the programme, which we will discuss with you when we get home.

The concert with Rachmaninoff to kindle enthusiasm for our cause in countless hearts stirs my imagination tremendously, and I long to be there more than language can express, but it is impossible to foresee the consequences of the operation which, as I have telegrammed, will take place tomorrow. I can only pray that I may be able to take part in that brilliant affair, if in nothing else. I have looked forward to it ever since I began working for the Foundation, and if I am absent on such a marvelous occasion, I shall consider it among my bitterest disappointment.

We were distressed to learn of your illness in Paris, but we are glad you are at home again safe and sound. What pleasant thoughts these golden autumn days must sing to you and Mrs. Migel as you move along the wood paths at Greenbraes or listen to the wind in the willows!

Here comes the nurse, imperatively ordering me to go to bed, and I must close with Polly's and my love to you both, and with the fervent hope that all may go well with you and the Foundation this winter.

Affectionately your friend,
Helen Keller

52   The Nazi Authorities Have Closed the Institute

December 2, 1938, letter from Helen Keller to John H. Finley, AFB.

Throughout the late 1930s, Keller continued to pay close attention to the growing European conflict, especially Hitler's rise to power. In this 1938 letter, she lobbied the now-emeritus *New York Times* editor, good friend, and Westport neighbor John Finley, to devote the resources of the *Times* to publicizing the devastating situation of Jews in Nazi-occupied territory. She asked him to highlight people with disabilities—who were targeted by the Nazis as "defectives," and then denied entry into the United States and other nations because restrictive immigration laws likewise labeled them as "defectives." European Jews, clients, and administrators of institutions for people with disabilities, desperately sought help. "The letters they send me,—and oh, I receive so many!—including one from a deaf-blind poetess, are full of pathetic faith in American goodwill and counsel."

Tragically the 1946 fire at Keller's home at Arcan Ridge destroyed those letters. Meanwhile in 1938, her lobbying efforts failed to bring the issue to the pages of the *New York Times*. She, however, followed her own suggestion to Finley by supporting an AFB effort to bring to the United States the head of the Vienna Jewish School for the Blind, under the guise of his learning English. In 1939, German police banned Keller's latest book, *Journal,* after she refused to delete sections expressing views favorable to Bolshevism. Lamenting Nazi restrictions on the use of braille, she wrote to her friend Walter Holmes in 1941, "news from Europe is like a stone ever heavy upon my soul." These repeated references remind us that many in the United States were not ignorant about Nazi horrors before and during the war.[2]

The warmest of welcomes to you, dear Dr. Finley! It gladdens me to learn that you are well enough to be back among your friends in New York. It is a comfort these sad days to think of you again presiding over the growth of human sympathy and good-will to every one, regardless of race or creed. May you be blessed with improved health and a sense of the peace that springs from your unselfish, brother-loving life.

Last month I said goodbye to the house in Forest Hills—the second home Teacher and I called our own,—and now I am settled with Polly for a while in this snug old New England farm-house at the end of a narrow road. We are deep in the country, away from steam heat and telephones. Everything here is very simple and rural, but big fire-places, stoves, sheep-skins which we brought from Ross-shire and the sun, when it shines, will keep us warm until spring.

I came here in quest of the undisturbed privacy essential to literary work. Already the materials are spread over the desk for a book about Anne Sullivan Macy as the liberator of my personality and for notes I jotted down while traveling through Japan last year.

However, it is extremely difficult to put my mind on matters which seem of small moment beside the tragic, sinister world situation. One passionately interested in mankind's welfare cannot but have a mind lacerated, heart wounded and imagination clouded by the breakdown of European democracy, the perfidy of France and Britain to Czechoslovakia, the folly and cowardice of governments which should have been far-seeing, fearless against dictatorship.

The other day I received a letter which, like concentrated fire, burnt deeper into my consciousness the meaning of the present crisis, for it brought the sense of a nameless shadow worse than blindness, a silence stabbed by inhumanity to defenseless handicapped fellow-beings under Nazi rulers. That is why I turn to you, Dr. Finley, a champion of the oppressed, a counselor of the bewildered.

The letter is from a seeing exile who used to be an assistant at the Israelite Institute for the Blind in Vienna. Heartbroken, ashamed because she cannot use her good eyes to save others, she tells how the Nazi authorities have closed the Institute and driven out the students to beg or starve. Deliberately, as part of a ruthless, calculating scheme, these ill-starred ones—adults and children—are being reduced to misery even worse than that of Jews who can see, since blindness intensifies every privation.

Before their expulsion many of the students had attained high credit in intellectual pursuits, excellent workmanship and a degree of self-support. That was their Light, their Manhood. Now this precious All of life has been snatched from them. It is as if we should rob the cripple of his staff or the drowning man of his life-belt or a thirsty person of the spade with which he digs in the desert for water!

Nature has been called cruel, but the sea that slays, the winds wrecking ships, the sun scorching the land to sterility are insentient, and think no evil. The wild beasts seek only to satisfy their hunger, they do not go out of their way to persecute the weak or cast them out of shelter.

Yet there are those Jewish blind wandering from place to place, exposed to the cold, shut out from all the associations of their "Christian" fellow-blind, denied the friendly hand and counseling voice that would render less desperate their search of bread and safety. They are refused the one compensation possible for loss of sight— using knowledge and will power to wrest victory from misfortune. They cannot expect aid from the Jewish communities who are also destitute.

Thought is paralyzed by such injustice without excuse, without a parallel—crushing mind and virtue in the afflicted and powerless. Before its wantonness philosophy staggers, and faith is sore tried. It has not happened among savage tribes—there are even cannibals with a code of gentlemen—it has happened in a country known during centuries for its civilization, art and learning. It is not a pagan but a Christian land where Jesus, the Inspirer of Hope for the Blind and the deaf, is crucified, and Judas Iscariot is rewarded. All this has been wrought by hate-crazed creatures—I scorn to call them fanatics or men or even devils since they are morally diseased.

How fearful is the responsibility resting upon governments and churches that thus allow ultimate misrule to hold sway over human beings normal and handicapped alike!

Unfortunately, as you are aware, it is impossible to assist these doubly stricken people individually, in view of the fact that other nations will not admit defectives to citizenship. But, Dr. Finley, is there no way in which we may hopefully approach this problem? Why we can not establish some agency private or public to create through collective action a more humane atmosphere for the Jewish blind—and the deaf too—in Austria and Germany? The letters they send me,—and oh, I receive so many!—including one from a deaf-blind poetess, are full of pathetic faith in American goodwill and counsel. They say that without any means they do not know what course to follow, but America does, and will befriend them once it is informed of their bitter plight. I wish I might lay their case before the NYT [New York Times]. However, you will know what is best at a time when thinking minds and loving hearts are overburdened with urgent problems and the world's unhappiness.

Please give my love to Mrs. Finley. It touched me to receive her beautiful letter giving news of you while you were in hospital last summer.

Hoping that Polly and I may see you the next time we are in New York, I am,

Affectionately your friend,
Helen Keller

53 This Time of Immeasurable Stakes

October 30, 1944, letter from Helen Keller
to Vice-President Henry A. Wallace, AFB.

With Jo Davidson, Keller attended a Madison Square Garden rally, sponsored by the Independent Voters Committee of the Arts and Sciences for Roosevelt, September 21, 1944. There Wallace's vision of postwar conversion, stressing racial and economic equalities, thrilled her. She also supported his efforts to establish a long-lasting peace with the Soviet Union. Despite her skepticism regarding the outcome of the war and of the 1944 elections, she expresses her faith in Wallace and her hopes for the persuasive powers of postwar liberalism in international politics. See document 76 for Keller's response to Truman's firing of Wallace in 1946.

Dear Vice-President Wallace,

This is the first opportunity I have succeeded in wresting from besieging duties to write the letter you requested with such irresistible benignity.

First I must tell you what a glorious event it was to meet you on an occasion altogether splendid. There was the immense listening concourse at the Madison Square Garden "Rally for Roosevelt." There were the noble music and the voices of the Arts and Sciences proclaiming the Republic of the Mind that alone can raise government to fellowship between the creative and the wise for the mutual advantage of all the people. There were the klieg lights illumining the myriads of faces full of hidden thoughts and choices as Destiny "passed with His back to them." Then came the civic fire of Orson Welles's speech, and he introduced you as one with "a perfect confidence in the capacity of the earth as a provider for all men and in the capacity of man to provide for man in a just abundancy." You arose—a new type of statesman for whom the times cry aloud—one who looks upon government not as politics in the sense of office-hunting but as skilful stewardship for the health and strength of the people, and almost before I knew it we were greeting each other.

Another wonder befell me some days later when Dr. Kingdom sent a copy of your address at the National Citizens' Political Action Committee luncheon. It touched me profoundly that amid world issues, colossal plans and the urge towards spiritual growth more mighty than any material movement you should mention my name, associating me in such beautiful words with the liberation of mankind.

Your understanding appreciation of the Soviet Union is refreshing to me especially because of the obstacles I encounter in persuading people to judge generously a country that has had only twenty-six years in which to achieve a stupendous social and economic renaissance. The stand you take on the all-importance of the Spirit is even stronger since you recognize the value of historic materialism as a science and how well the ideas of society based on it are working in Russia at present. Naturally when the Great Experiment began under Lenin, the people had sunk far down into the dungeon of the flesh through famine, disease, ignorance and oppression. They could not, and perhaps they cannot yet respond to the higher Light until their minds have been washed clean from the warping darknesses of twelve centuries. However, I am confident that the spirituality with which I believe some of them are endowed will increase and at last shed abroad its beauty in the nation's soul completing the triumph of its civilization.

What you say about most of us being "deeply encased in the flesh" brings back to my mind your talk on China at the Astor Hotel, after the rally, and on the imperative need to rehabilitate three-fourths of the race. I cannot but think of the postwar situation in terms of this need, and hope and anxiety alternate as I look futureward.

There is immediate hope such as I have not had before in the sanative agreements at Teheran, Moscow and Dumberton Oaks and in the many provisions to which they seem likely to lead for sufficient food, employment and physical well-being everywhere. My anxiety lies in the fact that three-fourths of mankind still lag behind in the rudiments of schooling they require if they are to lift themselves from a submerged, often animal-like status, exercise their human rights democratically and cooperate with the United Nations' postwar policies. What arrangements, I wonder, will be made to reach them extensively and as rapidly as possible in a campaign against illiteracy and mind-killing drudgery? China, in spite of its appalling misery, has a better fighting chance now because a large part of its people are literate, but what about India, Africa and the innumerable inhabited isles?

When these forgotten masses have once mastered the printed word and learned to a degree how to protect themselves against exploitation, what international safeguard will there be to put within their range the incalculable educative resources of the spoken word and personal stimulus through radio, motion film and television?

Only by these two basic kindred movements can we be sure that the Spirit will be released enough to overcome slavishness, intolerance and tribalism. Only by this direct viva voce power can a world unity rooted in the dwellers of the earth emerge that will crystalize our postwar ideals into a working friendship of peoples capable of withstanding reaction, trade rivalries and the partisan interests of each nation which still render any league or council of man insecure. The quicker we are in mobilizing our collective good-will towards mankind, the better chance we shall have to equip their minds to keep pace with their own inventions and their power to amass material advantages and the responsibilities they must assume as old institutions and governments crumble over their heads.

It is a bitter comment on the narrow scale of present-day education that the peon in the Latin Americas, the peasant of Europe and Asia's son of the soil contribute by their dumb incomprehension, inertia and fear of losing their livelihood to the continued evils of corrupt politics, war and plutocracy, and that is the truth you drove home so forcibly in your speech on the Century of the Common Man. What you are going to do, Mr. Wallace, is something beyond the limits of traditional or historic statecraft—helping to administer a mighty remedy to a vast suffering. Your premonition of unprecedented difficulties is just, but once the Spirit encased in all flesh breaks its shackles, how wondrous the change will be! Events and problems will be flashed from one end of the earth to the other, impulses to right disaster will not grow cold, and faith born of dynamic effort will multiply the unitive forces which will cement a peace never to be broken by recurring greed and barbarism.

As the 7th of November approaches I tremble. I will confess one of my heresies. The more I see of political parties competing for rule, the less I believe in them. Why should a national government be held up by the fury and smoke of their unthinking hysteria? And particularly at this time of immeasurable stakes, urgent work and destitution in the greater part of the earth!

Earnestly wishing you the richest happiness that can befall a man— the fulfillment of a faith-inspired mission, I am, with Polly Thomson's cordial greetings, (apart from her Scots loyalty she admires you tremendously)

Sincerely and affectionately yours,
Helen Keller

D *Friendships, Intimacies, and the Everyday*

54 The Battle of Eyes

June 24, 1929, letter from Helen Keller to M. C. Migel, Migel file, AFB.

This affectionate letter to M. C. Migel, the first president of the American Foundation for the Blind, emphasizes the concern for Anne Macy's eyesight that dominated much of Keller and Macy's lives in this period. She was the famous teacher of deaf-blind Helen Keller, but she also was visually impaired. As an educator and friend to Keller, Macy believed firmly that blindness should be no deterrent. Keller proudly asserted that Macy "believed in the blind not as a class apart but as human beings endowed with rights."[1] In contradiction to this, however, Macy responded to her own deteriorating eyesight with depression and isolation. Increasingly, she was physically incapable of performing the tasks she had undertaken, and increasingly, she was temperamentally unable to handle the changes in her own life. The pair depended more and more on Polly Thomson. Macy desperately hid her disability from public knowledge and retreated into seclusion. Nella Braddy Henney cooperated in this respect when she published her 1933 biography of the famed teacher and said little of the lifelong disability. The concealable efforts of both women have contributed to the dominant historical perception of Macy as sighted or only slightly visually impaired.

Dear Mr. Migel,

This sheet of paper is not large enough to express Mrs. Macy's and my appreciation of the friendly spirit of your letter. Your kindness is quite wonderful! The element of friendship in your check makes us willing and happy to accept it.

The trio has often thought how delightful it would be to take the St. Lawrence trip; but every time we have waved away the idea as being too emphatically good to be realized. The dream seemed farther off than ever when your letter put the magic carpet under our feet.

My reasons for being glad and grateful to you for making possible a real holiday for Mrs. Macy are too many to be set down here. You know how anxious I have been about her for a long time. Things have gone badly with her, there is no disguising the fact. I thought the Battle of Eyes was over, and was feeling happy, even though we had lost. But we saw Dr. Berens last Friday, and he told Mrs. Macy that her other eye would have to be operated on in September for cataract. He said she must take a complete rest during the summer months, and not worry!!! How does one not worry when there is a possibility of becoming blind in a few weeks? Without doubt, Fate lays relentless hands on some individuals. If Fate had perception, a soul, a heart, a conscience, it must needs blush for the pain it wantonly inflicts. But I am trying to keep such thoughts out of my mind, and the fascinating trip you are giving us will help to keep me brave and optimistic.

Besides being disheartened about Mrs. Macy, I am terribly distressed because I cannot go to Georgia. I promised Miss Rand I would do all I could to interest the Legislature in the blind; but under the circumstances it is out of the question; for Miss Thomson cannot accompany me, and I could not manage a public appearance without her.

There is something I have long meant to say to you; but always other things have got said instead. You have no idea how your interest in the blind keeps my spirits up. Without the encouragement of your understanding of what must be done for them, I should often feel unutterably weary of thinking, talking and writing about their problems. But when I think of your unfailing self-giving in our cause, it braces me, and I am ashamed to falter in my endeavors.

I have it on my conscience that I did not write to Mrs. Migel myself, instead of letting Mrs. Bond explain the situation. The truth is, I found it extremely difficult to put in writing Mrs. Macy's reluctance to accept her invitation to visit Rest Haven until the traces of what she had been through were somewhat less conspicuous. Personally, I cannot imagine any one feeling uncomfortable in Mrs. Migel's presence.

When I met her, she seemed full of loving and understanding. I suppose there must be more vanity in Mrs. Macy than in me. We hope, however, that Mrs. Migel will invite us again when circumstances are less unbending. The anticipation we have of visiting Rest Haven is a bright forerunner of the happiness that awaits us.

Mrs. Macy and Polly join me in this imperfect expression of our gratitude for the good time you have arranged for us. Certainly our thoughts will often be directed towards you while we are luxuriating between sky and water, and if this maddening weather continues, we will send up breezy prayers for you.

Wishing you and Mrs. Migel everything that can render your summer enjoyable, I am,

> Affectionately yours,
> Helen Keller

P.S. It is most dear of you to ask about our hospital bills; but we shall not send them. You may have heard of a golden windfall that dropped into our unexpected hands in the shape of a bequest from our lifelong friend Mrs. William Thaw. It will take care of the hospital bills and quite a budget of other obligations.

> Thank you once more, and bless you!
> H.K.

55 Discuss the Thousand and One Things

August 3, 1931, letter from Helen Keller to Amelia Bond, AFB.

Amelia Bond, secretary to the American Foundation for the Blind president M. C. Migel, frequently exchanged chatty letters with Keller. The Keller, Sullivan, and Thomson household appreciated her friendship. This letter reveals Keller's continued appreciation for brailled books.

Dear Amelia,

You have certainly displayed angelic patience towards an incorrigible procrastinator. I started a letter to you way back in the Tertiary Age, then let it fossilize while I exchanged letters and telegrams with Yugoslavia. Another geological period followed during which a mountain-slide of new experiences buried the fossil, one would think forever. But forever is a very long time, and many things may happen while it is passing. Your dear letters, to try again—not to revive life in the fossil, but to write a new one.

When we returned from Yugoslavia, there was your beautiful birthday remembrance awaiting me! I am delighted with the gloves, they feel like the caressing touch of your hand. I shall enjoy wearing them in Paris, where we shall go next month to be with Mr. Cromwell when the plans for the International Council for the Blind are expected to take a workable shape.

I had other belated birthday gifts, mostly books. Teacher presented me with Mrs. Caskell's "Life of Charlotte Bronte" in six volumes, which I haven't had time to glance at yet. Polly gave me "Japan," a curious and instructive history of old Japan and its ancestor-worship by Lafcadio Hearn. Her brother gave me a number of Balzac's stories, the finest one being "The Atheist's Mass," and her sister Margaret sent me Anatole France's delightful "The Crime of Sylvester Bonnard." No, no, no! I don't mean to say that the crime is delightful, but the octogenaire scholar with the spirit of immortal youth is adorable, and the crime he commits for sweet Jeane's sake is all to the good. Thus I defy the weather with plenty of reading, and keep my mind open to invisible sunshine. For there is little visible sunshine here, it rains and rains and rains!

We are glad that Mr. Migel is better. He wrote me a dear letter referring to his illness jocularly. We hope he is still improving, and that he has managed to find a cool refuge from the atrocious heat we read of in the newspapers. We look forward to seeing him in Paris. That will be a happy ending to our summer and a bright beginning for our voyage home.

It makes our hearts warm to know that you and Thomas go out to Forest Hills occasionally. We feel positively homesick as we read Andy's and your accounts of the good times we all have together.

I shall not say anything about Yugoslavia here because you should have a copy of the article I wrote on our visit by this time. I started it as a journal letter to Mr. Migel, then learned that "Good Housekeeping" wanted an article about some of my experiences abroad; so I sent what I had written to Leslie in the hope that he might sell it. Polly asked him to send you a copy of it as soon as possible.

I wonder what you will say to our decorations. They are very handsome. We are thinking of having them made into brooches. And his Majesty's photograph we shall have to put in the bank safe, as the frame is gold—and our little nest is under the shadow of the bandit terror.

Well, Teacher and Polly have kept you so well informed of our doings here, I can't make much of a show. I only want you and Thomas to know how often you are in my mind, and how constantly I keep you both in my affection. I can hardly wait until we are all together again, and discuss the thousand and one things "qui entretiennent l'amitie," but can't be written.

With the love of the trio in the House of the Moon, I am,

> Yours every affectionately,
>
> Helen Keller

56 These Adventures Under the Midnight Sun

August 21, 1933, letter from Helen Keller to M. C. Migel, Migel file, AFB.

Keller, Macy, and their new companion Polly Thomson frequently sought and found refuge in Scotland. Between 1930 and 1935, they traveled three times to Scotland for lengthy visits, this trip lasting fourteen months. All enjoyed the home of Polly's brother Robert, a minister in the Church of Scotland, and his family. The trips provided privacy, solace, and a slower pace. They also created and reinforced Keller's pattern of depending on travel as escape, refuge, and perhaps distraction. In this letter Keller expresses her concern for the lack of attention paid to the deaf-blind, her continued interest in dogs, and the difficulty of managing a home from across the Atlantic.

Dear Mr. Migel,

Last night I sent you a cablegram which I hope will not be too great a shock. After it was gone, I felt a qualm or two, but the deed is perpetrated, and there is nothing to do about it but let it go with the multitude of things that are impulsively started down the flood of the days.

This is the first time I have entered the ring of a cattle market. I must tell you how it happened. A herd of more than a hundred black Angus cattle graze in the fields of South Arcan. I have made friends with them. Some of them come to the fence a few feet from our door-step and take carrots and turnips from my hand. You should hear them bellow when tidbits are too slow coming.

One day as I fed them I thought of all the stories I had read about bullocks—how they ploughed the fields, drew pioneer wagons across continents, carried a lovely bride to church and Queen Bertha, who spun at her distaff seated high upon the bullock's back. It occurred to me that I might use the bullock in a new way—to interest the people of Scotland in their deaf blind. I had already talked with the Rotarians of Inverness on the subject, and promised to hold a meeting, the proceeds of which they were to use to assist the doubly afflicted.

There is to be a sale of cattle in Dingwall Wednesday noon. I shall appear in the ring with all the bullocks and offer for sale the one which has been selected as the best of the lot. The general public will be invited to make charity bids of half a crown, and afterwards the animal will be sold outright to the highest bidder. The newspapers have eagerly seized upon the bullock idea and given it wide publicity. Already a tremendous interest has been worked up. It looks as if all Ross-shire would come. There will not be room for the crowd in the usual market-place; so an open space is being prepared outside the building. The Provost of Dingwall will be present. I understand that donations are coming in thick and fast, some have been received even from London! That is why I cabled you, I thought New York should be represented.

It is astonishing how quickly the Scots can carry out an idea when they once get started. This country is so small, much can be done in a short time. I have a letter from the Town Clerk of Inverness expressing the hope that they will have all the facts about the deaf blind to present at the meeting which is to take place in that city the end of September!!! Amazing, isn't it?

We are having a wonderful summer, industriously doing nothing. For a month we slept, ate and sat in the sun. The weather has been marvelous—just enough rain to intensify the greenness of the pastures and the fragrance of the clover. For a time we were quite anxious about our water supply, the little River Orrin got so low, the cattle could step across it—and they did. Mr. McCrae had a hard time rounding them up. Now, however, the danger point is passed, we are having sufficient rain to feed the pipes.

Our only disappointment is your not coming here, we looked forward confidently to a visit with you. I know you would have enjoyed the Highlands, the hills and glens are so inexpressibly beautiful. We often picnic on the moors, sitting in the heather beside a chatty little burn or a slowly meandering river. Our last picnic was somewhat spoilt by the bleating of sheep whose lambs had been taken to market. Sixty thousand lambs were sold in Dingwall last week. That meant a turnover of about half a million pounds, but oh, the grieving of the sheep crying and milling about us—it was heartbreaking.

We have taken several charming trips with friends, the most interesting of which was a sail to the Orkneys and Shetlands. At Lerwick we secured the services of a seawise skipper and a staunch little boat and visited the island of Noss, the famous bird sanctuary of the North. When the skipper blew his horn, tens of thousands of birds rose from the tremendous cliffs and literally darkened the sky with their wings. Other thousands descended into the sea. It was a beautiful sight, they told me, to see them riding the white-capped waves and diving into the breakers after prey. I fed the herring gulls with their favorite delicacy. They took the fish from my hand, and their wings flapped about me like sails in a gale. A ship passed us crowded with young girls—herring-canners. They follow the herring round the coast of Scotland, weighing anchor when the catch is good. Fortunately, these girls are well taken care of, a doctor-nurse and a minister accompany them. The poor things often injure themselves in the process of packing the fish. What happens to their souls that necessitates the attendance of a minister I don't know.

After we left the Port of Scapa Flors, (you will remember the British fleet took refuge in that harbor during the War) we were told that the captain of the St. Ola manipulated the smoke from the funnel so that it traced a huge K in the heavens. Thus it is that fame goes up in smoke! But more of these adventures under the Midnight Sun when we meet.

August has been given over to visitors. The old farm-house has run with laughter and feasting. First Somers Mark and his wife came for a week, then a party of ladies—friends of Polly's—drove up from Stirling and spent a jolly evening with us. Polly's sister Margaret spent several days here, and we had her brother and his wife and four children to high tea. Dr. and Mrs. Love have just left us. They are delightful people to talk and go adventuring with. Dr. Love is preparing an article about me which he calls "The Mind of Helen Keller." It is by way of reply to current criticisms of Teacher's educational method and my presumptuous use of color terms in my descriptions of the visible world. He wants to bring out some fresh facts which he has elicited from Teacher and me. We both feel that he is most important to give a definitive answer to our critics; for he has a lifelong knowledge of the deaf and their problems.

We are putting off as long as possible the more or less formal visits we must make to friends before leaving Scotland. Lord and Lady Aberdeen are first on the list, then the Loves are having us for a week. The Duke and Duchess of Montrose have invited us to visit them at Buchanan Castle. I anticipate with interest exploring that historic castle—it has been a haunt of romance for more than eight hundred years. The Marchioness of Tweedale has asked us to tea tomorrow at Brahan Castle. This invitation is regarded as the highwater mark of our social triumphs.

You will be amused to hear that we are the proud possessors of two new dogs. One is a Shetland Collie which Lord Aberdeen gave me. His name is Dileas—Gaelic for Faithful One, pronounced "Gielis." He is a perfect beauty with a coat of gold brown and white trimmings. His little legs are like Dresden China. All the sheep lore his tribe possesses has been bred out of him and replaced by drawing-room manners which appeal to the eye and the delicate taste of fine ladies.

The other dog was given me by Mrs. Eager. She is a Lakeland Terrier, a breed of fox-hunting dogs that is just now very popular at the shows. She is called Maida. She is coal black, with a blue white tuft on her lower jaw which looks funny. Her legs are very long to run with the hounds. Her body is small, strong and agile, so that she can squeeze into narrow crannies after prey. The "Lakelanders" are endowed with great courage; for they must chase the fox to the very edge of precipices and up steep crags. Maida's tail is short and stubby—a long tail would be in the way when the pack hunts in bracken and heather. Altogether, she is a most interesting, fascinating little creature. Every time she and Dileas go for a walk, Polly brings back thrilling tales of partridges flushed, hares pursued, rabbits driven into their warrens, chickens and wild pigeons forced to roost precipitately in bush and tree. It is comical to see an old hare, who knows perfectly well that they are mere puppies, leading them in a dance in the corn-fields. We don't know what to do with the two dogs when we leave South Arcan, we already have more dogs than we have room for in Forest Hills.

Was there a streak of the "blues" in your letter? I hope not. I read that things are on the upgrade in America. The papers here are full of President Roosevelt's efforts to bring back prosperity. He is a very courageous and able man; his intelligence is above the average given presidents. I hope, though, he won't work his dictatorial powers to the bone. Some of his acts seem autocratic from this distance. One wonders if there is a shred of democracy left in the U.S.

It was good news about Mr. Markle's donations. It was Dr. Connelly in Dr. Berens's office who advised me to write to him. I did so at once, and received a nice letter from his secretary saying that Mr. Markel was ill, and could not see me then, but that when he was better, arrangements would be made for us to meet. I told "Jolly Boy"—I beg his pardon, I refer to Dr. Nagle—about the incident, and he began his siege of the poor man, and, I suppose, pantingly drove him to the River Styx. I trust he is at present enjoying the peace that cometh with the passing of riches and beggars.

I am naturally interested to know what the plans for next year are. If there is to be no money-raising campaign, there will not be much for me to do. In fact, we should be tempted to remain here and do some writing, were it not for a most vexatious situation at home. We left the house, garden and dogs in the care of Charlie, the husband of our maid. We were to pay him seventy-five dollars a month, (we thought that a large salary during these hard times) and he was to stay in the house nights. He was to buy his own food, but the bills we are receiving show that he is living on broilers, filleted sole, lamb chops, thick cream, fresh eggs and all the vegetables and fruits as they come in season—at our expense! The bills are simply outrageous. We are at a loss what to do. We fear that if we stopped his supplies, he might do something to the dogs. The house and the dogs are at his mercy. We thought of sending a policeman to put him out, but again it is a case of what he might do. There seems to be nothing for it but return to New York in October. We cannot well go sooner, as we are to speak at Inverness on the 28th of September and in London for the National College of Teachers of the Deaf early in October.

In the mean time I shall be happy if you feel like telling me something about your plans for the Foundation's future. I need not tell you how much I hope and pray that this may find you, as they say, in excellent health and prospect of a good year. I appeal to the softest corner of the softest part of your kind heart to make a sign of remembrance to "the three Musketeers" who appreciate and love you.

Sincerely,

Helen Keller

P.S. We have just received a cable from Dr. and Mrs. Berens. They arrive Wednesday, on the Manhattan, and we expect them up here soon after.

H.K.

57 My Only News Is Loneliness

Undated 1934 or 1935, letter from Helen Keller
to Anne Sullivan Macy, AFB.

Written probably during April 1935 when Macy received eye surgery, in this letter Keller uses news from home to attempt to cheer Macy during one of their few separations. She feared Macy's ill-health, but her death in October 1936 surprised no one.

Dearest Teacher,

Polly's letter has just come telling how wonderfully you stood the trip. I was afraid it might be too hard for you. I am glad you have a pleasant room. It is a relief to me to have you under proper medical care. Dr. Hunt will surely do all in his power to "make you over."

Blessings upon the Chatham Hotel for allowing dogs to stay! It must be a comfort to have Dileas with you.

My only news is loneliness, but I can bear anything that is a step on the road to your recovery. The woods talk to me about you with fragrant speech daily. Just think! You have not had a chance to see my walk or touch those beautiful trees that make it so beautiful! Well, if we cannot enjoy everything together as we used to on our holidays, we can love always.

The days glide along like soft music. It still rains heavily now and then, but most of the time the weather is delightful. Last evening it was clear and bright, and Herbert and I went fishing. Half an hour later we were caught in a downpour and had to hurry home without a fish for breakfast. We shall try again tomorrow.

The dogs are all well, and as good as gold, sunning themselves, dipping their feet in the water, chasing each other all over the place pretending it's a jungle, but seldom quarreling. You would have laughed at Helga the other night. It was raining hard, and she didn't want to go out. When we insisted, she suddenly began to run up and down the piazza, evidently in the hope of placating her gods. She is getting "cute" in her old age, isn't she? Sometimes Wendy and Jacqueline join me on my walks. They seem to miss you, they spend much time at the cabin.

Steffens's autobiography is intensely absorbing—and disenchanting.[2] I have long known about the terrible corruption that darkens American history, but I am only now beginning to grasp the details to some extent and realize the pressure which drove many to employ criminal methods. The wonder is not that they succumbed to bribery, but rather that they accomplished the great things they did for the people. It is a tragedy—the suffering of several intelligent bosses of city and state governments when they perceived that their measures yielded more evil than good because they had used unjust means for their purposes. There is inspiration, too, reading of the upright, courageous men who, often single-handed, fought for the people's rights. Emerson must have had such men as La Follette, Folk of Missouri and Mayor Cole of Chicago when he wrote "Self-reliance" and "Character."

Bob telegraphed that he had obtained money from the Federal Government for more talking-books.[3] I don't know how many men will be employed this summer. I don't think Bob can get away for a vacation for some time.

Theresa is sweet, and seems really interested in doing all she can for us including the dogs. Herbert speaks of you every day and wishes you could feel the warm sun or taste a particularly nice dish we have for lunch or dinner.

Anxiously awaiting Polly's next bulletin, I am, with love to you both,

Affectionately yours,

Helen

P.S. I am enclosing a letter which you can perhaps have copied so as to make sure it is free from errors.

H.K.

58 My Faith that Teacher Is Near Is Absolute

December 3, 1936, letter from Helen Keller, at the manse, Bothwell, Scotland, to M. C. Migel, Migel file, AFB.

Anne Sullivan Macy died on October 20, 1936, at seventy years of age. The book she had always said she would write remained unwritten. AFB officials and friends celebrated her life with a large funeral at the National Cathedral. The woman who spent her childhood as an orphan in the infamous Tewksbury Almshouse had traveled far.

Almost immediately after the funeral, Keller and Thomson made plans to return to Scotland and the sanctuary of Polly's brother's home. Aboard the ship *Deutschland* only two weeks after Anne's death, Helen wrote, "This is the first voyage Polly and I have had without Teacher. . . . The anguish which makes me feel cut in two prevents me from writing another word about these life-wrecking changes." The loss of such a vital partner made her "deaf-blind a second time"[4] (see also document 40).

The more than two months in "the manse," as they called the Scottish parsonage, soothed Keller. She ate good food, thrilled to the slow and earnest finger-spelling of Polly's nephews, followed European and U.S. politics closely, while the entire household obsessed about King Edward's abdication. At some points she despaired, writing once that "I have experienced a sense of dying daily. Every hour I long for the thousand bright signals from her vital, beautiful hand." At others she felt hope: "This morning I awoke positively sure I had seen Teacher, and I have been happier all day."[5]

During Macy's last months in 1936, Keller had received a visit from Takeo Iwahashi, an English-speaking Christian, the director of the Osaka Lighthouse (the primary school for blind people in Japan), and Japanese translator of *The Story of My Life*. He thrilled her by urging that she visit Japan. According to Keller, when Anne heard of it, she insisted that Helen "promise me that after I am gone you and Polly will be light-bringers to the handicapped of Japan." The AFB's M. C. Migel encouraged the trip.[6] In this letter, Iwahashi contacts her at the manse, urging her to visit Japan in the spring.

Dear Mr. Migel,

Your welcome letter has found its way here through the continued press of mail which Polly's two hands are hardly able to open and spell to me. How dear of you to assure us that you are thinking of the two "Musketeers" who, with your blessing, will carry high the banner of the blind alone.

My faith that Teacher is near is absolute, but as I take hold on things after all these weeks I find it even harder to be courageous when, forgetting, I call Teacher, and only silence answers me and emptiness touches my outstretched hands.

However, I am somewhat rested, and so is Polly. Usually we get up at half-past six and work until 8 p.m. when we stop for a cosy talk with her brother and family in his study.

I feel most fortunate to be in such a sweet home as The Manse. At first Polly came here intending to spend only a day or two and live like hermits the rest of the time trying to catch up with our correspondence, but Mr. and Mrs. Thomson's quick eyes and warm hearts found a better way. They persuaded us to stay with them and turned over to us the drawing-room, so that we could write in peace and spread papers and books over the floor if need be. With a good old-fashioned fire and warm clothes we are very comfortable. Better still, there are children in the family whose affection and bright talk put sweetness into my lonely heart.

As I have always said, you have a happy faculty of doing what will most satisfy me. Nothing could be pleasanter to my sense of oneness with the blind everywhere than to have you call me "Counsellor of the Bureau of National and International Relations." Proudly I accept this suggestive, much-informing title. Will you kindly convey to the Trustees of the American Foundation my thanks for this gratifying proof of their cooperative spirit?

The cable from Japan which I enclose explains itself. Certainly Polly and I are ready to go. You know how Teacher used to urge that trip upon me, and how willingly I should have undertaken it but for her broken health. Of course you know too how my heart yearns towards the handicapped in the East who remain friendless, untaught. A second time I thrill with the vision of you, dear Mr. Migel, preparing the way for us with your counsel, and—what a wonderful way to fulfill Teacher's wish it would be if you would be our Prospero on the enchanted Island of Nippon!

No doubt you have met Mr. Iwahashi. Polly and I are sure he will give the information required and arrange the programme wisely.

Hoping that you and Mrs. Migel are well and having a pleasant summer, I am, with Polly's love to you both,

Affectionately your friend,
Helen Keller

P.S. Polly has just found the mistake in the cheque-book, and will attend to the matter immediately. It happened through an oversight in the rush of departure.

H.K.

59 Bury Myself Deep in Thought

September 4, 1938, letter from Helen Keller to Lenore Smith, AFB.

In this fall 1938 letter, Keller clearly appreciates her friend Lenore Smith but continues to mourn the loss of Anne Sullivan Macy.

She seeks privacy in order to write a book that would honor Macy and mourns the many requests upon her. She would not finish the book *Teacher* until 1955.

Dear Lenore,

After the happy hours we spent at your retreat last Friday Polly [undecipherable] bulletin of the talk she had with you about our plans when [undecipherable] you should understand the circumstances in which I am placed. It is my avowed purpose to go to France quietly and bury myself deep in thought so that I may write the book I know I have to for mon cher's memory. It will be different from anything I have seen, and naturally I want to put into it my best workmanship as well as a fresh message for others who are engaged in healing the handicapped. This will mean—as it does with all writers who take their work seriously—solitude bordering on misanthropy, constant meditation and revising of what I have written, ideas dashed off on paper night or day before I forget them, ruthless exclusion of pleasures that would distract me to no repose.

As you know, for twenty years I have lived close to the center of importunate requests, interruptions and social functions. "Oh, please do this or that, and it will take only a few minutes"—these words are almost invariably accompanied by a call, a picture to be taken, an interview; and at the end of the day I have found myself with countless precious hours gone past recall. I wrote "Midstream" under mental and emotional stresses I cannot describe without a shudder, they were so nerve-wracking. Utterly discouraged, I preferred lecturing, although it tested me beyond endurance, to sudden, untamed breaks into my writing time.

Now I determined to put a stop to this kind of annoyance. That is why Polly and I are going away from America, away from family, friends and everything that exposes me to disturbances. I will not have mail forwarded—the American Foundation for the Blind and Nella will attend to it during my absence. Even aboard ship our names will not be on the passenger list—I especially insist on that. Then, only then can I humanly write as I used to at Wrentham—in peace and good humor.

Conditions will be such that I must have Polly day in and day out to help me read and reread manuscripts, look up passages I want and the countless little but important services that require sight. For that matter I shall need Herbert also in order to translate into Braille things to which I must keep referring as I write. Obviously it will be impossible for either Polly or me to see anybody or go on pleasure trips for a period whose duration depends upon my progress with the book.

That is what Polly tried to tell you the other day. It grieves me beyond words, Lenore, to seem inhospitable. I love young people as my own flesh and blood, and their gaiety renews my youth, but bitter experience has driven me to this hard self-denial, and I shall stick at the task until I have accomplished a too long deferred undertaking. At my age one cannot be sure of having a sufficiently long tether as in youth, and I have already sacrificed self-expression almost to the verge of self-stupefaction.

You will, I am sure, understand this outburst. Teacher suffered the same way, and the burdens she carried with such courage have fallen upon me pitilessly.

[undecipherable] love [undecipherable], and with memories of Lake Winnipegasset lovelier than ever, I am as of old,

  Affectionately yours,
  Helen Keller

60   You Inspire Other Women

January 30, 1939, letter from Helen Keller to Eleanor Roosevelt;
Folder: Helen Keller; Series 100; Papers of Eleanor Roosevelt,
Franklin D. Roosevelt Library, Hyde Park, New York.

Keller savored her relationship with Eleanor Roosevelt. She felt a kinship between them—of experience, of frustrations at the limitations placed upon women, of political ideology, and of shared hopes for a better world. Her decision to offer Eleanor Roosevelt a copy of her 1908 collection of political essays communicates her desire to establish a further political connection with the First Lady.

Dear Mrs. Roosevelt,

Since I am so fortunate as to know you personally, I cannot refrain from telling you with what very special interest I have read "This is My Story." It is a courageous record by—May I say the First Woman in the land? For it is a superb document of womanhood freeing itself from the countless social inhibitions, timidities, family paternalism and pleasant inertia so vividly portrayed in Edith Wharton's "The Age of Innocence."

Tenderly I sympathize with your girlhood aspirations to independence and the tremulous self-consciousness you overcame.—Oh, how that limitation still pursues me in my speech and public appearances! What unusual spirit you must have had to shape alone a life not out of dominating conventionalities but out of your concepts of women as human beings! The two lessons you took to heart we cannot learn too early—that power cannot last or preserve its beneficence without love for the people, that without serious acceptance of individual responsibility and cosmic righteousness wealth brings chaos "and weaves karma."

Because you have so bravely struck out on a self-chosen trail, you inspire other women with confidence in themselves and in life. You show them how through rightly directed intelligence and will-power they can evolve higher capabilities and raise the average of human accomplishment.

Sincerely I admire you for the courage with which you have declared yourself on the side of underprivileged and industrially oppressed women. Until we realize that we are all bound together—that we live by each other and for each other, we cannot create a better, more advanced world for our children to be born in or build up their leaves. I hope that some day in the quiet backwaters of private life you may write another autobiography. It would mean much to us in solving home problems and meeting unprecedented world changes which affect our very existence.

When I was in Seattle last October speaking for the blind, I had the privilege of meeting your daughter.[7] How happy and deeply complimented I felt when she took the time to call on me at the hotel! The President and you seemed very near as she spoke of you both and your warm championship of the people's interests. I was glad to hear how much better her brother James was. I marvelled at Madame Roosevelt's[8] zest in long journeys when Mrs. Boettiger[9] said she had just been out to Seattle for a visit. Your daughter gave me the same sense of vitality and vibrant responsiveness that your book did; so she was not a stranger to me, and I felt delightfully at ease in her presence. I told her how "This Is My Story" had been put into Braille, and how eager I was to read it. I said I would write to you after finishing it; and this is the earliest opportunity I have had to fulfill my intention.

These days my affectionate prayers are with you and the President as I read his soul-kindling summons to genuine democracy, his ringing defiance to dictatorship and his new ventures for America's healthful development. May God grant his wish, embodied in such mighty strivings, for democracy lifted up to the culture of the spirit that shall ensure both liberty and the well-being of all the people!

May I commit the indiscretion of sending you my "Out of the Dark?" It contains several chapters on the modern woman which I wrote when I was making discoveries somewhat similar to your own. Some of the things I said at the time are now out of date, but the spirit of revolt which animated us both remains.

With cordial greetings to the President, and with warm personal salutations to yourself, I am,

> Sincerely yours,
> Helen Keller

61 That Cup of Vernal Delight

March 21, 1943, letter from Helen Keller
to Katharine Cornell, Katharine Cornell file, AFB.

An ironic result of Anne Macy's death was that Keller's social, private, and political worlds expanded as she sought, and others sought to provide, friendship and intellectual camaraderie. This included a vigorous social network, emanating from Westport, Connecticut, the location of Arcan Ridge, the home to which she and Polly Thomson moved in 1939, and the New York world of her friend and literary agent Nella Braddy Henney. Keller grew to love the people of these active networks and valued them for their wit, sharp opinions, and knowledge of the political world. They were important for many reasons, not the least of which was her sense of self as a politically astute person. Integral to the network was the famed stage actress Katharine Cornell, as well as her husband director Guthrie McClintic.

A beautiful morning to you, dearest Katharine Cornell!—That is an item of undiluted good news extracted from a bitter world draught—that spring is here, and the sun warming me to the marrow is divine.

My mind is playing truant in tasks which require close thinking as I drink from that cup of vernal delight and recall the unique evening I spent with you while Polly descended into the shadows of "Die Götterdämerung." You "did treat me highly" as Pepys would say with that delectable dinner and fire-warm cosiness. And how Nancy's nimble spirits tripped through her rhymes telling Polly what she was missing![10]

It was a delicious independence that tingled through me as I piled into the taxi with you, Nancy, the two dogs and Shirer's "Berlin Dairy" and drove over to the theatre, then sat reading while you transformed your joy-radiating self brimming over with vivid interests into a sad, bored Masha. Then there was an adventure as romantic and full of dearness as when Beethoven played "The Moonlight Sonata" for the blind girl—in the full rhythm and absorption of your work you took me on to the stage before each change of scenery, so that I might breathe the atmosphere of the Prozoroff home. The drama as I had read it was heightened by the live characters with whom I shook hands as they moved through the gaiety of Irina's birthday party, the crowded, tense bedroom scene and the brave playing of the band as the regiment departed. Each scene was interpreted anew for me by the sweetness of Irina, Judith Anderson's amazing way of creating an embittered school-mistress, Ruth Gordon's vigor injecting a venom alien to her nature into that prisoner of the family life—Natalia, and the gallant bearing of the soldiers in their handsome uniforms. Also I caught the lovable idiosyncrasies of the old doctor with a newspaper in his pocket, the lifelong loving service in Anfisa's tremulous hand, the comedy of Kuligin's mustaches and the sinister slyness that imagination could conjure out of a friendly face into Solyony's "chick, chick, chick!"

Polly told me that the visit to Countess Tolstoy had been postponed, and I am indeed sorry about the cause. I can imagine the anxious moments you must have passed obtaining substitutes for the actors whom illness had laid low. However, I hope they are back in good health by now.

My heart aches for Miss Musgrave in that sudden separation from her loved ones. Please give her my tender sympathy. I pray that she may realize as I do that the greater our sorrow is, the more we find to be thankful for.

Until we see you again next Tuesday—and of course always—I am,

> Your affectionate friend,
> Helen Keller

62 Alas! I Am Incorrigible

April 28, 1943, letter from Helen Keller to Clare Heineman, Clare and Oscar Heineman file, AFB.

Keller also savored the friendship of her Westport, Connecticut neighbor Clare Heineman. This letter reveals the great fun and intellectual exchanges she experienced in the 1940s, despite the privations of World War II. As she wrote to Nella Braddy Henney, her most frequent correspondent, "After the intellectual hunger I often have felt since Teacher's going it is a priceless blessing to have such friends pour manna into my desert places."[11] These conversations and friendships provided a lifeline. In them she developed and sustained the political interests that were so vital to her own well-being.

Dearest Clare,

What a precious, touching Easter Remembrance! The letter so heavy with love that you and Mr. Heineman sent us was like spring fragrance gladdening our hearts, and for that we thank you more even than for the material blessing you enclosed.

The check will serve as an Aladdin's lamp to conjure up a new, very helpful addition to our resources as "farmerettes." Owing to rationing difficulties and the fact that we live so far from shops, it is a problem to obtain some foods we especially like. Besides the vegetable garden which we started last autumn Herbert is building a chicken-house down by the kennel, so that we can have hens to lay eggs and sometimes enjoy a satisfying dinner. It will be an especially interesting experience, as we have not raised chickens before. If it turns out well, we shall feel quite independent and rural.

Last Sunday the Easter sun shone out gloriously, and a south-wind caressed us softly, without the chill touch by which I always know a chilly night is coming. We spent the day charmingly with the Grummons.[12] There we met Mr. and Mrs. McCormack who have devoted their lives to reforming American prisons, Mr. Stuart Chase the historian and his wife.[13] It was an animated conversation we had about South America, the cordial relations which we feel should be fostered between the United States and Russia, history and books. To my great encouragement I learned that prison conditions are improving despite the War, and that many of the men are standing up splendidly to the defense service.

This spring I have had some delightful surprises. The end of March, while we were in the city we lunched with Katharine Cornell, and who do you think was with her? Countess Alexandra Tolstoy! She reminded me of Teacher in her dynamic vitality, impulsive moods and generous nature. She has not Teacher's large view of world events, and I had all I could do to curb my argumentative tongue when the Countess spoke of Russia as if it was hopelessly lost to Christianity and civilization. Otherwise her talk was illuminating, and I felt close to her father as she described his character and philosophy. She invited Polly and me, with Katharine, sometime in June to visit the Reed Farm up state where she has helped many White Russian refugees.

On April 13th Polly and I attended a luncheon and a musicale at the St. Regis Hotel during which I experienced one of the most beautiful moments in my life. For a long time I had wanted to meet Fritz Kreisler whom I honor because of his noble heart combined with a great soul poured out in harmony and championship of the unprivileged.[14] Suddenly the word flashed from Polly's hand into mine that Kreisler was there at the luncheon, and almost before I knew it a friend had introduced me to him! The warm graciousness of his presence and the cordial assurance of his friendship for me during many years will remain among my dearest memories.

Tuesday afternoon last week was memorable. Jo Davidson and his wife called on us, and with them came Van Wyck Brooks, author of "The Flowering of the New England Mind."[15] I had been reading that intensely fascinating book, and you can imagine what a pleasure it was for me who have loved New England since childhood to discuss it with Mr. Brooks. His power to grasp events as a true historian, his universal sympathy with artists, poets, writers and tenderness to youth imparted a rare quality to his talk. Jo Davidson told me about the figure of Henry Thoreau on which he is working at present, and I hope to have a chance of seeing it before long.

Saturday too we had the excitement of having distinguished visitors under our roof including Mr. Eby, the internationally known etcher, and Mr. Boyer who works at the Bridgeport Brass Company. Just now those two artists are working on murals which will serve as a pictorial history of the War. Besides art we discussed politics, "The Reader's Digest" (one of its editors, Mr. Waldron, was present) to whose pro-Fascist propensities I object, Mrs. Clare Boothe Luce for whom we have no use on account of her anti-British "campaign," and I spoke out my mind more than I intended to among guests some of whom were strait-laced conservatives.

Yesterday while in town we saw Mr. Migel for the first time in months. It shocked us to notice how far from well he still is. It is a marvel that he has pulled through two attacks of pneumonia. I can only pray that the warm weather and prolonged rest may renew his strength. There is always heartache for me these days—so many people I know are overworking or ill, or else they are summoned to the war fronts throughout the world. But God is mightier than all calamities, and if we only trust Him, we shall witness His healing for the nations as surely as we behold it among individuals.

After our call on Mr. Migel we dined with Guthrie McClintic and Mr. Koransky who had helped with the script of "The Three Sisters." The chief topic was Soviet Russia, and again I blurted out my views, that time in the presence of an unreconstructed White Russian. Alas! I am incorrigible, Clare. But what can one do when one believes that the truth is the highest compliment human beings can pay each other. So you see what new contacts are enriching our lives now that we stay at home. If you see Katharine Cornell, please tell her, with our love, what an enjoyable evening we had with Guthrie, and how happy we were to hear her voice on the telephone.

Polly joins me in dear love to you both. As ever, I am,

Affectionately your friend,

Helen Keller

63 Happy Heart-Throbs

June 19, 1944, letter from Helen Keller to Jo Davidson,
Papers of Jo Davidson, Library of Congress.

Sculptor Jo Davidson was one of the most important of Keller's friends and political dueling partners. He provided friendship and uncompromising access to the politics, intellectual debates, beauty, and joy of the rest of the world. For example, while the two were in Italy, he arranged for her to do a tactile viewing of Michelangelo and Donatello's sculptures (see document 78). With him she debated theology, politics, art, and literature. Unlike many others, he dared to disagree with her outright and bluntly. When they spoke, she said, "his whole soul flew to his tongue." He characterized knowing her as "a rich adventure." Davidson finger-spelled with skill, and when he and Keller met in 1942, a fast friendship grew between them that required no intermediary. He was one of the most noted sculptors in the United States and the world, widely known for his progressive and leftist politics. The two shared a love for sculpture, Tom Paine, Walt Whitman, anti-militarism, and a passionate interest in contemporary politics that resulted in vigorous debates and frequent letters. Twice she sat for lengthy, intimate periods as he made a bust of her and a sculpture of her hands. After she turned down his repeated requests for a public endorsement of presidential candidate Henry Wallace in 1948, he responded with an assurance of continued friendship. His death in 1951 was a great loss, as his friendship had provided a venue for wide political and personal expression.[16]

Dear Jo and Florence,

Wednesday the 14th was a unique, delightful evening for which I can only thank you in happy heart-throbs. It was a radiant Passage of

Friendship—not "a fair floating isle of palms eluding the mariner in Pacific seas," as Thoreau wrote mistakenly,[17] it seems to me, but rather minds alive at every point meeting each other with many-faceted sympathy, overleaping the frontiers of East and West, borders of custom and creed.

When I think of that occasion, the bow of memory will stir all the notes of inspiration, affection and beauty in my harp. For out of the multitudes with whom I have come into contact I have not found the likes of the group gathered around you in the studio which holds your sculpture history of a generation, and from which you still sail un-daunted to the new climates of human fellowship,

Polly and I still feel as if we were in a dream, so unlikely does it seem that we should have been part of such a felicitously blended galaxy of noble spirits—you two, Lin Yutang[18]—that rare union of profound philosophy, mocking whimsicality and warm humaneness, lovable Madame Hong whom he called "the real spirit of China," Van Wyck Brooks, Robert Flaherty[19] and Russell Lord. What impressed me so particularly was the quality of shining energy emanating from diverse, yet harmonious intelligences giving life and light to others' dormant thoughts, as Masefield would say. All of you, especially Jo and Lin Yutang, were caught up to the finest perception of life, which means to look unafraid upon the universe, its history, its individuals and nations and its potencies as they are in eternity—and friendship, wisdom and art springing from such celestial seeds cannot but be im-mortal.

That emotion came over me sweetly as I witnessed the big, fraternal embrace with which you exhorted Mr. Brooks to cast out the fear that he would not have time to finish his most deeply contemplated and travailed over history of American literature. And I was again led up higher when "Y.T." told the story of the man who set out to remove a mountain with his infinitesmal [sic] daily labor, and who replied to the scoffing of his neighbors, "I am limited, but my children are lim-itless, and this mountain shall be removed."

In eternity too I saw Mr. Brooks's bust and the intensity of creation upon his inward-thinking face. Usually it is a book by which I surmise a thinker's presence, and here I am rich both in a thrilling touch picture of Mr. Brooks's personality and a glowing premonition of his coming achievement!

Polly said she wished she had ten hands to convey to me all the sparks that flew from the striking of wit and repartee against facts too crudely interpreted, sarcastic comments on "the small beer of party politics," your flashing eyes, Jo, when you jested or leaped into the arena of controversy. Nor do I forget the stimulating side-lights on Henry Wallace I gained from Russell Lord's conversation. The presence of a man like Wallace, towering above nationalism and vote-getting, is daylight through a baffling maze of details that augurs little real good for the United States in the period immediately following the War. He appears to belong to a new type of statesman who will establish fresh starting-points of progress and high-water marks of public service and leave behind him an America more adequate to its world responsibilities.

Also I recall the delectable moments of dreaming of our journey to Russia and China. And to the tantalizing glimpses of Bob Flaherty's talk gave us of his wide travels, his penetrating insight into world events and the exquisite sympathy with which he had depicted primitive peoples in his masterly films that I was more than sorry not to have seen. Altogether that visit was a glorious acme of the blessed event when you two accompanied Polly and me through the Naval Hospital in Philadelphia and the trip back on the train when you and I tried to trace the spiral of life between reflection and action—a subject which I am still turning over and over in my mind.

We are plotting and planning. We have invited Dr. and Mrs. Robert Pfeiffer, Prof. Salvemini, Mr. and Mrs. Brooks to breakfast luncheon on Sunday July 2nd. We should love to have you and Florence spend the week-end of that date with us if you will come. The Pfeiffers want you to come to supper, where Prof. Salvemini will be present too, on that Saturday. There is a room all ready for you at Arcan Ridge.

Hoping that the weather and everything else will be just right for you to visit us, I am, with our affectionate greetings,

> Devotedly your friend,
> Helen Keller

64 My Public Acts and Utterances

*September 18, 1944, letter from Helen Keller to Nella Braddy Henney,
Nella Braddy Henney Collection, Perkins School for the Blind.*

In 1927, Nella Braddy Henney joined Keller's entourage. The manuscript that was to become *Midstream,* a continuation of her 1903 autobiography, was going nowhere. Ken McCormick, her editor at the publishing company Doubleday, sent Henney, a literary agent and assistant editor, to facilitate the writing of the book. Henney became an integral part of the Keller household, and this woman fourteen years younger than Helen remained an intimate friend until a bitter breakup in 1963.

This letter includes Keller's continued reflections on Franklin Delano Roosevelt. In the midst of World War II, he provided her hope. Since living in New York during his successful gubernatorial campaign, she had corresponded with him, publicly supported him, privately lobbied him on behalf of the AFB, and had met him and Eleanor several times. In August 1944, she had indicated to the *New York Times* that she would, for the first time, cast a ballot and that it would be for President Roosevelt. This letter indicates that Henney and possibly people from the AFB attempted to dissuade her from voting for him. Why she hadn't voted before wasn't discussed and seems contrary to her political interests.[20]

Also notable in this letter is Keller's self-reflections about whether or not the philanthropy she had advocated for decades actually mattered. Her insistence that she did not "conceal this awkward position from anybody" seems self-deceiving, as there is no evidence that she expressed disillusionment with philanthropy to any of those from whom she asked money. Nor did she publicly question whether her activities, and those of philanthropists, in general, addressed the fundamental issues facing blind people. The letter also includes a record of her friendship with birth control activist Margaret Sanger and novelist Pearl Buck, her visits to disabled World War II servicemen, and her ever-continuing efforts to finish her book on Anne Sullivan Macy.

Dear Nella,

Your letter was another evidence of the loyal friendship and conscientious care with which you lead me to weigh my public acts and utterances before I commit them irrevocably. Just to make sure that my "wild, strong will" does not run away with me and overturn the chariot of the American Foundation for the Blind, which drives it anyhow out of harm's path, I have again examined the possible consequences of casting my vote for F. D. Roosevelt, and I shall march up to the cannon's mouth just the same.

Seriously, Nella, my voting for Roosevelt seems to me no worse than taking part in this War after I had been a pacifist from my youth up. I still feel like a deserter, and I know that the conflict began as a rankly imperialistic one, but what could I do when it appeared to develop into a peoples' war of liberation?

Oh no! I do not mean to imply that I look upon Roosevelt as a leader of the masses. As I told you that day at the Harvard Club, I do not think America has had a genius people's president since Lincoln's day, and the people's party does not yet exist which would command my allegiance. Also I realize that it is impossible for even the greatest statesman or one nation to steer a frenzied world beating itself against destitution, rabid nationalism and ignorance. I am voting for Roosevelt because I believe he is sincere in advocating comprehensive policies for international cooperation out of which alone a stable, progressive world can arise. Reading his own words, "World collaboration must be the people's doing," I feel that he recognizes his limits and America's, and surely it does take a kind of greatness to make such an admission in a cruelly slanderous campaign.

Besides, despite apparent glaring inconsistencies in his attitude towards the people, I am sure if Roosevelt is reelected, his administration will continue at least tolerant of the labor movement whose steady growth is essential to America's higher democracy and closer union with other countries.

Yes, this seems to me the most critical period in human history, and every bit of courage and decency counts in grappling with it. You say the War crisis impresses you as "having been a-brewing for twenty years." Isn't that true of every momentous crisis? It has grown out of multitudinous seeds of error, stupidity and misrule until we realize that it must be uprooted, or it will strangle civilization. Anyway, this crisis grips me with the necessity of helping to quench an all-pervading conflagration. A bucketful of water is small, and so is a vote, yet how mighty the aggregate of votes may be to check appalling fascist influences in this country, carry on the War to complete victory and extend the international agreements we must have for post-war reconstruction. My conscience will not let me off from voting so long as I see an added chance of world betterment in Roosevelt's leadership during the next four years.

It is perfectly true that my work for the blind is a trust, and in order to fulfil its duties justly I must keep it as the centre of my external activities. But it has never occupied a centre in my philosophy or inner relations with mankind. That is because I regard philanthropy as a tragic apology for wrong conditions under which human beings live, losing their sight or hearing or becoming impoverished, and I do not conceal this awkward position from anybody. One can, and does dishonor one's trust through suave compliance quite as much as through lack of considerate caution. There is an even higher trust—to keep my essential freedom so that wherever possible I may release fettered minds and imprisoned lives among the blind, let alone those who see.

What I am going to say is not connected with the vote or the blind, but it may show you why I agree with Emerson that "our culture . . . must not omit the arming of the man, (but) let him take both reputation and life in his hand, and with perfect urbanity dare the gibbet and the mob by the absolute truth of his speech and the rectitude of his behavior." Of course his words are to be taken symbolically, as those extremes come to few outwardly, but millions upon millions are now facing them inwardly, and I bow to them reverently. They, not I, have become "world figures," even though their names may not be listed. Because they suffer long and perish rather than be slavish and treacherous under one tyranny or another, they wake faith that never slumbers again and nobility which we too easily allow to rust within us. Once those multitudes mostly followed a narrow, peaceful orbit, yet they tempered their characters to steel trueness by exercising simple, high instincts in humble duties. Even so I believe in firmly retaining sentiments that will strengthen me for the tumult or possible criticism by others in pursing an unusual path I may choose.

Last week Polly and I visited Margaret Sanger. We had met her before at Joseph Lewis's, and she had charmingly invited us to spend the night with her in her home on the Hudson. I had wanted to know her for many years, and when the "crisis" of contact came, her warm, rich personality justified my enthusiasm. She is indeed a truly great soul. Her instructive talk confirms my ideal as I picture her, despite imprisonment and calumny, choosing her own destiny and enabling unnumbered women to take independent charge of their lives and ensure the improved health and joy of their children.

Margaret was to give a birthday dinner in memory of her husband, Mr. Slee, who had died a year before. Polly and I were moved that she should include us in an anniversary so sacred to her. The setting in which we celebrated could not have been more satisfying. The house, Willowlake, was given Margaret by Mr. Slee, and is a replica of Shelley's picturesque Sussex home. The stones were carefully selected, and the glass-leaded windows were brought over from England. The grounds, contain a hundred and ten acres, beautifully wooded, slope down to the darling lake from which the place gets its name.

The festive ensemble was a delight—a cosy fire bringing out the soft colors of the stone walls, the laughter of Margaret's grandchildren playing from room to room, the tall candles and rose garlands on the table. As we ate turkey and drank champagne to Margaret's beloved "departed Guest," the conversation sped from one topic to another— birth control and the powers of darkness opposing it, distinguished negro writers, artists and scientists, the pros and cons of voting for F. D. Roosevelt. Margaret Sanger's antagonism towards the Roman Catholic Church as an organized despotism was plain to see, and I chimed in heartily, though privately. That is one of the perhaps too few pies into which I don't put my finger, for obvious reasons. I serve the blind of every sect, and I have a spiritual message of my own to impart. Besides, I think it will take the Catholics themselves to break up that deadly miasma which multiplies ignorance and faith without reflection. I have great confidence in the courage of men and women like Professor Salvamini, Mr. Estrada of Argentina, whom we met at Stuart Grummon's, and Constanzia de la Mora to achieve this new deliverance for western peoples.

The following day Polly and I met Margaret and Pearl Buck at the latter's apartment on Park Avenue, and I had my picture taken with them. A reporter interviewed Pearl Buck who talked most interestingly about the East-West Association and how it provides ways for orientals and occidentals to learn about each other and bring about a friendly understanding which may serve as a stepping-stone to world peace. You are no doubt aware of one reason why the peoples of the East and the West are hostile, because they are blinded by false propaganda and the prejudice it engenders. Here is another subject into which I long to put my finger, but I have already more interests than I can squeeze into a working day of fifteen or sixteen hours, and you know how the "Teacher" book hangs over my head like Damocles's sword. Saturday night Bob Irwin telephoned that he would get in touch right away with hospitals I may visit. You will sense what an element of uncertainty such a prospect throws into one's daily program.

Well, the weather here has done its damnedest, storming, deluging, disorganizing telephone wires and laying low many precious trees all through Westport. Arcan Ridge was hit hard too. Several big trees were broken in two, and we were without electricity until yesterday afternoon. Herbert is just back from a richly deserved two weeks vacation, and I am sorry for him as he goes over the place, the extra work to be done must discourage him after all the labor and care he has expended upon it. He feels that it is two steps forward and one back. Still, we shall manage, as we usually do. I wonder how it fared with you on Foss Mountain.

There is more to tell, but it will keep until we three can talk again, and I must send off one of the messages for the handicapped which elect to intervene when I am greedy to buckle down to the book.

With Polly's love, and hoping that your father suffers less now, I am,

Affectionately your friend,

Helen Keller

65 A Peal of Joy from My Heart Over the President's Re-Election

November 11, 1944, letter from Helen Keller to Jo Davidson,
Papers of Jo Davidson, Library of Congress.

In this letter, Keller updates her dear friend Jo Davidson on her opinions about President Roosevelt's reelection and her continued visits to disabled veterans in military hospitals. Significant in this letter are Keller's comments on Roosevelt's disability. She attended an October Foreign Policy Association dinner at which FDR spoke. International politics concerned her deeply in this period, and he held her hopes for a peaceable world. Despite this, her highest compliment to the president was that she "could not realize that he was being wheeled up to the speaker's table." Rather, she "sensed his powerful spirit striding among us." In her mind's eye, she saw him "not in his wheel-chair but walking out with an archangel might." To her, recognizing FDR's disability would have acknowledged a weakness that went beyond physical strength to be all encompassing. Throughout her life, she increasingly insisted that people with disabilities be considered individuals with potential, while she simultaneously considered them inherently damaged.

Dear Jo,

This is the first moment I have got away from under my tasks sufficiently to let out a peal of joy from my heart over the President's re-election and your glorious share in the victory. The American people have vindicated his and our faith in them, and that is the splendor of a lifetime, a new world of possibilities realized. May they go further than winning the War and refashion America as a vital democracy, an unshakable keystone in the arch of universal brotherhood!

Vincent Sheen is right. The people are responding to the limitless opportunities placed in their hands by the radio as the voice of an intimate friend, and soon it will be as a face looking upon them in television. If they only stand firm long enough, they will outwit the party machine and entrenched greed, and the unavoidably static framework of government will be energized a hundredfold by their dynamic will. Having witnessed such a nascent wonder of the ages, I could die fully content.

Polly gave me your dear telephone message. Nothing could have rewarded me more immensely than your wish that I keep on working with the Independent Voters' Committee to educate public opinion. I have felt that I was on the mountain-top doing my bit to tip the scales of destiny in favor of Franklin Delano Roosevelt and the international democracy he symbolizes, but after the whirlwind, the fire and the earthquake I must return to the quiet valleys of my own work for the handicapped and the "Teacher" biography. No, dear Jo, I cannot longer lend my name to the Committee. It is against my conscience to be a member of any organization unless I take an actual part in its enterprises. The "N.C. and P.A.C." have asked me to continue with them, and I must decline their request too, although it tugs at my heart-strings just as yours does. However, I shall be exceedingly with you always in your efforts to break down party bossism and instil civic responsibility and self-expression into the people that will keep their way of life progressive.

Never shall I cease to glow remembering the Foreign Policy Association dinner on October 21st. I have read many descriptions in history of royal progresses and august assemblies from every corner of an empire, but none has impressed me in quite the same way as the simple, yet regal atmosphere at the Waldorf-Astoria when the President addressed us. The flags everywhere, the imposing cohorts of police, guards and "FBI" officials with the dense crowds chatting and laughing unafraid in their presence, the tense minutes of waiting for the President and the magical way he put us all at our ease while he talked and enjoyed his repast—all these, though great, were only a setting for what I believe will go down to posterity as one of the decisive speeches of recorded history.

Somehow, Jo, when the President entered, I could not realize that he was being wheeled up to the speaker's table. Rather I sensed his powerful spirit striding among us and waving a trident over the sea of men's minds. Polly's racing fingers sought every adjective for the thousands of intent listening faces, the President's many facets of personality flashing out in his utterances, the laughter and the "boos" as he cracked his whip of sarcasm or warned against a wrecker of policies for world betterment. Again I saw him not in his wheel-chair but walking out with an archangel might when his last words were spoken, and the thunderous applause reached my feet. He was the very embodiment of the triumph I anticipate for afflicted humanity which will proclaim Heaven on earth. Since that evening it has been proved by crumbling forces and disappearing landmarks that "when demigods depart, gods arrive."

We shall be sorry not to bid you and Florence goodbye viva voce, but we are leaving Monday night for the long planned tour to visit

wounded soldiers in government hospitals. Our first two engagements will be in Hot Springs, Arkansas and Oklahoma. From November 20th to December 9th we shall be in Texas, then we shall
proceed to Santa Fe, New Mexico, Utah, Denver, Colorado. From
December 18th until Christmas Day we shall be in California. From
there we go to Oregon where we shall stay until December 30th. After
that we shall travel to Rochester, Minn., and down to Chicago where
we shall rest a week.

Do rest now, you two dears, and let us feel that life is good to us
when we come back and find you both strong and equal to all things.

With our Thanksgiving, Christmas and New Year Blessings
lumped in one big embrace, I am,

Affectionately your fellow-pilgrim towards the Dawn,
Helen Keller

66 The Tidings of the President's Death

*April 22, 1945, letter from Helen Keller to Jo Davidson,
Papers of Jo Davidson, Library of Congress.*

When President Roosevelt died in the spring of 1945, Keller had
just finished greeting disabled veterans at a naval hospital and was enjoying tea with the hospital commander. It was as if, she explains to Jo Davidson from her hotel in Atlanta, "the beneficent luminary in whose rays
civilization was putting forth new leaves of healing for all people was
seemingly extinguished forever." FDR's death sorely tried her optimistic
nature.

Dear Jo,

This is one of the times when only a silent embrace can express the
anguish of overflowing hearts, and you and I are absent one from another.

How greatly and violently the world has been bereaved since Polly
and I last saw you! It seems but yesterday that we heard Archibald
MacLeish speaking at the luncheon and listened to you and the Committee at the press interview discussing plans to enlighten the American people further on Frank Delano Roosevelt's foreign policy and

the objectives of the San Francisco Conference. Full of confidence we anticipated a fruitful campaign that would strengthen and deepen the cooperation among the States so essential to the triumph of international unity and constructive peace.

Then as in a moment the beneficent luminary in whose rays civilization was putting forth new leaves of healing for all peoples was seemingly extinguished forever. Polly and I received the appalling news in Charleston, South Carolina. We had been working all day at the Naval General Hospital, whose commanding officer is Captain King. We were among a number of people whom he had invited to tea in his home. It was a happy, animated company. We discussed G. B. Shaw. . . . All at once a guest, Rear-Admiral Julius James, came straight to us from the telephone with the tidings of the President's death. Everybody grew limp and silent. Soon church bells were tolling, and flags were at half-mast.

How Polly and I longed to be with you, to hear your wise thoughts born of an intimate friendship with the President and long views of the changes that must needs take place in our Government and the relations between Russia, Britain and the United States. Of course I remembered mankind's matchless champion, Soviet Russia, and the growing power of the workers in Britain. Thankfully I thought of great, noble hearts still throbbing against the world's own—Eleanor Roosevelt and Henry Wallace. But, Jo, I have an uneasy feeling about America at present, it is such an aggregate of conflicting elements— generous Promethean instincts, cruel isolationism, abysmal ignorance, individualism which often is criminal irresponsibility in disguise, race prejudice, obstinate adherence to the Divine Right of big business, anti-social politics and the two-party system.

What personalities are likely to dominate the San Francisco Conference? What creative brains will breathe a soul into the machinery of world reorganization? Perhaps Mr. Truman may act as a needed balance-wheel now that the War has reached its greatest momentum. Lowell Mellett's article on Mr. Truman's qualities of good sense, integrity and willingness to accept experienced counsel in foreign affairs relieves me somewhat, but I cannot say that the prospect of the next four years is very inspiring to me. However, Roosevelt was always saying that any great chance for the better must "be the people's doing," and if we no longer have a dynamic genius to infuse electricity into our administration, then we the people must inspire his successor with a critical interest and constructive demands in the policies he is laboriously trying to follow until one more gifted than he can assume inventive leadership in the experiment of global reintegration; and I have faith that there will be powerful beacons shining along Mr. Truman's path.

Then came another sorrow in which Polly and I tenderly feel for and with you. We were shocked to learn how Ernie Pyle had been killed on the firing lines. Yet I cannot imagine him as "hid in the tomb of dateless night," so intensely did his soul glow the day I met him at your studio. His blade-straight courage, passionate love of humanity, lightning fury against their violators are eternal. Your moulding hands, too, Jo, have made him immortal, and in that sense he will ever be a living presence to us who cherish his rare personality.

As for myself, the President's passing has left a void which causes me to ache in the larger work I have undertaken. Not only was Roosevelt the greatest American, he was also our most valiant victor over physical handicaps. It was a beautiful experience to have his unfailing sympathy in my efforts for the blind, and his tireless zeal for rehabilitation was a staff in my hand visiting the hospitals. But you and I know how inexorably life goes on tugging at us.

Thomasville, Georgia, May 7th

It is only now that I have had a chance to thank you and Florence for your precious telegram. The anxiety we have felt about you both can be measured only by our love. That will make you realize what a weight the telegram has lifted off our minds. Throwing our arms around you in thought we beg you to spare yourself as far as possible. Your inexhaustible spirit is a merciless taskmaster, and we are glad of the enforced rest prescribed. Reluctantly Polly and I have submitted to this necessity, and we accomplish more, paradoxical as that sounds. How much bigger is your importance in the lives of uncounted human beings!

Our trip through Georgia has been a wonderful trail of warm friendships and inspiring fortitude among the servicemen. This section is fascinating—tremendous, romance-filled plantations extending down to Florida, a wealth of mimosa—and magnolia blossoms, the spring chorus of southern birds. But all this beauty, Jo, cannot make me happy, knowing as I do how the long curse of racial oppression broods over the land. The ignorance of the negroes is incredible, and the unsanitary conditions under which the whites permit them to exist and labor is a disgracing witness against those who call themselves a democracy and a Christian society. I tell you, "the serpent fury" of accusation will hiss far into America's future. Even the sober joy over the end of the war in Europe does not soften my bitter rebellion.

Tomorrow we leave for Jacksonville and Pensacola, and from there we go to New Orleans. While in New Orleans we shall visit the National Leprosarium at Carville. It is surprising how a labor of love leads us through one of life's desolate areas and strengthens us for the next.

Please excuse me, Jo, if this letter seems disjointed, and is cluttered up with mistakes. At least it takes our affection to you two, and tells how we look forward to seeing you the middle of June.

Devotedly your friend,
Helen Keller

FOUR 1946–1968

A Major Works

67 Teacher

New York: Doubleday, 1956, chapter 5.

Keller began writing her memorial to Anne Sullivan Macy in 1939, not three years after her death. In the early 1950s, motivated perhaps by the constant assessments of her life and perhaps aware of her own age, Keller focused on completing her nearly thirty-year effort to write the book. The 1946 fire that destroyed her home, and in it all her correspondence and notes for *Teacher,* had made the process even more difficult. Where and how the poetry remnants included below survived is not clear. Nella Braddy Henney thought the forced reflection drained Keller emotionally. She had asked Nella, "How can I bear the burden of this sacrifice?" and cried over all Anne had given her. Henney helped with editing and thought *Teacher* (1956) a true accomplishment. Keller wrote that she hoped the book "may convey to my readers some gleams from the opal fires in the nature of a woman with a heart for glorious living and an eye for the 'beauty beyond dream.'"[1]

Teacher was twenty-nine years of age and I fifteen before I could form an idea of her personality apart from her vocation as devotee of loveliness. As I grew more mature, she let loose upon me all her varied moods, and because of this I was not taken unawares by the storms of destiny.

At fifteen when I could observe her more closely, I learned that her moods changed continually. "Don't repeat what I am going to say to you," she would say, and I listened to her tales of weariness with women who inflicted upon her their witless little dramas and social inanities. Together we saw life in all its different aspects and were often in the society of the great, the gifted, the influential, among whom were women beautiful both in mind and body whose conversation intrigued Teacher. What irritated her most were idea-less talk and deportment and actions without grace of individuality. She excused the ill-starred poor and the untutored defective, but never those who had means to be educated and acquire refinement.

Teacher also suffered, thought not long, from a melancholy which bred a wretched incapacity to respond even to the kindest approaches from her intimate friends. She would fly from them to the woods, or if she was near the water, she would conceal herself for hours under a boat on the shore. But then she would come back to her friends asking forgiveness. One time when she had erysipelas[2] she hid from everyone, even me, for the whole day, and it was not until suppertime that mother found her lying quietly in her bed. Alas! I have met some fools who will not be enlightened about such human ills, and therefore I cannot tell the whole truth, though I say nothing that is not true. No doubt those dark moods appeared in Annie's youth at Perkins, and they continued to harass her every once in a while until her death: and they did not help her sight. She gallantly rallied each time, and though she often fretted, she never lost the free exercise of her mental faculties and suspended them except when she slept, and that merciless taskmaster, the brain, steered her helm at its own sweet will. Awake, she analyzed her difficulty with diamond clearness, and soon was her buoyant, wholesome, teasing self again. From the multitude of letters she was obliged to compose and which I typed for her I saw how she could keep her mind on matters requiring minute attention and build such long-range plans as those which made my college education possible.

Many years later Teacher and I visited Ireland together, and now I see her in my remembrance of the country that gave her to me—a land full of moisture and hard, gleaming rocks, washed with sunshine and tremulous with fairylike bloom and greenness, a land animated with people active, overflowing with images, combative and ironical, a touch of the fantastic about everything, all these qualities combined or eclipsing one another according to the rhythms of an amazingly changeable climate.

Teacher was not logical. Yet she was the only woman I have known intimately who could engage in the rough and tumble of argument and come off victorious. One had to beware of her impetuous rejoinders when she spoke too positively or enthusiastically in support of this or that. She was bored by the commonplace on any subject—education, politics, religion, or any other area of social intercourse. A drawn-out talk on science or philosophy was a trial to her nerves, but the art of delightful speakers like Mark Twain or Dr. Alexander Graham Bell sufficed to keep her mind on a deep theme long enough for her to feel refreshed and uplifted. She frowned upon rhetoric, yet she was sensitive to every expression of a person's higher faculties.

I tried not to argue with her—and I seldom succeeded—for I knew that she would have me nonplused and speechless, especially when her imagination was on fire or she was angry. Her comments flew out spontaneously, highly colored and pithy, leaving me "dazzled, delighted, and dumbfounded all at the same time." She did not talk as a poet except when she described to me breath-taking natural beauties, but secretly she jotted down bits of verse as they occurred to her. Most of these were burned in the fire that consumed our first house at Arcan Ridge, but a few have survived. Here is one:

When God unhinges the gates of light,
Wild little fancies perch on the edge of the moon
Like the ghosts of birds.
The dark stream of life flows
Through time and space carelessly;
No one recognizes the light
Entering the wide eyes close to their doom.
All things move in a great sea;
Thoughts from another silence pour
Like flowers opening in the night.
They fall in space like April rain,
Colored and shaped of self
Like the pearl in the oyster-shell.

Then hands unseen dip into little pools of Heaven;
There, and there again
The hands of the mind are wet
With silver rain-drops;
With all her wonder-feelers the mind marks

With wind's changing flight,
Dropping pearls on the walls of night,
Driving the rain-drops through the dark,
The mind advancing on the world of light.

If Teacher's eyes had been normal, I am sure she would have reveled in contemplating space, the stars, and planets as a stupendous, ever changing spectacle. As it was, she preferred the universe of books —and what a pitifully small portion of it her undependable sight could absorb! Poetry and music were her allies. In her fingers words rang, rippled, danced, buzzed, and hummed. She made every word vibrant to my mind—she would not let the silence about me be *silent*. She kept in my thought the perceptive, audible, and other qualities of every object I could touch. She brought me into sensory contact with everything we could reach or feel—sunlit summer calm, the quivering of soap bubbles in the light, the song of birds, the fury of storms, the noises of insects, the murmur of trees, voices loved or disliked, familiar fireside vibrations, the rustling of silk, the creaking of a door, and the blood pulsing in my veins.

Here is another of her fragments:

Hands, understanding hands,
Hands that caress like delicate green leaves,
Hands, eager hands—
Hands that gather knowledge from great books, Braille books—
Hands that fill empty space with livable things,
Hands so quiet, folded on a book—
Hands forgetful of words they have read all night,
Hands asleep on the open page,
Strong hands that sow and reap thought,
Hands tremulous and ecstatic listening to music,
Hands keeping the rhythm of song and dance.

B *Travel*

68 The Beauty and the Tragedy which Endeared Greece to Me

February 10, 1947, letter from Helen Keller to Eric Boulter, AFB.

The numerous international trips Helen Keller made between 1937 and 1948, especially the 1948 trip to Japan, began a rich international life and transformed her from a tourist into an ambassador. From that point forward, she traveled abroad, in a semiofficial ambassadorial status, virtually every other year until 1957, at which point the seventy-seven-year-old woman retired from international travel.

Keller considered her 1946 tours of war-torn Greece, Italy, France, and England an extension of wartime service. Accompanied by Eric Boulter of the Foundation for the Overseas Blind, she visited civilians and service personnel blinded and otherwise disabled by the war. Her trip succeeded in drawing media attention and in raising funds to provide medical and educational programs. It also highlighted visits with personal friends, international dignitaries (including Queen Elizabeth and the pope), as well as the suffering of Europe. As a tragic finale to the trip, she received news that the Arcan Ridge house had burnt to the ground. The fire destroyed everything, including all her correspondence and notes for her long-planned book *Teacher.*

Once home in November 1946, Keller found her friends, supporters, and trustees battling over the finances of rebuilding her house at Arcan Ridge. They didn't like one another, nor did they agree with each other's and her politics. She lamented the state of U.S. politics, characterizing it as a "bitter period of retrograde." Home provided little pleasantness—and *no* home. She and Polly stayed with various friends until the new house was completed in September 1947.

Dear Eric Boulter,

Before the wrath with which my conscience has taken me to task for not sooner writing to you I quail as I start this letter. I can only blush and be grateful for the understanding charity so evident in the heart-warming letters you have sent both Polly and me. Rather than recite futile apologies, I prefer to tell you right away that Polly's and my visit to Athens was a superlatively moving event for us which I still find difficult to distil in words.

It was charged with such loveliness and tragedy in the atmosphere of such poetic power that it illumined my emotions and sensations as Athens has illumined world history. It was a whirl of glory, and the glory had many elements—the gleam of deities descending from Olympus, the thundering diapason of the "Iliad" and the mellow surge of the "Odyssey," storms of light in philosophy and oratory, paeans of genius in architecture and sculpture, the final darkness of conquest by Roman and Turk, and the Renaissance rekindling culture throughout Europe while Athens, itself a beacon, lay in chains.

But there were other elements even more stirring—the love with which the blind of Athens received me, your genuine enthusiasm and tireless efforts to ameliorate their lot in an impoverished land, your constant helpfulness that carried my broken speech further in every task we undertook, the evenings we spent together discussing everything under the sun. Polly and I emitted many a spark, I fear, as we argued about politics and economics, and I appreciated your patience listening to us. While we were as full of animosity towards any kind of dictatorship as Athens once was towards the Thirty Tyrants, we honored the sincerity of your friendship and selflessness in seeking the best interests of the sightless. If only there were more men and women as skillful and forceful as you are in administration, how much sooner the handicapped would reach their goal of true rehabilitation.

Both Polly and I were touched by your generous praise then and afterwards in your letters, and we wish we might have deserved it by large accomplishment. The tears come to my eyes as I recall the gallant response of the blinded servicemen in the old building when we begged them to master Braille and take up trades and handicrafts. Alas. There are still many shadows of agelong ignorance to pierce, but the miracle you helped to bring about in the reorganization of the

School for the Blind at Athens and the renewed ambition of the pupils to make the most of their powers will, I am sure, send its rays far along that desolate coast of Darkland. My spirit overflows with a fervent prayer for everything good to the new school for blind children when it is opened at Salonika, and may that be very soon. Despite countless difficulties the Lighthouse at Athens to which you and the Near East Foundation have given such a hopeful start will in undreamed ways lead the exiles of the dark into the radiance and freedom of soul growth.

Thanks ever so much for all the information you have taken pains to send me. It will be precious in my efforts to open the hearts of the American people to the needs of the blind in Greece. Already arrangements are under way for Polly and me to raise funds. A tea is contemplated the second or third week in March at which I am to launch the campaign. Whenever possible, Polly and I will call on large givers likely to contribute generously.

A month ago I wrote to Mr. Cambadhis as you suggested, pointing out the unwisdom of having blind people in Greece trained as masseurs at present, and expressing the hope that the American Friends of the Greek blind would send their money to the Lighthouse at Athens. No reply has been received.

We called on the Near East Foundation in New York and spent a delightful hour with them. Certainly they are a forward-looking group with the high intelligence demanded by their mission. They were cordially sympathetic as we told them what we know about the work for the blind in Greece, and they were pleased that we admired the splendid achievements of their organization in Athens.

Also we spent an afternoon at the American Foundation for the Blind office talking about our experiences in Europe, and great interest was shown. I spoke to Mr. Irwin of you, urging upon him the desirability of meeting you, and he said he would plan to do it. I believe he is going to England next May.

Not long ago we attended a tea for aid to the college at Anatolia, and met many Greeks.

After having been so close to the beauty and the tragedy which endeared Greece to me, I am even more distressed by its unhappy political situation. I boil over considering the criminally stupid policy of the

Allies restoring the monarchy in Greece when ninety recent of the people want a republic. For it meant bringing back reactionary forces that trample upon the liberties for which WWII was fought—free speech, a free press, freedom from fear and tyranny. The nations who wrought this shame will some day be scourged by serpents of retribution.

Here in America we are living through a bitter period of retrograde. Since Franklin Delano Roosevelt's death an uninspired, short-sighted administration has made havoc of the far-seeing, beneficent global policies for which he gave his life. Race discrimination is rampant. Every effort is being put forth, as in Greece, to stifle radicalism. Liberals are not allowed the use of any broadcasting stations. The manufacture of bombs continues, and it dismays me to see how little the people are doing individually to prevent atomic warfare. How it will all end it is impossible to predict. I can only hope that the people may be aroused to a sense of their danger before it is too late to assert their human dignity and put to office men who grasp the supreme issue—"one world or none."

I can imagine your sadness over the terrible state of affairs in Britain. My heart bleeds for the mass of the people enduring drastic cuts in fuel and electricity which, it seems to me, a little foresight might have rendered less severe. But their spirit is unbreakable. I am confident they will gather new forces from within and learn higher wisdom as a commonwealth and as the centre of a federation of free peoples.

Oh the riches in Braille books I am receiving from the National Institute for the Blind in London. Every time I touch them I feel like weeping; for I know they are gifts out of the very limited resources of the Institute at one of the hardest times in Britain's history.

By the way, the honey has not arrived, nor has the fragment of the Parthenon presented me by Mr. Mantoudis, Director de Belles-lettres, and the delegates from the women's unions of Greece. However, I shall write to him just the same.

Polly and I treasure the Cretan dagger and the ear-rings you and dear Mary gave us. From a world of white loveliness we send our love to you both in the balmy warmth of Hellas.

     Devotedly yours,
     Helen Keller

69 Hiroshima's Fate Is a
Greek Tragedy on a Vast Scale

October 14, 1948, letter from Helen Keller to Nella Braddy Henney, AFB.

Energized by the success of her 1937 trip to Japan, Keller had planned to continue her international efforts and return to Japan in the early 1940s. The war in Europe had made that unlikely, but the Japanese attack on Pearl Harbor made it impossible. When her Japanese friend Takeo Iwahashi reestablished contact in 1946, she responded without hesitation. She planned a three-month stay in Japan, and Iwahashi had secured the preliminary approval of General Douglas MacArthur, Supreme Commander for the Allied Powers and the de facto ruler of Japan during the years of U.S. occupation. For Keller, the trip signified a new, purposeful, and expanded focus on the world's blind people. After a ten-year interruption, she could begin to fulfill the international agenda she had only begun to define with the 1937 trip to Japan.

The enthusiastic reception given her by the Japanese public, the thrilled response of the U.S. government to this reception, the intensity with which she enjoyed the trip, and the profound unease generated in her by Hiroshima and Nagasaki, called her to international action. Yet she remained relatively quiet in public about the personally most profound aspect of her trip. On October 13 and 14, 1948, she visited Hiroshima and Nagasaki, the sites of massive U.S. atomic attacks. The devastation of the atomic attacks strengthened her commitment to international cooperation. She felt herself and her nation reproached and sought absolution.

The trip also had physical consequences for both women. Polly Thomson's health had previously been fragile, and it should be no surprise that her blood pressure caused the trip to come to an end only days later.

Keller's rich description of the cities and their people leaves no question about the depth of her ability to perceive or to "know." Since *The Story of My Life* (1903), critics had maligned her use of visual imagery, arguing that she had no direct access to visual knowledge. In this letter she describes the uneven ground, the mangled remnants of buildings, the lingering smell, the melted face of a fellow human being, the overwhelming solemnity and weight of a grave of ninety thousand, and conversations with those who knew they were dying.

Dearest Nella,

At last I have captured some free moments to write to you—a meager return for your wonderful letters—but you will at least feel in these few lines how lovingly Polly's and my hearts throb for you, and how often we are at your side in spirit, though unseen. Your voice, coming thousands of miles from home, was a blessing to hear, Polly declares. We are both well, though very weary at times, and we derive great satisfaction from our work. Our one desire is that we may keep strong to finish the tour next April.

Now I simply must tell you about our visit to Hiroshima yesterday. We are still aching all over from that piteous experience—it exceeds in horror and anguish the accounts I have read. Polly and I went to Hiroshima with Takeo Iwahashi to give our usual appeal meeting, but no sooner had we arrived than the bitter irony of it all gripped us overpoweringly, and it cost us a supreme effort to speak. As you know, the city was literally leveled by the atomic bomb, but, Nella, its desolation, irreplaceable loss and mourning can be realized only by those who are on the post. Not one tall building is left, and what has been rebuilt is temporary and put up in haste. Instead of the fair, flourishing city we saw eleven years ago, there is only life struggling daily, hourly against a bare environment, unsoftened even by nature's wizardry. How the people exist through summer heat and winter cold is a thought not to be borne. Jolting over what had once been paved streets, we visited the one grave—all ashes—where about 8:30, August 6, 1945, ninety thousand men, women and children were instantly killed, and a hundred and fifty thousand were injured, and the rest of the population did not know at the moment what an ocean of disaster was upon them. They thought that the two planes—when they bombed they always came in numbers—were reconnoitering planes; so they were not prepared for the flash of light that brought mass death. As a result of that inferno two hundred thousand persons are now dead, and the suffering caused by atomic burns and other wounds is incalculable. Polly saw burns on the face of the welfare officer—a shocking sight. He let me touch his face, and the rest is silence—the people struggle on and say nothing about their lifelong hurts. We saw a memorial to the ninety thousand who perished—a simple wooden shrine where people of all sects lay flowers, and the Shintoists place food, wine and incense.

And it was to those people that I made the appeal! Yet, despite the consummate barbarity of some military forces of my country and the painful wreckage upon the survivors, they listened quietly to what I had to say. Their affectionate welcome from the moment I arrived until two hours later, when we left by ferry for Miyajima, will remain in my soul, a holy memory—and a reproach.

After the meeting Polly and I went to the City Office, and there gifts were poured upon us out of the people's destitution and sorrow. My pain made me almost mute, but I managed to tell the Governor, the Mayor and other representatives of the welcoming committee that a city which has such magnificent will to give cannot really perish. "Hiroshima will rise mightier, fairer and more thriving than before," I said, "because the agelong, dauntless courage of Nippon is in you, and will renew your deep instincts of home, workmanship and civic order. You will give with a higher motive, and with insight, so that all the unfortunate of your city may be helped, and the capable ones may take their places as useful members of the community, and know the sweetness of God's Gift of Life."

Polly tried to convey to me the sadness and horror in the eyes of the people we passed. Only the children smiled. Altogether, Nella, Hiroshima's fate is a Greek tragedy on a vast scale, not a modern one, carrying with it the burden of deliberate wrong-doing or the far-seeing moral responsibility that inexorably summons our democracies to the bar of Judgment.

From the City Office we drove out to the Peace Tower in what is to be a memorial park. What a tragic, noble symbol the Peace Tower is of new ideals and aspirations in a people trying to start life afresh! A few years ago some of the Japanese people really believed that they were destined to conquer the world by war and to change the world for the better. Now Hiroshima has experienced the utter futility of war, as General MacArthur told me, and all Japan is reaching up to a loftier courage—that of peace. Many people stood with us beside the Tower. Their unsmiling silence seemed to call for a word of comfort. My message was to the effect that the city had undergone an ordeal of fire, but the unsubduable spirit of Nippon was strong in its shattered body, and by adopting the principles and practices of true democracy it would attain a higher greatness, and the Tower rising before us above the desolation was a challenging evidence that Hiroshima was leading Nippon in the way of disarmament and good-will. That meant that the world, stirred by such a heroic example, would take a long stride towards lasting peace, and then indeed Hiroshima's tragedy would become a purification of its soul through brother-hood. I left with a conviction that the splendor of a genuine victory would belong to Hiroshima, not to America. Today I learn with deep humility how touched the people of Hiroshima were by my few words, and as a result they are trying to put up a bell on the Peace Tower which will ring to remind the city of its new mission.

It will require more time than I have at present to express my emotions and thoughts on the subject as I want to, but I believe that I have written you the truth nearer than what most of us Americans know. Certainly I am raw thinking about yesterday's events, and more determined than ever to do what lies in my power to fight against the demons of atomic warfare and for the constructive uses of atomic energy.

Now we have been to Nagaski, and it too has scorched a deep scar in my soul. Only one-third of the city was demolished, but the testimony to the atrocities of atomic combat is equally damning. We saw a monument marking the spot where the Bomb fell. We walked through the mangled corpse of one of Japan's beneficent enterprises —the medical college and the clinic where the patients were killed by the bomb. Some of the buildings are being partially repaired and the hospital restored, but the wreckage still sends up its dumb accusation, even as the blood of the righteous Abel cried unto the Lord.

I should say, the college was a fifteen or twenty minutes' drive from where the bomb struck, but the concussion was frightful. Although the buildings which were of stone withstood the shock in some measure, yet everything inside had been swept away. I felt the walls bending like a reed in the wind. We stumbled over ground cluttered in every direction like foundation-stones, timbers, broken pipe-lines, bits of machinery and twisted girders. I felt sure that I smelt the dust from the burning of Nagaski—the smoke, of death. In that graveyard of a splendid establishment twenty-four professors lost their lives. Surgeons were operating at the time, and they and their patients perished together.

We shook hands with two professors who came to show us around. Also we met a wonderful scientist, Mr. Nagai, who is slowly dying from atomic radiation.[1] Yes, Nella, Polly saw him dying with her own eyes, and was almost unable to speak or spell. Yet out of his lighted face smiled a great, gentle spirit as he talked with us. When I said to him, "How you inspire us, lifting your soul up above the miseries of the flesh!" he replied, "My body is consuming away, but I am free spiritually, and today, beside being happy, I am fairly well because the sun is warm and pleasant." With that towering faith in God and a virile mind he is writing his diary, in which he calmly notes the effects of his disease, and he hopes that the journal may be of vital service to science when his hand can no longer hold the pen. He is not expected to be alive after Christmas. This is murder indeed—taking not only the physical life of a young man, but also of the potential work wrapped up in him that would have thrown its light far into the future.

Polly says there has never been such revolt in her soul before, and life will not be the same for her after Hiroshima and Nagasaki. For many years I have sensed profoundly the war-made wrongs and crookedness of mankind, but now it is more than a feeling, it is a concrete knowledge I have gained and a stern resolve to work for the breaking of barbarism and the fostering of universal peace.

October 27th. Now a sudden change has taken place in our plans. As you know, Polly and I have been ordered home by the doctors on account of Polly's serious physical condition. General MacArthur's physician, Major Canada, has told her that the strain of the tour has overtaxed her strength, and that if she continued it, she would perhaps not return to America alive. You can imagine how the news fell upon us both like a bombshell, and how anxious I am to get her home as soon as possible. It will mean a quiet life for Polly the rest of her days on earth. Truly we have been fortunate in having such wonderful friends and medical advisers all the way from Australia to Japan.

We are leaving tomorrow morning on the army transport Shanks. Everything is being done to facilitate our departure, even to the length of having a young sergeant accompany us and see to it that we are kept incommunicado. We hope to see Herbert on the dock at Seattle and get reservations on the Great Northern. Then we shall stop off at Minneapolis and be "checked up" at the Mayo Clinic. When we do return to New York, it will be such a happiness to see you!

With our united affection to you and Keith, I am,

> Lovingly your friend,
> Helen Keller

70 Hiroshima Is Beginning to Flourish Again

Undated speech from 1948 trip to Hiroshima, Takeo Iwahashi file, AFB.

Regarding Hiroshima and Nagasaki, the contrast between Keller's public and private statements is marked. In her public speech, she acknowledged the "cruel nemesis that overtook" the city, but told its citizens that "tragedy generated new forces of healing." The new Japan espoused by the United States provided the solution and the redemption. She publicly praised democracy as the solution to Japan's problems, but privately lamented that the bomb "summons our democracies to the bar of Judgment." She went on, "We are still aching all over from that piteous experience—it exceeds in horror and anguish the accounts I have read," she wrote (document 69).[2]

The contrast reveals her unease with making public statements of political importance in this period. It reflects her affirmed and newly adamant conviction that war is wrong, and her belief that she should and could do something about international hostilities. It also reveals her understandable inability to comprehend and make sense of the devastation caused by her own country. Never again would she think of U.S. military force or her international citizenry in the same manner. Hiroshima shook her understanding of the place of the United States in the world and caused her to question U.S. involvement. Publicly, however, she remained silent on these issues.[3]

Helen Keller horseback riding in California during the filming of *Deliverance,* 1919.

Helen Keller amid vaudeville preparations, 1922.

Helen Keller at the back door of her Wrentham home, 1909.

Anne Sullivan, 1881.

Helen Keller and Polly Thomson aboard ship en route to Scotland, 1930.

Helen Keller on board ship near Orkney Island, Scotland, 1932.

Helen Keller at Arcan, Scotland, 1932.

Formal portrait of Helen Keller and Polly Thomson, 1938.

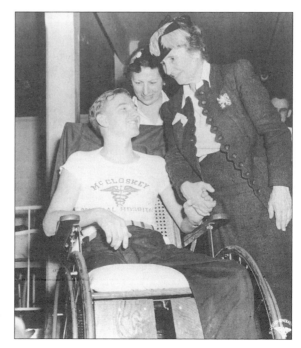

Helen Keller (on right) and Polly Thomson (middle) visit Sergeant Jasper Pennington of Solon, Iowa

Helen Keller and Polly Thomson, Hokkaido, Japan, 1937. Keller is on the left side of the photo; Thomson on the right.

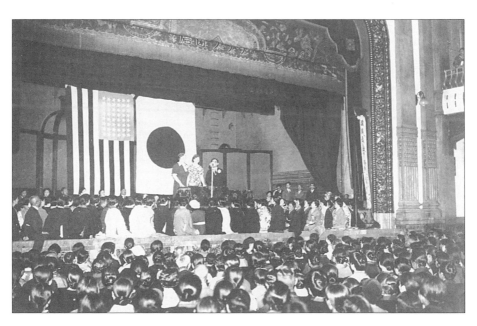

Helen Keller and Polly Thomson, Osaka, Japan, 1937, at the Central City Hall with approximately 4500 women.

Katharine Cornell, Helen Keller, Polly Thomson, and unidentified woman (left to right), undated.

Jo Davidson, Florence Davidson (top), and Helen Keller at the Davidson home in Becheron, France, 1951.

Helen Keller and Polly Thomson shopping for hats, 1954.

Helen Keller in Brisbane, Australia, 1948.

Helen Keller in military vehicle, Japan, 1948.

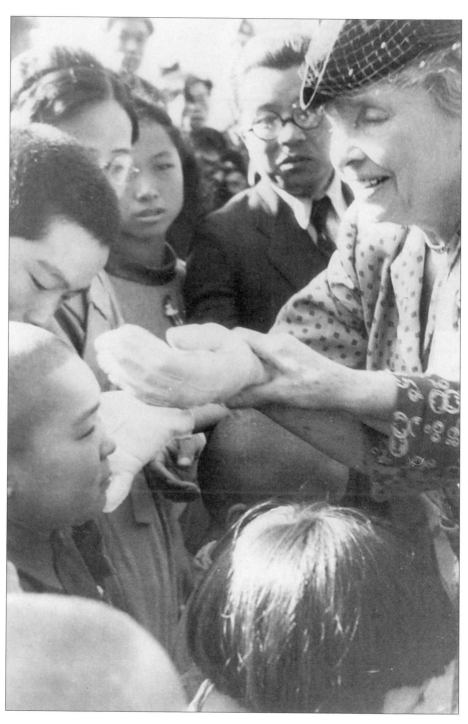

Helen Keller greeting children in Fukushima, Japan, 1948.

Helen Keller and Polly Thomson at the Zeitoun School for the Blind, Egypt, 1952.

Helen Keller, playing the Japanese instrument shamisen, and Polly Thomson in Japan, 1955.

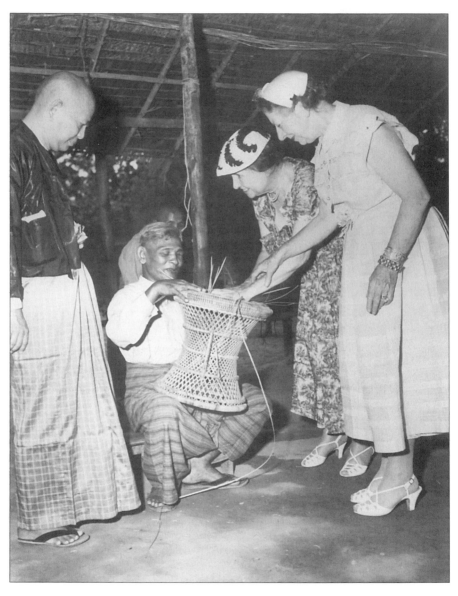

Dr. U Thein, unidentified man, Helen Keller, and Polly Thomson at the Home for the Blind, Rangoon, Burma, 1955.

His Excellency the Governor of Bombay, his unnamed daughter-in-law, Helen Keller, Polly Thomson, and unidentified man, 1955, Bombay, India.

Helen Keller and Polly Thomson in Calcutta, India, 1955.

Helen Keller reading braille with dog Tinka, 1960.

Dear Friends,

It is with affectionate emotion that I greet you once more. Lovingly I remember the beauty, the strength and the joy of your sea-girt city that was, and above all, the warm friendship with which it welcomed me eleven years ago remains to me a touching memory.

It is not easy to thank you all for the dear words you have spoken or the gifts (if any are presented) which you have put into my hands on my second return to Hiroshima—the glow of a rare generosity reaching out of its bitter fate to embrace me. That is the most sacred part of the—friendship that life's vicissitudes cannot destroy. I pray that God who smiles in every gift from brave hearts may keep me strong to encourage and cheer your handicapped. It was a cruel nemesis that overtook Hiroshima—as it has overtaken many mighty cities before now. But even as the city collapsed, and thousands of lives vanished in the fires of atomic war, the tragedy generated new forces of healing. Your splendid qualities which have times without number helped you in bygone days have triumphed, and Hiroshima is beginning to flourish again through your devotion and self-denial. It will rise too in the new sense you are gaining of personal freedom and responsibility for the welfare of others and your adoption of the principles and practices of democracy. Then truly will your tragedy be a purification of your souls through public spirit and brotherhood.

71 Our Tour of South Africa

August 1, 1951, letter from Helen Keller to Jo Davidson,
Papers of Jo and Florence Davidson, Library of Congress.

When Keller went to South Africa in 1951, she wanted to confront the racism of South African society directly but felt she had to be very careful. At a news conference immediately prior to her departure, she mentioned the racial disparities among the opportunities available for blind people but focused instead on drums and zebras (the zebras she would encounter at Kruger National Park). Newspaper reportage noted that she "radiated enthusiasm" as she spoke of her desire to "catch glimpses of the tribal life and of the great hills and wonderful plains. To me it is all novel and full of enchantment."[4] Her personal preparations for the trip are described in document 79.

Keller criticized racial apartheid publicly and privately. Yet she was unsure that she had sufficiently aroused the conscience of anyone. She kept her strongest opinions on the country and its race relations private. As nearly always, she addressed them to her dear friend Jo Davidson. The omnipresent "bitter racialism" clashed with the beautiful South African countryside. It took "all the courage and fortitude Polly and I could command" to make public pleas for education and employment for the indigenous blind and deaf people. Frustration caused her to have dreams of "bang[ing] my head against an impenetrable wall trying to discover a break-through." While at Radcliffe in 1900, Keller had written a college paper describing white South Africans as "the heroic Boers" (see document 6). Clearly, by the time she returned to the United States in August 1951, she had changed her mind.

Dearest Jo and Florence,

What darlings you were to send Polly and me letters that made us feel strongly embraced by you, unseen but none the less real and adorable friends! With equal warmth we have reciprocated your sentiments in silence. But ever since our homecoming July 1st I have lived in such bewilderment, trying to clear away months of piled-up mail on the desk, the couch and the study floor, that each night has found me all hollowed out mentally, and I see no end to this chaos yet, but I shall come out of it in good time, I am sure.

We were grieved to hear about Florence's being held captive by her sprained ankle. And poor "Whuskey" struck by a car![5] She and he are so active from morning until evening, looking, listening and each chasing after a special interest, that it must be "tough" on them remaining quietly in one spot. We are glad that he has licked himself into walking again, and earnestly we hope that Florence too has improved greatly. How we should have loved to sit by her speeding the time in talk and reminiscence!

It delighted us to read the news that your autobiography has actually been finished and pushed out of the house into the hands of the publisher. Through all your doubts and hesitations, your sighs over the manuscript, Jo, and Florence's sturdy proddings of your genius I never lost confidence that you would complete the book. Proudly we join the host of friends who behold your triple laurel crown as a sculptor, a painter and an author. Polly and I remember the hours at Becheron full of the scents of lavender and honeysuckle from the garden, while you read some of the manuscript aloud to us, and how in fear and trembling I discussed this or that matter of literary crafts-manship with you. Always I was impressed by the masterful way you moulded the clay of words when we read "Between Sittings." Three cheers for Jo Davidson the writer!

It pleases us much that you have been out to Israeli [sic] at least. Sometime I hope I may touch the heads of the eminent men you met there. All you say about the vigorous new life and the cleanness of Palestine gratifies me as a confirmation of the inspiring articles I read on the subject. Polly and I still dream of going to Israeli, but there is no one near to make the necessary arrangements, since Van Wyck is abroad. Perhaps when he and Gladys come back, we can go over with him the letters and papers relating to Palestine and decide upon the time and the plans for the kind of visit we wish to make. My travels through the world would indeed be incomplete unless I breathed the air of that land, tiny of bulk but spiritually mighty, where the Hebrews have fearlessly rallied to build a future that shall unfold in sevenfold radiance God's fulfillment of their agelong dream of liberty, justice and brotherhood everywhere.

We envy Van Wyck and Gladys the privilege of being with you two and forgetting the world in the tranquil loveliness of Becheron. When they are back in America, we shall devour their news of you both and reminisce about the delectable times and thought-filled conversations we had together last year.

It would be much easier to talk over with you our tour of South Africa than to write. It is to me at once a unique experience in my travels and an ultimate expression of world problems and the hopes and terrors that beset man in his efforts to solve them. Naturally, my first impression when we reached Cape Town was the warm reception we had there, and the generosity with which the people responded to my appeals for the blind and deaf. But I had known about the real structure of society for many years, and I quickly detected beneath the mask of European ways and professed adherence to the ideals of

Western civilization the domineering, self-willed, at one time slave-owning whites who call themselves "Afrikaaners"—the Boers. Nothing has made me more ashamed of my own race than that creature depicted in a book, "White Man Boss" by Adamastor which I am at present reading in Braille. It took all the courage and fortitude Polly and I could command to face newspaper interviewers and audiences and ask them to provide education, employment and hope for the natives blind or deaf. Many times my heart sank as I observed how apathetic many of the public had been towards those unfortunates, and occasionally in dreams I banged my head against an impenetrable wall trying to discover a break-through. The gorgeous bouquets of flowers and fruits we received could not put out of our minds the bitter sense of racial discrimination and injustice that may, and do neutralize the beneficent efforts of those who sincerely desire the well-being and self-support of the native handicapped. However, we threw ourselves into our work resolutely, and had the satisfaction of being told again and again that I had touched the hearts of the people.

Polly and I held three or four meetings almost every day, which was part of the racial problem. (The whites, the colored people, the natives and the Indians refuse to assemble in one place.) We traveled constantly by ship, rail, aeroplane and automobile. We visited schools and workshops for the blind and the deaf, and I pleaded to have a lot more opened for native children deprived of sight or hearing.

We had two fascinating, though fatiguing days in Kruger National Park. From dawn until sunset we drove in a car to catch views of lions and graceful giraffes with their heads over tree-tops. Herds of impalas were everywhere, and how nimbly they leaped over the car! Also we saw kudus, zebras, wildebeests, wart-hogs and many beautiful birds of all colors. We got out of the car to look at the hippopotami in the river. Our guide knew it was safe for us to visit that spot. The tall grasses rustled against me, and I drank in the sweet, clean air and the sense of four hundred miles where wild animals were free to roam in. Despite Kruger's glaring defects, I honored him for his vision and sagacity in setting aside that vast natural park to instill reverence for life which God has created in man and beast alike.

We also flew over Victoria Falls in Rhodesia, and when we alighted, I was covered with its spray. I was disappointed not to feel its roar—the voice of Africa, but its immensity remains with me, an unforgettable experience.

It was awesome to traverse unmeasured plains of rocks and the karroo, to climb winding roads up rugged, austere mountains and to fly over vast lengths of the Indian Ocean. Amazement swept over me as I realized what untold cataclysms of volcano, flood and drought Africa has survived and what bursts of greenness and fragrance can yet be found in some of its valleys and jungles.

While we were in Kimberley, Polly and I visited the great mine and the Big Hole.[6] By the way, Jo, I have learned that we need not be terrified by the fabulous, "futile" wealth passing through Kimberley. Ninety-five percent of the diamonds found so far serve as abrasive in industry—an enormous use to mankind. Five percent are kept for the world's jewels. I was enchanted as I felt diamonds in the natural state and heard about their variety of colors, but oh, the desolation that inundated me as I considered the Big Hole—an immeasurable symbol of misery, ill-paid labor and wasted lives.

Here I am reminded that at Johannesburg a tea was arranged for us at Sir Ernest Oppenheimer's beautiful home.[7] He entertained us pleasantly. That was one of the numerous occasions on which we had to keep watch over our mutinous lips. Sir Ernest talked much about General Smuts with evident admiration, and told us that they had been close friends for many years. Afterwards he sent me—not a diamond but a photograph of Smuts and himself, which, as you can imagine, I acknowledged with mingled emotions.[8]

Stuart Cloete called on us at Cape Town.[9] His delightful personality and the word-picture he conjured up of his retreat made us long to run away with him for a day or two, but the inexorable manager in charge of our lectures carried us off to another meeting that evening.

Johannesburg is a truly astonishing city, considering the fact that it has been in existence only sixty-seven years. We did not like it at all on account of its brutality, its ugliness in some sections and its "gold fever." But I believe there is a nobler spirit growing up that will direct its wealth ultimately towards the true welfare, education and brotherhood of all races within the city. Certainly the people I personally met were charming and alive to the ideals of genuine citizenship.

The finest expression of Johannesburg's spirit is the University of Witwatersrand from which I received a degree—Doctor of Laws—an honor equal in importance to one from Oxford. At first I thought I should refuse, as I have said "no" to degrees from colleges for ever so long, but it seems that Witwatersrand conspired in friendly secrecy to capture me, and now I am glad. For it appeals to me in everything it champions—open-mindedness to the best thoughts in religions and philosophies, equality between students of different races and pursuit of knowledge that will promote world betterment.

We are thankful to be at home where we can compose our ruffled thoughts. The heat is devastating, but we enjoy the fragrant coolness of early mornings working in the garden.

Polly has asked Miss Dunham of the American Foundation for the Blind to write to Dick Whittington regarding the two thermos Florence and you so thoughtfully slipped into our lunch bag when we went to Portofino. They are the best thermos we ever had, and we hope we can get "refills" for them from Paris. They were broken recently when we went blueberrying at James Melton's place. We cannot obtain the "refills" here because they are foreign-made.

Van Wyck and Gladys docked yesterday, and we are to have them for tea Saturday afternoon.

Our big Ettu is well and as destructive as ever of our "ballees." We shall be happy if you can find one for her as large as "Whuskey's." We have tried everywhere in New York, but can't get one of that size and make.

This letter is heavy with our love to you both shaken down, pressed together and running over.

Devotedly your friend,
Helen Keller

72 Our Trip Through the Near East

July 2, 1952, letter from Helen Keller to Nella Braddy Henney, Nella Braddy Henney Collection, Perkins School for the Blind.

This letter chronicles Keller's continued travels throughout the 1950s, as she entered her seventies. She and Thomson joined in the Paris celebrations of the one-hundredth anniversary of Lewis Braille's invention of braille, where she figured prominently. This was their first trip to France since Jo Davidson's death in late 1951, and she missed him.

The height of their AFB travels was a three-month expedition to Egypt, Syria, Lebanon, Jordan, and Israel in the spring of 1952. Keller's visits thrilled U.S. embassy personnel. The public affairs officer of the U.S. embassy in Egypt reported to the State Department that "so poignant and so universal was her appeal that Miss Keller received by far the widest press coverage of any recent American visitor to Egypt." In Syria, an embassy staffer reported with delight that twenty-three daily newspapers, five weeklies, and one monthly magazine covered the visit, devoting 1,792 inches to the visit. Reports submitted from embassy personnel in Jordan and Arab Jerusalem were similar. Her disability and her miracle status, perhaps her gender, and certainly her willingness to avoid explicit mention of politics, rendered her a powerful political propagandizing tool.[10]

Dearest Nella,

Here I am at last sending you a letter just for the pleasure of writing it.

Until now, as you so well understand, I have been obliged to rest after the despotism of my work—it is a blessed privilege to me, but it has exacted every bit of energy I could put into it, and "duty letters" have been all I could manage.

Polly and I returned last Monday with Florence from Becheron where I spent a happy, peaceful birthday, and where for days I enjoyed to the full the "dolce far niente." The only thing lacking to make complete my visit to Becheron was the joy of having you with us. I did want you to share with us the utter loveliness of dear Jo's "Sans Souci" which we were perhaps seeing for the last time. Poor Florence, I fear that it will be too great a burden for her to keep Becheron with all the responsibilities and expenses it entails.[11] We will tell you all about it when we see you.

When everything at Becheron blooms, shines and sings, it is a bit of Heaven on earth. It was wonderful just to sit in the courtyard during the day and let the motions of the air play upon my face. The lavender hedge beside the door of Jo's studio swung on every breeze, discharging its odor mingled with the sage and thyme. Roses and honeysuckles everywhere poured out their souls in cascades of delight. Day-lilies, pungent marigolds, arbor vitae and scented leaves on some of the shrubs gave a peculiar quality to the soft sighing of the wind. I understood then what Hudson meant when he described his passivity as he sat hour after hour with his power of collected, purposeful thinking suspended. Instinctively he was waiting for new life to be poured into him. He believed, and so do I, that this is one of the static goods of the mind which we must cultivate sometimes in order to lessen the strain and nervous irritation of mental effort.

Now, after giving you a picture of one of my blessed states, I will speak of the emotional "eblouissement," as Victor Hugo would say, that I had at the Sorbonne. It was thrilling to have Polly describe the venerable college, the audience crowding the hall of learning to the rafters, the powerful Kleig lights and the blind near us who were on the programme. Pierre Henri and several others paid tributes full of spirit and warmth to Louis Braille. Between the speeches blind musicians played exquisitely on the piano and the violin. You can imagine my joy when M. Henri and several other distinguished blind persons had the decoration of the Legion d'Honneur pinned on their coats. After my little talk, which the audience received with affectionate fervor, I was decorated too, and oh the applause, Nella! It did not seem possible that the tremendous volume of vibration had burst forth just for me, causing the rafters to ring again. It was, and still is like a dream. Such a magnificent compliment awes me, but since it has been so willed, I hope that I can deserve it a little by finding new ways to serve the handicapped before I depart from earth.

My emotions reached a high pitch again when Polly and I were in the Pantheon on Sunday the 22nd. That noble building impressed me powerfully as a memorial to the best and the greatest men and women. We had been invited by a descendant of Louis Braille—a good-looking, distinguished man—to sit with him and his family during the ceremonies, and I felt that nothing could have honored me more than such an intimate contact with kinsfolk from Coupvray which Louis Braille loved so passionately. Everything was conducted with supreme elegance and dignity—the glorious music, the colorful costumes of the Republican Army which raised their sabres every time an important personage appeared, and through which the bier was borne. The Minister of Health made an eloquent speech on Louis Braille's contribution to the fellowship of mind and spirit which has united the seeing and the blind. He dwelt on the amazing simplicity of the alphabet which enables more and more of the sightless to read and write, and he ended by saying that Civilization has been brought a step nearer, since the inventor of the dot system was recognized by the world. I was introduced to President Auriol, and I sensed real gladness in his hand as he clasped mine. (He was a friend of Jo's.) Afterwards M. Braille, the descendant, asked me to take his arm as we walked down in to the crypt, and Nella, the silence was awe-inspiring —one of the experiences that occur once or twice in a lifetime. It was a marvelous service untouched by creed or dogma, sanctified by an element of universal worship. It was Georges Raverat whose big-hearted devotion and vigorous efforts made it possible for the blind to appear at the Sorbonne, and it was he too who arranged for the removal of Louis Braille's ashes to the Pantheon. I hope that now the people of France may become blind-conscious and push forward the long delayed process of integrating their capable sightless into normal society.

I have just been reading M. Henri's "La Vie et l'Oeuvre de Louis Braille," and I am able to tell you, Nella, that my first impression of Mr. Kugelmas's book was correct. We cannot condemn it too strongly as a mass of errors, anachronisms, inventions and "invraisemblances." It does not serve its avowed purpose of communicating knowledge to young people if it deforms the personality of Louis Braille by wresting facts from the framework of his quiet life and putting in figments of the imagination.

July 5th. Dear me, we see by this morning's paper that Sophie Tucker is in town. How often she has followed or preceded us on our tours!

This week Florence, Polly and I spent a marvelous evening with Monsieur and Madame Dignimont who were among Jo's close friends. M. Dignimont is the well known French artist whose charming painting of Becheron hangs on the wall of Polly's office. While we were there, we met Michele Simone, who is regarded as the greatest actor in France. From the dimples in his beaming face I should not have known that his role is that of tragedy, but when I saw his hands aquiver with understanding of human sorrow and joy, I was profoundly stirred. Their exquisite sensitiveness is another form of speech.

Polly and I are bringing home a film for Nancy which we had "made" here in Paris. We did our best to follow her suggestions, but we are afraid that the film may not be all she wants.

The mondial heat wave has all but prostrated us the last few days. However, we managed to refresh ourselves at several restaurants outdoors—one at the end of Avenue Foch at the beginning of the Bois de Boulogne, where it is always cool and delightful, another on the Champs-Elysees and the Pre Catalan.

Wednesday morning we went to the Louvre where I was permitted to touch some works of art. Among them were marvelous friezes from the Parthenon which enabled me to feel the beautiful forms of youth and maidens and follow the rhythm of their bodies. Thus I could fill out a bit more of the mental picture of the Parthenon that has thrilled me ever since Polly and I climbed the Acropolis. There were impressive giant stone statues, badly broken and defaced, but eloquent of ancient Greek art. A moving representation was two friends before death shaking hands with a long last look. My fingers thrilled as they passed over an adorable Eros, a dancing-girl who seemed to me one of the Graces, an appealing image of a young athlete who had met his death at the Olympic games and his boy slave and two dogs looking up at him most affectionately. I wish that something would move you, Nella, to come to Paris with us sometime, learn to know and love it as we do and feast your eyes upon the treasures in the Louvre.

At present I am reading "Les Miserables," one of the countless books I have not found leisure for all these years. It contains twenty-eight Braille volumes. It is an amazing book, and if Victor Hugo had had Tolstoy's power of suggestion and compact writing, it might have ranked with "War and Peace." As it is, Hugo deserves eternal gratitude for his mighty fulminations against degrading poverty, the convict system that used to exist in France and ecclesiastical despotism.

Well, well, I have not said a word about our trip through the Near East. You will learn much from Karl Meyer's diary and the many fine photograph [sic] we have to show you. He took great pains to bring out the meaning of our work, and we ourselves are astonished at the enormous amount we accomplished. Some error on the part of the American Foundation created an impression abroad that I was to address universities and schools for the seeing as a sort of missionary, beside visiting the institutions for the handicapped, and that is why our program was so crowded. However, thanks to the capacity for more intense living that some of us develop towards the end of our earth-life, I have garnered a wealth of memories which will shine upon me until Eternity. There is the awful sense of a whole civilization entombed when I visited the Museum in Cairo, a glorious remembrance of the Mosque of Light to which Madame Marzouk took us and the bird's-eye view we had of the city old and new from the heights occupied by the mosque. It is a poem to recall the night we spent on the desert under the shadow of the Pyramids. I could feel the silence of the desert, intense, primal, hostile to all growth, extending over the noiseless sand in every direction. On several occasions we met charming Egyptian women, progressive in their ideas, with whom it was a delight to discuss various aspects of history and who, I believe, will exercise a potent influence on the higher development of their country. One of them said to me, "The Egyptian people have a strong will-power, but you must make them believe in a movement before they attempt it." And how true that is of the work for the blind and the deaf! The good school and workshop for the blind at Zeitoun and the splendid institute for deaf girls opened by the Government owe their existence to the untiring perseverance of Mr. Sayyed Fattah, a jolly, lovable man, an undiscourageable optimist, whose jokes made me laugh away difficulties when we met.

And there was the unforgettable hour which Taha Hussein Pasha spent with me at the Semiramis Hotel in Cairo. He could not speak English, but his son—the true son of his mind and a dear, charming boy, interpreted for us both. We talked about many things—Homer, Aeschylus, Euripides and other Greek poets and dramatists, the liberating power of the mind, Taha Hussein's studies of the great blind Arab philosopher of the tenth century and his summer home on an island in the Nile, and how responsive and tender he was to me! I plucked up courage to ask him what he had done for the blind while he was Minister of Education, and he told me that he had worked quietly helping capable blind people to go on to a college or a university. He said that one of the chief needs of the Egyptian blind was secondary schools from which they could go to finish their education in a college. It was a precious boon to feel his strong personality behind me when I pleaded with different ministers of the Government to establish those secondary schools. Finally the Minister of Education said definitely that the schools would be opened, and Mr. Fattah beamed his assurance that the promise would be fulfilled. Nous verrons—you know how dilatory the officials of the Middle East are.

We were most hospitably entertained at Beirut, and everybody was wonderful to us. Beirut is a sweet, clean city, packed with schools, colleges and Christian missions. At some distance is the Lebanon range of mountains where we had a glorious drive through peaceful pastures and villages that recalled Bible times, and we found one or two places where every man sat under his own fig-tree and his own vine, and no one made him afraid. I was disappointed not to see the ancient cedars of Lebanon, but I touched many young ones and reveled in their fragrance.

Damascus was absorbingly fascinating and exciting too. We could feel how terribly the Syrians are stirred up over the Arab refugees from Palestine, and it was not prudent for us to leave the hotel unless some one from the American Embassy accompanied us. We understood that Damascus is the oldest continuously inhabited city on earth. We saw many handsome buildings, mosques and picturesque old shops, and I walked on the oldest street in the world. I learned that the women of the city are moving rapidly towards social maturity and independence, and that more of them go to the University than men. We attended a meeting of the Arab Women's Federation, and I was sure, judging by their warm-hearted response, that they would at least start one school for the blind. We had a public meeting, and I will say to you, Nella, that I gave them the devil because their blind had been utterly neglected. I had been wrong in my ideas of Arab psychology. They had little sense of social responsibility, and must be pounded and pounded before they adopt an attitude of helpfulness towards the unfortunate. There is an appalling economic and social gap between the poor and the rich in all the Arab countries through which we have traveled, and any attempt to remedy the situation is put down ruthlessly by their rulers.

We often passed the camps of refugees, and I turned sick at the inconceivable misery and helpless animality in which they live. Yet the wealthy Arabs who own rich, beautiful lands throughout the Near East do little or nothing for those pitiful creatures but fill the world's ears with their complaints and wrongs, while the United Nations uses every possible means to solve their problems. It was heart-warming for us to meet all the way from Egypt to old Jerusalem American delegates who are working with all their might on Point Four. As we listened to the thrilling story of their efforts, the endless obstacles they encounter and their slow but steadily increasing triumph in convincing the backward peoples that self-help is the sure way to salvation, the world atmosphere vibrated for me with new energy and hope. Despite the tragic blunderings of America in its foreign policy, just to hear and look at those young men and women absorbed in their global endeavor was a revelation to me of the growing intelligence and spirit of service to others that will yet establish Civilization for all peoples.

It was the golden season of harvest, and on all the roads over which we drove from Beirut to Israel I smelt the blessedness of plenty. Polly described to me the endless processions of camels, donkeys, men and boys carrying the wheat to its destination. As a whole, except for several cities and towns, the land was quite as pastoral as when Abraham and his men tilled it. For mile after mile thousands of sheep and goats browsed by the roadside, and the primitive solitude spoke volumes to my imagination.

In Jerusalem I was bored stiff "sight-seeing." We went to the Church of the Nativity and the alleged tomb of the Virgin Mary, and Oh, the sickening commercialism of it all! We climbed every step of the Via Dolorosa and heard every detail of the vicissitudes which had befallen those sacred places. The smells of the ancient city were horrible, and nearly drove me crazy. It was all I could do to keep from exclaiming out loud, "How can any sane person call places containing such filth sacred to any religion?" However, there was a satisfying spiritual experience that brought Polly and me happiness. Early one Sunday morning we visited the garden sepulcher of the Lord. As you probably know, when General Gordon was in Jerusalem, he discovered what he felt sure was the real site of the Lord's tomb—the new sepulcher not yet finished in which Joseph of Arimathea laid the body. What a forceful symbol of God's Work, unfinished, going on forever! We walked down a path bordered with tall sage, thyme and other sweet herbs and wild-flowers that must have gladdened Jesus's heart, and as we entered the tomb, I was full not of sorrow but deeply felt joy. For there, as always, God's Presence was an exalted reality to me. We sat down at the entrance and gave ourselves up to an inundation of virgin morning fragrances, sunshine soft and tender—a reflection of His revivifying Love, the song of birds, and I was more than ever confident in the Resurrection.

When we at last crossed the area of bombed territory between the two parts of Jerusalem, I was speechless at the desolate ruin around us. But in another moment we had entered the electric, stimulating atmosphere of Israel, so different from the putrescent decay of civilizations not yet buried. Really, Israel is all that I have read, it is clean, vigorous and rejoicing "like a strong man to run a race." Everybody in Israel is working with a will to found a commonwealth on the highest ideals of the Prophets. From one end of the Republic to the other Polly and I saw and touched the fertility that the hands of the people have wrought in the bare hills and plains. As we went from one kubbitz [sic] to another, we observed how happy and healthy the children and youths were, and how wisely they are being trained not only for agriculture and industry, but also for constructive citizenship. We were delighted with the good roads and bridges in process of construction everywhere, and we passed the gigantic irrigation projects on which Mrs. Roosevelt has commented. But what we saw in a country surrounded by enemies and involved in difficult financial problems is so wonderful that doubters will hardly believe our report.

The work for the blind and the deaf in Israel has not been exaggerated. I was impressed by the intelligence and alertness of the teachers of both groups. Their imagination and resourcefulness help the pupils to overcome lack of equipment and of apparatus that bypasses their limitations. It is touching to reflect that this want of proper educational materials and shortage of housing for the handicapped are partly due to the necessity of ministering to all the homeless Jews who responded to the generous invitation of Israel to settle in the land.

Every time I think of Israel, the loving hospitality and courtesy of the people will smile upon me. They were generous with the little they had to give. For instance, I was presented by the Director of the Jewish Institute for the Blind with a beautifully bound Bible adorned with silver "crowns," and I received a handsome metal guide dog from the blinded ex-servicemen.

We had the privilege of meeting Ben-Gurion—a titan in courage and vision, Golda Meyerson who is responsible for the fine roads in Israel, Mrs. Weizmann, the wife of the President of the Republic, (he was ill at the time we called) Ruth Kluger, whom Jo knew and admired, and who went with us to meetings. She is among the heroic group who rescued many Jews from Dachau and Buchenwald and brought them "illegally" to Israel.

Now it is time for us to go to the airport, and I must stop. Florence sends you her love. We have done our best to divert her mind from her many troubles, but God alone can touch a sacred sorrow like hers. With Polly's and my love until we see you, I am,

Affectionately your friend,
Helen Keller

73 The Blind in Chile

April 25, 1953, speech at the University of Concepcion, Concepcion, Chile. Helen Keller Archives, Awards, General-C, AFB.

Throughout May and June 1953, Keller visited Brazil, Chile, Peru, Panama, and Mexico. Again, her schedule was frenzied. Secretary of State John Dulles told diplomatic officers to assist with trip arrangements, and State Department and embassy officials had nothing but praise for her visit. The public affairs officer in Sao Paulo, Brazil, wrote that the publicity she generated exceeded in both quality and quantity that given the previous year's visit of Secretary of State Dean Acheson. Embassy personnel in Lima, Peru, reported that "no private individual" had received as much press attention as Keller in the last year, and that the favorable press would benefit the United States. From Mexico, embassy personnel reported similarly that "no other visitor of any nationality has attracted as much attention from the press or as much public recognition in Mexico during the past several years." The positive press reports she received in "the anti-American, Communist organ *El Popular*" were those most noted by embassy personnel.[12]

Professors, students and friends, it is an honor to me to be among such a warm-hearted, hospitable people in a marvelously fascinating country with great mountains, fruitful valleys and turbulent rivers.

I welcome this opportunity to speak to you about the blind. As you are aware, there are many blind children in Chile growing up helpless, un-trained. The major cause of blindness in this country, I am told, is ophthalmia neonatorum. I understand that a law exists requiring doctors and midwives to put a solution of silver nitrate in the eyes of every new born baby, but from thirty-five to forty percent of babies receive no attention from either doctor or trained midwife. You, professors and students will, I hope, keep this sad fact before the public until the scourge of blindness in the new-born is abolished.

Besides this pitiful group, there is a large number of those who go blind in active life. They want to support themselves, but they are debarred from this vital, human right because there is a prejudice that, because they are blind, they can do nothing. Yet we know that if prompt action is taken after loss of sight, full readjustment can be achieved, and resettlement through training accomplished. In this amazing era of technological progress, undreamed of advances are made in devising appliances whose use promises wide, new vistas of cultural activity, social integration and vocational opportunity. The blind do not want charity, but the kind of help that will give their lives a goal, their frustrated selves a purpose around which to reintegrate their personalities, regain their inner health. They ask only for training that will keep them alert and enable them to occupy an honorable status in service to society.

Have you ever tried to imagine how you would feel if you lost your sight tomorrow? Can you picture yourself stumbling and groping at noonday, as in the night, your work, your independence gone? In that bitter hour would you not cry out for an experienced friend to teach you how to live in the dark. This is a friend you can give the blind of Chile by providing them with skillful workmanship and social competence.

You will be glad to hear of the new, national school for the blind that is to be built in Santiago—it will have skillful teachers, qualified personnel and a well-headed staff. A National Commission for the Blind is being appointed to coordinate all of the work for the blind in Chile. If this is to become a great center of well-being and constructive effort, it must have the cordial cooperation of all who have the interest of the blind at heart; whatever divides destroys, but unity is strength.

Smooth the path under the feet of the blind and they shall stride forward with new courage in the desire of self-fulfillment.

74 One of the Numberless Instruments in God's Hand

February 1, 1955, speech at the farewell dinner sponsored by the American Foundation for the Blind. Foreign Travel file, AFB.

While Keller worked desperately to finish her nearly thirty-year effort to write a book on Anne Sullivan Macy in 1954, she, the AFB, and the State Department continued plans for an early 1955 trip to India, Pakistan, Burma, the Philippines, and Japan. The AFB, Nella Braddy Henney, and others used the February 1955 departure to stage a Helen Keller love fest, always noting that she would return only days before her seventy-fifth birthday. Harvard bestowed her an honorary degree. The AFB kicked off the trip with a February 1 farewell banquet for 400 at the Waldorf Astoria Hotel in New York City. The U.S. ambassadors from each of the countries she was to visit spoke briefly, followed by effusive praises from Eleanor Roosevelt. In her farewell speech reprinted below, Keller, as always, spoke humbly.

Mrs. Roosevelt, Your Excellencies and Friends,

Your tributes are most eloquent and touching, and I thank you for them warmly.

But I am especially grateful for the encouragement and good-will with which you are sending me on my mission to the handicapped. I believe that I am just one of the numberless instruments in God's Hand carrying out His Plan of Good. And what thought can be more precious to me than that he has guided me in my share of the work for His disabled children? And what humility as well as joy I feel that He has permitted me to be a part of the world-wide movement for their welfare? If I only fulfill my mission with both good intent and good effect in helping to eliminate blindness and deafness from the earth, my heart will sing with joy that is Heaven indeed.

75 The People of India Most Hospitable

March 14, 1955, letter from Helen Keller, Madras, India, to Eric Boulter, Helen Keller Archives, Foreign Travel file, 1955 India, AFB.

India impressed Keller. She made her usual visits to schools for blind children, laid the cornerstone for the first workshop for blind adults, and made the rounds of receptions and government officials. Prime Minister Jawaharlal Nehru, claiming the difficult policy of neutrality between the Soviet Union and the United States, charmed her. For pages and pages, she did nothing but praise him to Henney, calling him the "most electrifying expression of India we met." She joined him and his daughter Indira, who would eventually be prime minister herself, for dinner at their home, where they spoke of poetry, philosophy, and economic development.

As in Keller's other travels, the AFB and the State Department continued its involvement in her 1955 trip to India, Pakistan, Burma, the Philippines, and Japan. The AFB had added Burma to the itinerary at the request of the State Department, which was apparently concerned by pro-Communist and anti-American sentiments in that country. Embassy personnel characterized her weeklong visit as having "an enormous psychological impact favorable to the United States." She berated the Burmese government for its lack of support for blind and deaf citizens. Embassy personnel noted that these comments from anyone else would have generated "grievous resentment" but had prompted action and support when stated by Keller.[13]

Dear Eric,

Polly and I were glad to hear from you, and we appreciated the time you took from your crowded days to write to us. The appeal you enclosed for the blind of the Far East pleased me very much, and I was gratified that you had attended to it, knowing in what a hurry it had to be sent out under my name. May the returns from the contributors show an understanding of the tremendous task which the American Foundation for the Overseas Blind has undertaken. Every day a heavy sense of responsibility lies upon me as I try to rouse enthusiasm in my audiences for affording greater facilities to the ten million blind living in the countries I am traveling and more extensive means for preventing loss of sight.

I have found the people of India most hospitable, affectionate, lavishing their fragrant garlands which they heap upon me wherever we go. Our three days in Delhi were exciting. Meeting Nehru[14] was a thrilling event, and the evening we dined with him I imagined that I felt as the climbers did when they reached the top of Mt. Everest. In Nehru I saw a man able to give the people confidence in themselves, and I am sure that under his leadership there will be swift economic and social changes in India the next twenty years. I was disappointed not to find a program of meetings or to obtain definite information about the work for the blind in Delhi. However, I hope that when we go back there on April 6th, we may do some real work.

Our visit to Bombay was delightful, though strenuous. The interest of the Governor, the ministry and the city in the welfare of the blind was stimulating. Great crowds attended the meetings and even came to the schools for the blind where we spoke. It was a great experience for me to lay the foundation stone of the first sheltered workshop for the blind in India. Of course, as I said to the people, it was a tiny seed sown for the two million blind of their country, and I begged them to continue opening new workshops until the public was convinced of the capabilities of the blind. By that time I hoped big employers would be willing to draw upon the labor of those who, though blind, can keep abreast with those in the industrial world.

Here we are the guests of the Governor. We are in a beautiful palace with five miles of forest, a wonderful lawn and a lovely garden. Yesterday the Governor gave a great garden party, then I addressed the Guild of Social Services which includes many affiliations not only in India but also throughout the world. They responded warmly, and said they would do their best to carry out my message.

The Governor has a charming personality and a mind rich in beautiful thoughts gathered from the poetry of India and Britain. Although he works very hard, he comes to see us every day and bestows many delightful kindnesses upon us. You should see him walking round with us in the middle of the day holding up a big black umbrella to shade our heads from the blazing sun. This place is decidedly English, a combination of garden, fruit orchard, deer park and fruit orchard [sic]. We sit out evenings and relax deliciously while the fragrances from many trees and flowers enchant me. So far the heat has not killed us. We are going to Mysore for two weeks' holiday, and I shall be able to catch up with my relentlessly accumulating correspondence and recast some of my speeches for different situations that arise from country to country.

Polly and I wonder if you will mind our taking Ann with us to Pakistan. We realize the additional expense to the Foundation for the Overseas Blind, but a capable, educated girl is a tremendous help to us both with the multitude of details which demand our attention. Besides, Mr. Mortimer is not going to Pakistan with us.

With warm love from us both, I am,

    Affectionately yours,

    Helen Keller

C Friendships, Intimacies, and the Everyday

76 Another Abyss of Evil

September 22, 1946, letter from Helen Keller to Nella Braddy Henney, Nella Braddy Henney Collection, Perkins School for the Blind.

In the 1940s, Nella Braddy Henney, who had provided friendship and editorial assistance to Keller since 1927, became an increasingly important friend. In this letter, written immediately before she left for Europe, Keller laments her upcoming travels, U.S. racial relations, the firing of Vice President Henry Wallace after he criticized President Truman's Soviet Union policy, and the general state of the world. In concert with the Marshall Plan and U.S. efforts to provide assistance for civilians and military officials attempting to recover from the war, Keller was going to Europe to foster support for European blind people. The Foundation for the Overseas Blind, part of the AFB, hoped her visits to war-torn Greece, Italy, France, and England would draw attention to the dire postwar conditions, particularly of those who were blind, and consequently raise funds in the United States.

As civil rights campaigns developed in the post–World War II period, she also paid increasing attention to racial inequalities in both the North and South. This letter chronicles her participation in a Danbury, Connecticut, rally "to urge justice to negroes of Connecticut." There she met black and white activists, including opera singer Marian Anderson.

Dear Nella,

The summer has come and gone bringing us your welcome, news-crammed letters, and not a word have I written you! But your heart tells you, I know that you are never far from my thoughts, and I will not waste words uselessly trying to appease my scolding conscience with apologies.

First, Polly and I thank you for the proud joy we had reading the citation in honor of Robert Braddy for his fine achievement as commander of the "Mansfield," his high strategic skill and devotion to his men. More than ever I glow at the memory of the commissioning of the "Mansfield" in Boston. I was sure then that Robert would grandly cleave his way through other seas of difficulty, and I can divine his satisfaction of having given his all as he again steers his course in home waters.

We are glad you are at last getting some rest in the health-giving aura of Foss Mountain. You will, I am sure, need every bit of that heavenly ozone to keep pace with the exacting tasks and rich interests that crowd your days in Garden City. We can hardly wait until we see you on October 5th, and hear the thoughts with which your mind is evidently brimming over, and cover in talk distances of emotion and experience that outrun epistolary limits.

How happy I am over the news of your friend's generosity to the handicapped in whose release my own freedom is blessed! If the money is allotted to my work for the deaf-blind, it will be as dew upon my sore tried spirit in the too slow process of drawing one of the last and least noticed groups whom good-will seeks out into the fold of human fellowship and restorative self-help.

Now for the flight to Britain. I cannot say the prospect elates me.

It will mean heartache as I sense over there gusts from the world's distress, famine, hope of peace deferred and international discord. But I feel a deep necessity of going. The American Foundation began early this year a drive through the Foundation for the Overseas Blind to aid the destitute sightless of Europe, and I am expected to make further appeals on their behalf. I receive constantly piteous letters from the European blind begging help, and by going to England and Paris, where the headquarters of the Foundation for the Overseas Blind are, I think I can gather firsthand information which I must have in order to lay their desperate needs before the American public effectively and raise funds for their relief.

As Polly told you, we are flying by Pan-American Air-ways to London, October 16th, and later to Paris where I shall no doubt obtain valuable counsel from Mr. Raverat, who is in charge of the work for the Blind of Europe, and perhaps meet a number of the war-blinded servicemen. We do not yet know what our program in London will be, but we shall probably visit the National institute for the Blind and St. Dunstan's. We shall also run up to Scotland to see our friends and Polly's family, to whom I am bound by such tender remembrance and grateful affection. Our return to America will be on December 20th. I imagine it will be another pensive Christmas, shadowed by a fuller realization of the wreckage, human and moral, strewing earth, but the thoughts it evokes will surely prove the grass-roots of better service to others and happiness in driving darkness further back everywhere.

The gathering at Danbury to urge justice to negroes of Connecticut was impressive. Leslie Carter made a splendid speech that encouraged me more than anything I had heard or read on negro emancipation for a long time. Another able man, Rabbi Molino, spoke eloquently. It was sweet to think of your responsive sympathy when I gave my little talk, which seemed well received. To my delight Marian Anderson was in the audience, and I was introduced to her. We all had supper together with Stuart and Sandra Grummon. There was no opportunity to have Marian's moving voice vibrate in my fingers, but perhaps there will be if Polly and I can accept her invitation to her house before we leave.

As you can easily surmise, what I said at the Danbury meeting was only a sign of the unquenchable shame I feel over the situation of our colored people today. This revolt has never slumbered within me since I began to notice for myself how they are degraded, and with what cold-blooded deliberation the keys of knowledge, self-reliance and well-paid employment are taken from them, so that they may not enter the gate of social competence. I cannot forget my humiliation when a colored teacher of high culture and noble dignity who called on me at a hotel in a Southern city was ordered into the freight elevator. It stabs me to the soul to recall my visits to schools for the colored blind which were shockingly backward, and what a hard struggle it was for them to obtain worth while instruction and profitable work because of race prejudice. The continued lynchings and other crimes against negroes, whether in New England or the South, and the unspeakable political exponents of white supremacy, according to all recorded history, augur ill for America's future.

Then I have had a glimpse into another abyss of evil learning how a police officer blinded a colored veteran, reportedly "in self-defence." An atrocity of such an ultimate nature is not only an impeachment of the inertia through which it occurs, it also indicates an undercover of moral infection by traitors to Christianity and to the whole democratic spirit in the best tradition of America—a sinister danger of our being dragged down to the standards of the Middle Ages when torture and mutilation were openly practiced and legally approved!

No sooner had I heard that report than there blazed up in me the concentrated horror and fury that I experienced as a child reading in "King Lear" the scenes where the Duke of Cornwall says to Gloucester,

> "Upon these eyes of thine I'll set my foot.
> . . . .
> Out, vile jelly!
> Where is thy lustre now?"

and Gloucester replies to the crazed King when asked to read a challenge,

> "Were all thy letters suns, I could not see."

But I cannot bear to pursue longer the similarity between Shakespeare's drama and the diabolical reality at Aiken, North Carolina.[1] However, I cannot help adding that the rights of the blind, the deaf and other handicapped groups are invaded wherever brute force defies the law to maim a limb or put out an eye, then calls its conduct "self-defence."

Friday night I was stunned by the radio announcement of Henry Wallace's forced resignation after the President had publicly approved the Madison Square Garden speech, and professed respect for the right of the Secretary of State to express his views. The indignant remarks of various commentators bore out my feelings with regard to the Administration, which has never given me the slightest cause to renounce my extreme left-wing views. I have long suspected that both the Democratic and the Republican parties, backed by high financiers and other powerful vested interests, are working towards imperialism, and now the proof glares me in the face. You know what potential explosions that trend contains. The American people including myself have, I think, been ignominiously slow about supporting Wallace in his struggle to check the disgraceful squabbles between the supposed Allies and restore F. D. Roosevelt's magnanimous foreign policy as a counselor and friend of mankind. True, it is hard for a war-weary generation to stand on guard against those whirlwinds of reaction, but vigilant steadfastness is our only sure citadel from which we can break the force of their onset. Now we must pay for our weakness of the flesh by facing a worse affliction. For a protracted season, I fear, the dark gods whom Alexander the Great, Genghis Khan, Hitler and Mussolini invoked will again try to break open the sanctuary where a new humanity is being moulded to spread over earth, renewing an outworn social order, and to use it in their own combat for dominion. Regardless of Fate's warning, "One world or none," they will bribe some with the slogan, "victory and plenty!" others with "plunder!" and still more with "Race superiority!" while they lay their nets to capture the resources multiplied by a thousand years that science and invention are amassing everywhere. Yet mightier giants will appear in the earth and reach out rapacious hands unto the daughters of men. Under the circumstances it seems blasphemy to talk about "making sacrifices" while the magnificent ones wrought during the recent War are disappearing into the maw of power politics. The thunder and lighting of the Prophets are around us as the spectacle they beheld unrolls before us—conquerors dividing the peoples as booty, prelates of pelf and fear, learned men prostituting science to devise still deadlier weapons, all of them arrayed in the splendor of victory's spoils torn from the nations' storehouses, the depths of the sea and the very atmosphere, blood-red with myriads of lives wasted on battle-fields, in persecution and famine.

But outraged spirit and nature will surely reassert themselves and set aright the plumb-lines by which alone society's new structure can be reared. It is not faith I lack, it is the dizzying nearness of the precipices above which man's nobilities rise that appalls me at present.

We had the interview with the representative from "Coronet" last week. Now she wants a colored photograph of me to go with the article.

We are trying to see Jo and Florence Davidson after their return.

It is a relief to know that it was not necessary for your dear mother to have an operation. I trust she keeps as well as can be expected.

Too bad about the trouble Ann had over transportation facilities when she was taking Robert's children back to Seattle. But I know she was refreshed by her holiday with you.

Oh dear! the "Teacher" book will be at a standstill again. However, as Iphigenia says, "Any road to any end may run," and in some way past hoping I may regain undisturbed leisure for the biography. I am enchanted by the beauty of Euripides' "Iphigenia in Aulis." When I was in college, I read Goethe's play on the same subject, and, while paying him the warmest homage, I consider it far from equal to Euripides' drama in the colorings of Greek life, ritual and philosophy.

Until we see you, and Keith also, I hope, I am, with our love to you both,

        Affectionately your friend,
        Helen Keller

77   How You and I Will Talk

December 6, 1949, letter from Helen Keller to Jo Davidson,
Papers of Jo Davidson, Library of Congress.

Until his death in 1951, Jo Davidson continued as one of Keller's most valued friends. This letter exemplifies his importance to her. It also illustrates the continued merging of Keller's personal and political relationships in this period. With Davidson, she could discuss, be silly, debate politics, and enjoy art. Here she discusses shared friends, the weather, international and domestic politics, as well as poetry. This discussion of South African politics contrasts well with document 71, in which she tells Davidson of her trip to South Africa.

Davidson was also one of the most noted sculptors in the United States and the world and widely known for his progressive and leftist politics. The two shared a love for sculpture, Tom Paine, Walt Whitman, antimilitarism, and a passionate interest in contemporary politics that resulted in vigorous debates and frequent letters. Twice Helen sat for lengthy, intimate periods as Jo made a bust of her and a sculpture of her hands.

Dear Jo,

How Polly and I welcomed your letter full of news and vibrations from the centre of mondial events whose excitement has all these months surged through your life! As we read, we were delighted by your renewed vitality and zest in work, and hopeful that you and dear Florence would settle down in the peace of Becheron[2] for a winter rich in satisfying accomplishment.

Certainly you had a great adventure doing that bust of Tito. Vividly I imagine the fireworks of comment, wit and sarcasm that must have shot back and forth between you two. It is a fascinating spectacle—the factions and schisms, now tragic, now comic, that divide peoples of the same race and faith. Of course my sympathies are with Yugoslavia in its rebellion against what seem arbitrary measures to take away its raw materials for the profit of another country—measures which no real democracy will tolerate. Yugoslavia will, I am sure, lift itself up by its bootstraps with the unbreakable, tough courage that enabled the people to liberate themselves. Great already in the application of revitalizing ideas, full of the spirit of noble self-sacrifice, they only need higher education, social reorganization and a government based on individual and collective liberty to become a constructive power in world progress. I have read a condensation of John Gunther's "Behind Europe's Curtain" in the "World's Digest," printed by the National Institute for the Blind, London—the most radical article about the Balkans I have yet seen in that magazine—and I feel nearer to the truth about Yugoslavia. If this book has come into your hands, Jo, you will notice Mr. Gunther's candid admiration of Tito with a just reserve in regard to Yugoslavia's party politics. If you can write your article on Tito with such a generous attitude—and I know you can—it will be splendid. Not only will it be among the most interesting records in your autobiography, it may be a substantial aid indirectly to the United Nations in its difficult task of creating world harmony.

Glowing memories crowd upon me of the July in 1931 when Teacher, Polly and I visited Yugoslavia, as guests of its Government, in behalf of the blind. Even in Belgrade, under the dread shadow of the throne, the women delighted me with their fine public spirit, civic fire and determination to assert their rights as human beings and to work aside with men in all capacities of service to society. Proudly I reflected that they would be an aggressive force in the regeneration of their country. When we were in Zagreb, I was thrilled to sense an upsurging radicalism in the young people and their lusty outreachings to a new, brighter future. In fact they impressed me with the exultation of free spirits. Now it is a joy to see my prophecies of Yugoslavia's upward ascent at least on the way to fulfillment. I behold

> the frontiers and boundaries of the old aristocracies broken,
> I see the landmarks of European kinds removed,
> I see this day the People beginning their landmarks![3]

By the way, friends have taken us twice to visit the United Nations at Flushing Meadows. Of course as a Leftist I never forget the extreme dangers to which that mighty global organization—the first of its kind in history—is exposed or the persistent bourgeois tendencies always on the alert to pull down the mounting dream of true civilization, but at present it seems animated by a genuine feeling that its triumph means world peace, and its defeat would be a catastrophe, and every possible effort is being made to reach agreements on questions vital to mankind such as atomic energy control. As we listened to the deliberations, my heart throbbed warm with the conviction that the "elite" of all lands—men and women equipped with creative education, public spirit and knowledge extending beyond their own frontiers—are laboring to achieve universal peace. It was our privilege to be introduced for a moment to such personalities as Ralph Bunche, Mr. Malik, Mr. Warren Austin, the Haitian delegate, two ladies from India, and we had luncheon with the sweet wife of Ambassador Jessup. We were sorry not to see Mrs. Roosevelt there, as her Committee was not meeting that day.[4]

One of the discussions at which we were present was concerning a clergyman from South Africa, Mr. Scott, who wished to bring before the United Nations the wrongs and grievances of the natives. The Haitian delegate pleaded Mr. Scott's cause eloquently, but some other members said that, since Mr. Scott was not a representative of South Africa, he was "self-appointed," and it was not in order for him to speak there. The British opposed such action vigorously, declaring that there was no precedent for it. My heart, as always, goes out to the African negroes, but I am not acquainted with all the ins and outs of this question.

Polly and I are negotiating for our trip next year, but our plans are still hanging in the air. Bartley Crum has written inquiring if I was willing to go to Israeli [*sic*] on the basis of payments for articles to be published. Of course I would not dream of undertaking the trip on such a basis, and I have declined. As for my Cousin the Contessa, she wrote me a charming letter asking if Polly and I would stay in her home at Besozza either in April or May. I told her May would suit us admirably. She has not replied since. Her eyes are giving her such serious trouble that her doctor has ordered her to use them as little as possible. So we are not yet sure just what we shall do, but happen what may, we shall be with you and Florence at Becheron in June. Then how you and I will talk, and how I shall drink in the loveliness and peace of the French countryside!

Last summer was not to our liking—extreme heat and the longest drought in New England history—and it continues. We just kept the garden alive, weeding, clipping and watering morning and evening. Our multifarious tasks insisted on being done at once without fail while our bodies dissolved in perspiration. Finally, August 11th, we struck and ran away to spend a few blessedly idle days with Katharine Cornell at Vineyard Haven. There was never a sweeter or more understanding hostess than Katharine. We just slept, ate and walked with her arm-in-arm along the beach. She invited Van Wyck and Gladys over, and we all had a marvelous time talking and admiring the artistic quaintness of Katharine's summer home, "Chip Chop." She was rehearsing Kate O'Brien's "That Lady," and she permitted us to read the manuscript. On November 22nd—the opening night—we were the guests of Eddie and Ethel—we saw Katharine as Ana de Mendoza. Whatever the critics may say about it as a stock comedy, Katharine's acting is magnificent as always, and we were overcome emotionally by her interviews with King Philip II and her heroism when, faithful to Antonio Perez, she was finally walled up in dark silence.

We see Van Wyck and Gladys often. We have been over to their pleasant new house, and they lunched with us ten days ago when Nella Braddy was visiting us. Your ears must have burned, we spoke of you and Florence and rejoiced that you were writing your autobiography. That will indeed be a sublime act in your life so brimming over with the drama of your dynamic personality. Don't let anything entice you away from your book, Jo, all your friends are waiting for its appearance.

At a big gathering in Ethel Clark's house last summer we saw Frederic and Florence March. They were bearing up wonderfully under the wicked practices of the witch-hunters. Also we met Mr. Luce's sister and Sara Churchill, who was playing at the Westport summer theatre in "The Philadelphia Story."

Hot anger leaps up in me as I consider the cruel ordeal which David Lilienthal has endured, and which has led to his resignation. We could ill spare a man of such noble character and distinguished abilities from the service of the nation, but now he will be able to give an opinion when it is necessary on atomic energy without the tension which his position has entailed upon him.[5]

Pitilessly I am pulled away from this letter by the demands of work, and I must stop. With Polly's and my affection to Florence and yourself, and with a heartful of Christmas Blessings, I am

> Devotedly your friend,
> Helen Keller

78 The Hearts of True Friends

July 24, 1950, letter from Helen Keller to Jo Davidson,
Papers of Jo and Florence Davidson, Library of Congress.

As one of the most important of Keller's friends and political dueling partners, Jo Davidson provided friendship and uncompromising access to the politics, intellectual debates, beauty, and joy of the rest of the world. This letter reveals the joy Keller found in the friendship, particularly during her visits with him and his wife Florence at their home in Becheron, France, where Davidson had gone in order to escape possible McCarthyite attacks.

Dear Jo and Florence,

I am going to make sure of this letter by writing to you precious friends the first thing today. Ever since our homecoming, I have been trying to express what you both meant to Polly and me in a letter that would communicate the quality of our visit with you and the extraordinary charm of your unique personalities, but I shall never be able to say how wonderful you were to us. I can only say with all my heart that you gave us abundantly of yourselves and of your home, and that the spontaneity in everything you did and said warms us.

A strange loneliness came over me as you left us aboard the "America." That very night I had flown over the lengthening miles between us and Paris in my dreams, and I was throwing my arms around you. The aura of your affection still holds us in its close embrace. There are friends the thought of whom stimulates one like Spring sunlight, and that is how Polly and I felt under your roof.

What an illuminating experience it was for us to be among the many people surrounding you in Paris! Your conversation full of expansive good fellowship, humor, the generous desire to understand views different from your own and the gay laughter that rippled in your presence are memories that will ever be radiant in my mind. And there also Florence's perceptive soul, the fire of her individuality, the countless attentions she paid us.

Then what an adorable way you had of heaping up our pleasures yet higher, no matter how much occupied you might be entertaining artists, writers and wits and introducing us to them! Like the birds and butterflies among the luscious berries and the honeyed blossoms at Becheron, I had through you many a choice taste of the intimate life, beauty and history of Paris that will sweeten my tasks at the desk when I must live without dreams to raise me above the dullness of the work-a-day world. The delightful cafes at which we lunched or dined —the open-air markets you showed us—the parks and small circuses in almost every quarter of the city that afford its children a happy playtime—an old house with narrow-paned windows or a row of noble trees shading the street within a stone's throw of the traffic and the shops, our drives to St. Germain and Fontainebleau Forest, the Eiffel Tower and Montmartre where my spirit mingled as never before with the vibrant, versatile, indefinable soul of Paris speaking out of the vicissitudes of centuries and diverse civilizations.

The memory of you and Florence visiting Italy with us makes me all the happier that my dream of almost a lifetime was fulfilled. Your enthusiasm for all great art and knowledge of the times in which artists lived gave wings to my imagination as I inspected masterpieces by Michelangelo and Donatello or the glories I could touch in the cathedrals and palaces of Florence. Absorbed in observing sculptures, paintings and buildings, you never forgot to share your delight with me, and I wish I could command scintillating words to thank you. Alas, I have not Prospero's art to release in a letter the exquisite Ariel that keeps singing to me of the magnificence of the "Flowering City" during three centuries, of its persistent struggle until the people were recognized and the hope that it may rise in a new role—a habitation fit for a healthy, free population contributing to the welfare of Italy and the whole world. But I feel as you do that as long as that city's past works of genius last they will shower fertility upon life's barren places, a rich largess of loveliness and creative faith upon those who pay sincere homage to that illustrious city—the city of Michelangelo, Galileo, Savonarola and Dante.

The drive with you two from Florence was tantalizing in the views we had of the mountains and the enchanting Mediterranean coast and lovely places all through sweet Provence to be explored and the still more interesting things you had to tell us. St. Paul in a region which had never known the yoke of a grand seigneur and the ruins of the Roman amphitheatre in Orange thrilled me with a sense of old France that I had not experienced even in reading. Despite the ruinously delectable luncheon you gave us at the "Pyramids," I was sorry not to have more time to get acquainted with Lyons, one of the citadels of the free spirit with which I had become familiar in books.

But O, the heavenly weeks Polly and I passed at Becheron! O, the uniqueness of everything—the old rambling, hospitable manoir with its wealth of historic associations, quaint stonewalls and floors and plants in every window—your studio with the lavender tall and odorous at the door where for the first time I was happy having my portrait painted, and the additional gratification of Polly's being in it—the huge cherry tree where I refreshed myself after each sitting—the garden with its handsome espaliers and grand old trees where you, Jo, and I walked arm-in-arm among the boxwood hedges, flowers and vegetables. It was unforgettable the way Florence reflected in her soul the hill where she sat in front of the house, the miracles of light and shadow in the tranquil fields or the loveliness of the placid Indre as we drifted along in the boat. Wherever we went I had an exquisite sensation of odors thronging about me as if Aphrodite were near,

> Her neck refulgent, and disheveled hair,
> Which, flowing from her shoulders, reached the ground,
> And widely spread ambrosial scents around.[6]

Besides, there were the evenings when Polly and I had the dear privilege to read chapters from your autobiography, sympathizing by turns with your patient, scholarly father and your vigorous mother whose amazing energy has survived in you, sighing over your obstacles and disappointments, laughing over the comical adventures that befell you, rejoicing in the recognition that lifted your genius into the light. Jo, you have lived greatly both in art and in mind, and I believe that when your book finally emerges from the forge of your craftsmanship, it will impress deeply those who read it and ultimately be a source of pride and satisfaction to you. You have a tremendous worthwhile message embodying a philosophy of sculpture, and delivering it will be another of your works of inspiration and far-reaching influence.

Our discussions over a glass of wine and hors'd'oeuvre or at teatime or dinner about human nature, freedom, art and the nemesis of the Roman Catholic Church were to me a mine of independent thinking. I could not always avoid clashes between our points of view —not antagonistic, but varied in their angles and methods of approach. However, I always wanted to understand your attitude towards world problems. Not having read Karl Marx had enabled you to maintain a fresh outlook and discourse with luminous instruction on one subject after another. I had never had a tolerant view of the character, objectives and flaws of capitalism as you have, Jo, and I fear I am incorrigible. A very few of the rich whom I meet appeal to me eloquently, and are ready to surrender their all for the good of humanity if need be, but I have never felt close to them even before I became a

Socialist. So you see the beneficent effect your wise, charitable ideas had upon my wayward, impetuous mind, and what a precious stream of wisdom your talk was about Lincoln Steffens and H. G. Wells. Your courageous optimism encouraged me in holding fast to the faith that out of the appalling blunders, stupidities and aggressions of the present humanity will yet evolve justice and harmony.

And I learned wonderful things from books as well as from your conversation. I had never expected to find Anatole France's "l'ile des Pengouins" and "La Revolte des Anges" or Voltaire's "Candide" in Braille, and it took you to get them for me! It was more than I could have hoped—having you there while I read them and hearing your comments upon their significance and their influence upon France. I shiver as I reflect the power that their dynamite will have when they are dropped into the unthinking minds of humanity.

Oh, I could say much more, but the hearts of true friends are the best interpreters of the deeds of good and the deep-down thoughts that underlie their affection. I just wanted you to know what lavish libations of happiness you both poured upon us. It was hard to part from your household—Marceline, Julie, Colette, Ginette and Gino. No wonder I am not quite at home yet, I have so often a vivid consciousness of being at Becheron.

We had a very calm passage home, and were warmly welcomed by a few friends besides Herbert—Ethel Clark and representatives of the American Foundation for the Blind, and Mr. G. A. Pfeiffer who took us back to Westport in his comfortable, big station wagon. Ever since our arrival we have faced an eruption of mail that no one could answer for us, and the servant problems remain unsolved. But Polly and I are trying to take things easy and keep the balm of Becheron. Every morning we are out at half-past five working in the garden, and the peace of those hours settles upon me like dew that does not vanish during the day.

Your letters, Jo and Florence, have come, and they fill us with gladness—and nostalgia too. We can just see your portrait in your beautiful frame, and its high praise by your friends is sweet flattery to us, especially as you, Jo, created our likenesses. But you have confirmed our feeling that those who know you will not permit you to abandon sculpture into which the best of your life has been expended.

The pictures you took on the Italian trip are here too, and Polly is delighted with them. It is good news indeed that the President of France is sitting for you. May other orders for busts rain upon you before long!

Your marvelous birthday gift, Jo, is on my desk beside Passionnara, and I know that if my "Teacher" book is half worthy of the subject, it will be thanks to Walt Whitman. Every time I use your perfume, Florence, I shall think of you and the sweet celebration of my birthday we had together in your home—more beautiful than any publicity, however splendid, could have made it.

Please remember us warmly to your household, and give a big love-pat to Whiskey. It was darling of you, Jo, to tell us that we are beloved by every member of that blessed family.

With our affectionate embraces for you both, I am,

Devotedly your friend,
Helen Keller

79 Beneath the Fun and Gaiety There Was a Serious Motif

January 31, 1951, letter from Helen Keller to Jo Davidson, Papers of Jo Davidson, Library of Congress.

Christmas 1950 was the first holiday season Keller spent since 1936 without Herbert Haas. In September, Haas, the man who had served as the household caretaker since the years of Macy's illness, died. Keller and Polly Thomson loved and depended on him. When Keller first wrote of his death to Davidson, she described not only the loneliness that had descended on the household but also referred obliquely to the question of who was going to perform his former tasks, such as lawn-work, snow shoveling, shopping, and general household maintenance. Haas's death made more difficult the already complex household arrangements. Nella Braddy Henney, other friends, and Keller's financial trustees worried almost constantly about what would happen when Polly Thomson died. Polly's niece Effie tried to join the household, but the new relationships didn't work.[7]

Jo and Florence Davidson's gift of perfumed blankets is an example of their thoughtfulness. Keller enjoyed scent, and the pair often gave her scented items. For the results of Keller's planned trip to South Africa, see document 71.

Dear Jo:

How adorable you and Florence were to remember Polly and me so fragrantly last Christmas! We love the perfumed blankets, and whenever we catch a whiff from them, it will gladden us to know that they were a gift from two precious friends who are always in our hearts. Thank you ever so much.

Polly was delighted with the snapshots you sent. How I envy her the faculty of seeing their excellence! They make us long more than ever to be with you, they call up such intriguing memories of us all standing on the steps of the Roman Forum in Orange, France, and of you, Florence and Whiskey at Becheron. In fact they are so significant and charming that we shall put them in the "Helen Keller Files."

Florence's note about Ettu[8] warmed us. It was pitiful to see Ettu's helplessness while it lasted, but by now she has regained her old vigor, and is as full of importance as of old bossing me. Her zest is marvelous playing with a splendid ball that "Uncle Gus" as we call Mr. G. A. Pfeiffer sent her in anticipation of her recovery.

We were interested to hear that Larry Adler was to give a concert in Paris and that you would be present. What wonderful folks you are, always giving aid to artists in need! We hope the concert was a gratifying success.

But—and you know the butt is the big end of the log, you must stay quietly at Becheron and complete your autobiography. From your letter which I greatly enjoyed I was glad to learn that the book "is on its last lap," and that Florence is seeing it through. You gave me a good laugh describing Steffens as Atlas carrying the world on his back with your assistance, and yourself ducking under, stepping aside and watching, "and nothing happened—the world stayed where it was."—

No, it continued its celestial travels, and according to the latest reports it is still traveling towards Jupiter, not deigning to rest upon any support of mortals! Seriously, writing out your memories, thrilling or tragic, of the Madison Square Garden Rally for Franklin D. Roosevelt, the formation of the Progressive Citizens of America and other world events will be a satisfaction to you and, I trust, quiet whatever disturbing voices may come to you from the past.

Naturally, the last Yule-tide was a sad one in our home, as Herbert has always been with us during the festivities. But Katharine Cornell —bless her beautiful heart—invited us to the picturesque old Dutch house at Sneden's Landing—which she has rented from the Tonetti family many years—for the weekend. The fire of huge logs blazing away, a great Christmas tree in the corner, Katharine in her long plaid robes and the happy friends who foregathered there gave us a sense of joy in the season that had not seemed possible before. Among the guests were Brenda Forbes who was playing in "Ring Around the Moon." We saw the play not long ago, and were enchanted with it. How nimbly Christopher Fry, who translated it, caught the spirit of la comedie francaise. Beneath the fun and gaiety there was a serious motif—conveying the futility of wealth and self-indulgence and the preciousness of work as a preservative of happiness. We were sorry that it was found necessary to close that delightful play.

I am glad you liked my speech at the United Nations celebration in Hartford. The present world situation does not look favorable for peace, and I am much worried over the censorship of news from Korea, but I hope against hope that Great Britain, India, and the large peace party in France may steer our storm-tossed earth ship into quiet waters. As you know, some say that the Korean war cannot be localized, but history gives me reason to think it can. A military man of unusual intelligence once told me that after Napoleon had been banished to St. Helena in 1815, everybody talked long and anxiously about the imminence of a general war which never broke out for a hundred years. So I hold fast to my belief that the United Nations is still "a platform where," as you say, "men of different races and languages can meet and be heard," and ultimately avert a third world war.

Naturally Polly and I are finding out all we can about South Africa before we sail on February 16th. Two weeks ago we went to see Mathilde and Robert Pfeiffer in Cambridge, and they introduced us to a Mr. Marshall, who had visited South Africa. He held us spellbound talking about the native tribes, especially the Bushmen whose innate goodness and independent spirit, he hoped, would enable them to build up their own civilization without imitating the vices of the whites. He showed us an appealing carving of a native with—not a pick or shovel in his hand, but an adorable baby on his arm. We looked at some wonderful pictures he and his son had taken of the flora and fauna of Africa. Even the shy zebras they had managed by photographing them from a hiding place in the tall grass.

I learned more from the historic point of view when Polly and I attended the colored debutantes' cotillion in Harlem the other night. As you know, Dr. and Mrs. Clayton Powell[9] are among our friends—Dr. Powell is editor of the Amsterdam News—and it was they who invited us to the cotillion. Dr. Bunche[10] was the guest of honor, and it was my good fortune to talk with him about his visit to South Africa and his checkered impressions of the country. He told me that he found the native workers in mines, factories and on the land more than a century behind the progress of the workers in Britain after the industrial reform legislation of 1832. You know, Jo, how miserable and overworked they were before that date, and how Elizabeth Browning was moved to write "The Cry of the Children." From what Dr. Bunche said, I fear that it will be a long while yet before an enlightened attitude is adopted towards the native workers in Africa, but I am inspired by his brave faith in the forward movement of mankind, even if often interrupted, and in the dissolving force exerted by higher ideas and sentiments that will exceed our small anti-social feelings of today. There is no royal road of logic to world-change, as you so wisely said, speaking of Tito and his fight for Yugoslavia's independence of all foreign interference. What I hear about the speeding up of the human brain during the past three centuries, I anticipate mightier works of religion, science, art and philosophy than anything we have dreamed.

We see Van Wyck Brooks and Gladys now and then. Then your ears must burn, we always talk about you, our magical visit with you and Florence and your book.

I am enclosing a letter to Ambassador Ristic. You may be interested to read it before you forward it to him.

Oh dear! I must turn to other letters and wind up my home correspondence before we start our voyage. With our heartfelt love to you both, I am

Affectionately your friend,
Helen Keller

80 All that Is Greatest and Most Beneficent in American Womanhood

August 5, 1957, letter from Helen Keller to Eleanor Roosevelt; Folder:
Helen Keller; General Correspondence, 1957–1962; Papers of
Eleanor Roosevelt; Franklin D. Roosevelt Library, Hyde Park, New York.

Eleanor Roosevelt's weekly newspaper column, "My Day," was one of the most successful in the United States. In 1957, she used the power of her column to celebrate Keller's seventy-seventh birthday and to praise Nancy Hamilton's film, *The Unconquered*, which would ultimately win a 1955 Academy Award. This recognition by a woman she so admired thrilled Keller.

Dear Mrs. Roosevelt,

It was wonderful to have my birthday celebrated with such generous praise in your column, "My Day." I cannot feel that I deserve such beautiful tributes. For I have seen the war-wounded and many others overcoming handicaps far greater than any I have known, and their heroism has electrified me as no ambition or faith in myself could have done. But I am deeply grateful for encouragement from one whom I love and look up to as representing all that is greatest and most beneficent in American womanhood.

Truly I am thrilled to hear how enthusiastically my film is appreciated everywhere in America. If it arouses widespread desire among the people to assist all the qualified handicapped to develop their abilities and gifts, I shall be in the seventh heaven of happiness.

With affectionate greetings from Miss Thomson and myself, I am,

Sincerely your friend,

Helen Keller

NOTES

Notes to the Introduction

1. Keller, *Midstream*, 313.
2. Keller, *Midstream*, 313.
3. March 9, 1900, letter from Helen Keller to Alexander Graham Bell, Alexander Graham Bell Family Papers, box 131, Library of Congress. Copyright dedicated to the public.
4. Keller, *Story of My Life*, 32.

Notes to Part One, Section A

1. Philanthropist John Spaulding.
2. Helen Keller, *The Story of My Life*, 44.
3. Sophia Hopkins served as Anne Sullivan's housemother while she was a student at Perkins. Hopkins continued as a confidante and correspondent of Sullivan's.
4. Henry Wadsworth Longfellow's poem "Hymn to the Night" includes the stanza: "From the cool cisterns of the midnight air / My spirit drank repose; / The fountain of perpetual peace flowers there,— / From those deep cisterns flows."
5. Sir Walter Scott, "The Lady of the Lake."
6. Eleanor Hutton, the wife of wealthy Princeton resident Laurence Hutton, served as a principal fundraiser and donor for Keller and Sullivan.
7. Agnes Irwin.
8. Most likely Henry Drummond's *The Ascent of Man*, a collection of the Lowell Lectures he delivered in Boston in 1893.
9. Ida Chamberlin.
10. Helen Keller, *The Story of My Life*, 63. For more on Keller's relationship with Bell, see Nielsen, *The Radical Lives of Helen Keller*, 1–3, 41.
11. For more information on Bridgman, see Freeberg, *The Education of Laura Bridgman*; Gitter, *The Imprisoned Guest*.

Notes to Part Two, section A

1. Keller, *Midstream*, 34.

Notes to Part Two, section B

1. *New York Times Magazine*, February 27, 1938, 13.

2. This comes from James Russell Lowell's 1844 poem against slavery, "The Current Crisis."

3. *New York Times*, May 6, 1913. Keller's endorsement and participation in suffrage parades and rallies led by the National Woman's Party, the radical suffrage organization led by Alice Paul that picketed the White House almost daily for several years, allied her with the radical elements of the suffrage movement. For more on Keller's socialism, see Nielsen, *The Radical Lives of Helen Keller*, 24–28, 32–33, 35, 43, 58.

4. Emmeline Pankhurst, a British suffrage activist.

5. Einhorn, *Helen Keller, Public Speaker*, 107.

6. Lodge was a British physicist and spiritualist.

7. Colossians 4:11.

8. Arturo Giovannitti to John Macy, October 2, 1913, Arturo Giovannitti file, AFB.

9. This is likely Herbert S. Bigelow, a Cincinnati minister and Progressive Era politician who preached a social Gospel message.

10. Frank Little was an IWW labor organizer lynched in 1917.

11. John Brown was hanged for raiding the Union arsenal in Harpers Ferry, Virginia, in 1859. Of his hanging, Ralph Waldo Emerson wrote that his "martyrdom if it shall be perfected, will make the gallows as glorious as the cross."

Notes to Part Two, section C

1. Act I, scene 5 of Shakespeare's Hamlet reads "For every man hath business and desire, / Such as it is, and for my own poor part, / I will go pray."

2. Keller, *Midstream*, 36.

3. *Mathilda Ziegler Magazine* was a leading monthly braille publication of news and literature.

4. This refers to Keller's *The Song of the Stone Wall*, a lengthy poem published in small book form in 1910.

5. Here she's referring to Wilkins Micawber, a Charles Dickens character of eternal optimism.

6. Biographer Joseph Lash characterizes the surgery as undescribed. Dorothy Herrmann argues it to be a hysterectomy. Lash, *Helen and Teacher*, 378; Herrmann, *Helen Keller*, 182.

7. Keller, *Midstream*, 141.

8. The placement of this section is unclear, though most likely occurs here.

9. Keller, *Teacher*, 126. For more on the Macy marriage, see Nielsen, *The Radical Lives of Helen Keller*.

10. 1 Corinthians 13.

11. Keller, *Midstream*, 34.

12. This is from the poem "The Birth of Galahad" by Richard Hovey.

13. Foner, *Helen Keller*, 73; *New York Times*, December 20, 1915.

14. Foner, *Helen Keller*, 83–84; Snyder, "Women, Wobblies, and Workers' Rights." See also Foner, *Helen Keller*, 57, 91–93, 94–97.

15. Keller, *Midstream*, 216.

16. March 28, 1920, letter from Kate Keller to Helen Keller, AFB.

17. Keller, *Midstream*, 223.

Notes to Part Three, section A

1. Lash, *Helen and Teacher*, 553. For more on Keller's religious views, see Nielsen, *The Radical Lives of Helen Keller*, 10, 20–21, 39, 64, 86, 100.

2. Keller, *My Religion*, 122.

3. Keller, *My Religion*, 46, 47, 122.

4. Lash, *Helen and Teacher*, 560–561; Nielsen, *The Radical Lives of Helen Keller*, 54–55.

5. Keller, *Midstream*, 6; Lash, *Helen and Teacher*, 566.

6. The omission of the name of this group is significant. It is likely the radical and highly controversial Industrial Workers of the World (IWW).

7. Keller referred to March 3 as her "soul birthday," for it was the anniversary of the day in 1887 that Anne Sullivan entered her life.

8. John Greenleaf Whittier.

9. Mr. George A. Pfeiffer, Trustee of the American Foundation for the Blind.

10. Robert Louis Stevenson, "Virginibus Puerisque and Other Papers," chapter 3.

11. Matthew Arnold, "Tristam and Iseult," part I.

Notes to Part Three, section B

1. Ned Holmes, an architect and inventor they had known from Cambridge days.

2. Address by M. C. Migel, November 14, 1932, AFB.

3. Keller, *The Story of My Life*, 63.

4. HK to Walter Holmes, November 19, 1938, Walter Holmes file, AFB. See also Nielsen, *The Radical Lives of Helen Keller*, 53, 79–80.

5. Nielsen, *The Radical Lives of Helen Keller*, 77–79.

Notes to Part Three, section C

1. Clipping from *The Japan Advertiser*, July 6, 1937, HK, President's Personal File 2169, Franklin D. Roosevelt Library, Hyde Park, New York.

2. Helen Keller to Walter Holmes, May 17, 1939, AFB; *New York Times*, August 15, 1939; Helen Keller to Walter Holmes, May 9, 1941, AFB.

Notes to Part Three, section D

1. Keller, *Teacher*, 180–181.

2. Lincoln Steffens, *Autobiography of Lincoln Steffens* (New York: Harcourt, Brace and Company, 1931).

3. Robert Irwin of the American Foundation for the Blind.

4. Keller, *Helen Keller's Journal*, 9, 35. For more on the relationship between the two women, see Nielsen, *The Radical Lives of Helen Keller*.

5. Keller, *Helen Keller's Journal*, 80, 83.

6. Keller, *Teacher*, 222. Nella Braddy Henney told the same story: Henney, *With Helen Keller*, 7. Lash, *Helen and Teacher*, 636.

7. Anna Roosevelt Boettiger, Franklin and Eleanor Roosevelt's daughter.

8. Sara Roosevelt, Franklin Delano Roosevelt's mother.

9. Anna Roosevelt Boettiger, Franklin and Eleanor Roosevelt's daughter.

10. This likely refers to director Nancy Hamilton. Hamilton's film on Keller, *The Unconquered,* would ultimately win a 1955 Academy Award. The film is known both as "The Unconquered" and "Helen Keller—in her Story."

11. Helen Keller to Nella Braddy Henney, January 4, 1943, AFB.

12. Westport, Connecticut neighbors Stuart and Sandra Grummons.

13. Stuart Chase, actually an economist, was married to author Marian Tyler.

14. An Austrian violinist.

15. Van Wyck Brooks would later write a biography of Keller in 1956.

16. Helen Keller to Nella Braddy Henney, June 23, 1950, AFB; Davidson, *Between Sittings,* 333; Jo Davidson to Helen Keller, March 6, 1948, Papers of Jo Davidson, Library of Congress. See also Brooks, *Helen Keller,* chapter 9.

17. This comes from Henry David Thoreau's "A Week on the Concord and Merrimack Rivers."

18. A Chinese philosopher and theologian.

19. A film producer.

20. *New York Times,* August 24, 1944.

Notes to Part Four, section A

1. Nielsen, *The Radical Lives of Helen Keller,* 116–118; Lash, *Helen and Teacher,* 746; Keller, *Teacher,* 36.

2. Erysipelas is an uncomfortable skin infection.

Notes to Part Four, section B

1. Keller met Takashi Nagai, a physician and scientist who had survived the attack, but now lay dying of radiation sickness. The famed Christian, widowed by the attack, authored books that reflected on his imminent death, on what would happen to his young children, on the future of Japan, and on the attack's theological significance. Like many others, Keller visited his deathbed in a small iron hut near the center of the explosion. Nielsen, *The Radical Lives of Helen Keller,* 93.

2. Osaka speech to social workers, 1948, Iwahashi file, AFB; address to women, Foreign Travel 1948 Japan, AFB.

3. For more on this trip, see Nielsen, *The Radical Lives of Helen Keller,* 87–97.

4. *New York Times*, February 8, 1951.

5. Whuskey was one of the Davidson's dogs.

6. This is a diamond mine.

7. Sir Ernest Oppenheimer, a German-born South African philanthropist and industrialist, invested heavily in mining.

8. Jan Christiaan Smuts, a defender of South Africa's racial divisions, became president during World War II.

9. Stuart Cloete was a South African novelist, many of whose works were banned by the South African government.

10. For more on this trip, see Nielsen, *The Radical Lives of Helen Keller*, 106–112.

11. Jo Davidson died late 1951.

12. Nielsen, *The Radical Lives of Helen Keller*, 113–114.

13. Eric Boulter, Field Director, AFOB to Mr. John Stegmaier, Public Affairs Officer, Bureau of Far Eastern Affairs, December 18, 1954, General Records of the Department of State, 1950–1954, Central Decimal File. 032 HK; Foreign Service Dispatch from U.S. Embassy Rangoon, June 3, 1955, General Records of the Department of State, 1950–1954, Central Decimal File. 032 HK.

14. Prime Minister Jawaharlal Nehru.

Notes to Part Four, section C

1. In 1946, police officers in Aiken, South Carolina (not North), beat and blinded African American veteran Isaac Woodard.

2. Becheron, France.

3. Walt Whitman, "Years of the Modern," *Leaves of Grass*.

4. Eleanor Roosevelt chaired the United Nations effort to write the Universal Declaration of Human Rights.

5. Lilienthal opposed continued atomic weapons development and proposed that an international body be established to monitor research on atomic energy in the hopes of avoiding rivalry between nations. The growing Red Scare and accusations of Communist sympathies made the approval of his nomination increasingly unlikely. Jo Davidson and Nella Braddy Henney also supported Lilienthal. Nielsen, *The Radical Lives of Helen Keller*, 84.

6. This is from Virgil's Aeneid, I, 402–405.

7. Undated letter from HK to Jo Davidson (the first written since Herbert's death), Papers of Jo Davidson, Library of Congress; Lash, *Helen and Teacher*, 714–718, 722.

8. Ettu was one of Keller's dogs.

9. Rev. Dr. Adam Clayton Powell, Sr., minister at the Abyssinian Baptist Church, one of the largest and most dynamic congregations in Harlem.

10. Ralph Bunche was the first person of African descent to be awarded the Nobel Peace Prize (1950, only months previously), a leading U.S. expert on African and colonial affairs, and a fierce advocate of decolonization.

SELECTED BIBLIOGRAPHY

Books Authored by Helen Keller

Keller, Helen. *Helen Keller's Journal*. London: Michael Joseph, 1938.

————. *Light in My Darkness*. Revised and edited by Ray Silverman. West Chester, Penn.: Chrysalia Press, 2000 [Revised version of *My Religion*, 1927].

————. *Midstream: My Later Life*. New York: Greenwood Press, [1929] 1968.

————. *My Religion*. New York: Citadel Press, 1927, 1960, 1963.

————. *Out of the Dark: Essays, Letters, and Addresses on Physical and Social Vision*. New York: Doubleday, Page and Company, 1914.

————. *The Story of My Life*. New York: Dover Publications, [1903] 1996.

————. *Teacher*. New York: Doubleday, 1956.

————. *The World I Live In*. New York: Century Company, 1908.

Books and Articles Pertaining to Helen Keller

Barrick, Mac E. "The Helen Keller Joke Cycle." *Journal of American Folklore* 93/370 (1980): 441–449.

Blaxall, Arthur William. *Helen Keller Under the Southern Cross*. Cape Town & Johannesburg: Juta and Company, 1952.

Brooks, Van Wyck. *Helen Keller: Sketch for a Portrait*. New York: E.P. Dutton, 1956.

Clark, Brett, and John Bellamy Foster. "Helen Keller and the Touch of Nature." *Organization and Environment* 15/3 (September 2002): 278–284.

Cohen, Paula Marantz. "Helen Keller and the American Myth." *Yale Review* 85/1 (January 1997): 1–20.

Cotton, Carol. "Helen Keller's First Public Speech." *Alabama Historical Quarterly* 37 (1975): 68–72.

Cressman, Jodi. "Helen Keller and the Mind's Eyewitness." *Western Humanities Review* 54/2 (Fall 2000): 108–123.

Crow, Liz. "Helen Keller: Rethinking the Problematic Icon." *Disability and Society* 15/6 (2000): 845–859.

Einhorn, Lois J. *Helen Keller, Public Speaker: Sightless but Seen, Deaf but Heard*. Westport, Conn.: Greenwood Press, 1998.

Fleming, Mary M., and William H. Ross, "On Behalf of the I.W.W.: Helen Keller's Involvement in the Labor Movement." *Review of Disability Studies* 1/1 (2004): 70–79.

Foner, Philip S., ed. *Helen Keller: Her Socialist Years*. New York: International Publishers, 1967.

Giffin, Frederick C. "The Radical Vision of Helen Keller." *International Social Science Review* 59/4 (1984): 27–32.

Harrity, Richard, and Ralph G. Martin. *The Three Lives of Helen Keller*. Garden City, N.Y.: Doubleday, 1962.

Henney, Nella Braddy. *Anne Sullivan Macy: The Story Behind Helen Keller*. New York: Doubleday, 1933.

———. *With Helen Keller*. North Conway: North Conway Publishing Company, 1974.

Herrmann, Dorothy. *Helen Keller: A Life*. New York: Alfred A. Knopf, 1998.

Hickock, Lorena. *The Touch of Magic; the Story of Helen Keller's Great Teacher, Anne Sullivan Macy*. New York: Dodd, Mead, 1961.

Klages, Mary. "What to Do With Helen Keller Jokes: A Feminist Act." In Regina Barreca, ed., *New Perspectives on Women and Comedy*. Philadelphia: Gordon and Breach, 1992: 13–22.

Kleege, Georgina. "Blind Rage." *Southwest Review* 83/1 (1998): 53–61.

———. "Helen Keller and 'The Empire of the Normal.'" *American Quarterly* 52/2 (June 2000): 322–325.

———. "Letters to Helen." *Michigan Quarterly Review* 37/3 (Summer 1998): 371–391.

Lash, Joseph. *Helen and Teacher: The Story of Helen Keller and Anne Sullivan Macy*. New York: Addison-Wesley, 1980.

Nielsen, Kim E. "Helen Keller and the Politics of Civic Fitness." In Paul Longmore and Lauri Umansky, eds., *The New Disability History: American Perspectives*. New York: New York University Press, 2001: 268–290.

———. *The Radical Lives of Helen Keller*. New York: New York University Press, 2004.

Pelka, Fred. "Helen Keller and the FBI." *Ragged Edge* 5 (2001): 19–22, 35, 36.

Porter, Edna, ed. *Double Blossoms: Helen Keller Anthology*. New York: Lewis Copeland, 1931.

Smith, J. David. "The Challenge of Advocacy: The Different Voices of Helen Keller and Burton Blatt." *Mental Retardation* 35/2 (April 1997): 138–140.

Snyder, Robert E. "Women, Wobblies, and Workers' Rights: The 1912 Textile Strike in Little Falls, New York." In Joseph Conlin, ed. *At the Point of Production: The Local History of the IWW*. Westport, Conn.: Greenwood Press, 1981: 27–48.

———. "Women, Wobblies, and Workers' Rights: The 1912 Textile Strike in Little Falls, New York." *New York History* 60 (January 1979): 29–57.

Swan, Jim. "Touching Words: Helen Keller, Plagiarism, Authorship." In Martha Woodmansee and Peter Jaszi, eds., *The Construction of Authorship: Textual Appropriation in Law and Literature.* Durham: Duke University Press, 1994: 57–100.

Wolfe, Kathi. "Helen Keller." *Mainstream* 20/10 (August 1996): 33–39.

———. "Helen Keller, Radical." *Utne Reader* (July/August 1996): 16.

———. "War Work." *Mainstream* 19/10 (August 1995): 17–23.

Young, Iola. "Helen Keller Came." *Pacific Historian* 24 (1980): 55–59.

Autobiographies

Davidson, Jo. *Between Sittings: An Informal Autobiography of Jo Davidson.* New York: Dial Press, 1951.

Steffens, Lincoln. *Autobiography of Lincoln Steffens.* New York: Harcourt, Brace, 1931.

Theorizing Disability and Disability History in the United States

Baynton, Douglas D. "Disability and the Justification of Inequality in American History." In Paul K. Longmore and Lauri Umansky, eds., *The New Disability History: American Perspectives.* New York: New York University Press, 2001: 33–57.

———. *Forbidden Signs: American Culture and the Campaign against Sign Language.* Chicago: University of Chicago Press, 1996.

Bodgan, Robert. *Freak Show: Presenting Human Oddities for Amusement and Profit.* Chicago: University of Chicago Press, 1988.

Bragg, Lois, ed. *Deaf World: A Historical Reader and Primary Sourcebook.* New York: New York University Press, 2001.

Buchanan, Robert M. *Illusions of Equality: Deaf Americans in School and Factory, 1850–1950.* Washington, D.C.: Gallaudet University Press, 1999.

Burch, Susan. *Signs of Resistance: American Deaf Cultural History, 1900 to World War II.* New York: New York University Press, 2002.

Davis, Lennard J. *Bending Over Backwards: Disability, Dismodernism and Other Difficult Positions.* New York: New York University Press, 2002.

———, ed. *The Disability Studies Reader.* New York: Routledge, 1997.

———. *Enforcing Normalcy: Disability, Deafness, and the Body.* New York: Verso, 1995.

Easton, Terry. "Identity and Politics in the *Silent Worker* Newspaper: Print Publication and the Laboring Deaf Body." *Women's Studies Quarterly* 26/1&2 (1998): 56–74.

Gallagher, Hugh Gregory. *FDR's Splendid Deception.* New York: Dodd, Mead, 1985.

Groce, Nora. *Everyone Here Spoke Sign Language: Hereditary Deafness on Martha's Vineyard.* Cambridge: Harvard University Press, 1985.

Fleischer, Doris Zames, and Frieda Zames. *The Disability Rights Movement: From Charity to Confrontation.* Philadelphia: Temple University Press, 2001.

Freeberg, Ernest. *The Education of Laura Bridgman: First Deaf and Blind Person to Learn Language.* Cambridge: Harvard University Press, 2001.

Garland-Thomson, Rosemarie. *Extraordinary Bodies: Figuring Physical Disability in American Culture and Literature.* New York: Columbia University Press, 1997.

―――. "The FDR Memorial: Who Speaks from the Wheelchair?" *Chronicle of Higher Education* (January 26, 2001): B11–B12.

―――. "Integrating Disability, Transforming Feminist Theory." *NWSA Journal* 14/3 (Fall 2002): 1–32.

Gerber, David A., ed. *Disabled Veterans in History.* Ann Arbor: University of Michigan Press, 2000.

Gitter, Elisabeth. *The Imprisoned Guest: Samuel Howe and Laura Bridgman, the Original Deaf-Blind Girl.* New York: Farrar, Straus and Giroux, 2001.

Goode, David. *A World Without Words: The Social Construction of Children Born Deaf and Blind.* Philadelphia: Temple University Press, 1994.

Hillyer, Barbara. *Feminism and Disability.* Norman: University of Oklahoma Press, 1993.

Joyner, Hannah. *From Pity to Pride: Growing Up Deaf in the Old South.* Washington, D.C.: Gallaudet University Press, 2004.

Klages, Mary. *Woeful Afflictions: Disability and Sentimentality in Victorian America.* Philadelphia: University of Pennsylvania Press, 1999.

Koestler, Frances A. *The Unseen Minority: A Social History of Blindness in America.* New York: David McKay, 1976.

Krentz, Christopher, ed. *A Mighty Change: An Anthology of Deaf American Writing, 1816–1864.* Washington, D.C.: Gallaudet University Press, 2000.

Kudlick, Catherine J. "Disability History: Why We Need Another 'Other'." *American Historical Review* 108(June 2003): 763–793.

Lane, Harlan. *The Mask of Benevolence: Disabling the Deaf Community.* San Diego: Dawn Sign Press, 1999 [1992].

―――. *When the Mind Hears: A History of the Deaf.* New York: Vintage Books, 1989.

Linton, Simi. *Claiming Disability: Knowledge and Identity.* New York: New York University Press, 1998.

Longmore, Paul K. "A Note on Language and the Social Identity of Disabled People." *American Behavioral Scientist* 18/2 (January/February 1985): 419–423.

―――. *Why I Burned My Book and Other Essays on Disability.* Philadelphia: Temple University Press, 2003.

Longmore, Paul K., and David Goldberger. "The League of the Physically Handicapped and the Great Depression: A Case Study in the New Disability History." *Journal of American History* 87/3 (December 2000): 888–922.

Longmore, Paul K., and Lauri Umansky, eds., *The New Disability History: American Perspectives.* New York: New York University Press, 2001.

Matson, Floyd. *Walking Alone and Marching Together: A History of the Organized Blind Movement in the United States, 1940–1990.* Baltimore: National Federation of the Blind, 1990.

Mitchell, David T., and Sharon L. Snyder, eds., *The Body and Physical Difference: Discourses on Disability.* Ann Arbor: University of Michigan Press, 1997.

―――. *Narrative Prosthesis: Disability and the Dependencies of Discourse.* Ann Arbor: University of Michigan Press, 2000.

Noll, Steven, and James W. Trent, Jr. *Mental Retardation in America: A Historical Reader*. New York: New York University Press, 2004.

O'Brien, Ruth. *Crippled Justice: The History of Modern Disability Police in the Workplace*. Chicago: University of Chicago Press, 2001.

Ott, Katherine, David Serlin, and Stephen Mihm, eds., *Artificial Parts, Practical Lives: Modern Histories of Prosthetics*. New York: New York University Press, 2002.

Padden, Carol, and Tom Humphries. *Deaf in America: Voices from a Culture*. Cambridge: Harvard University Press, 1990.

Pernick, Martin S. *The Black Stork: Eugenics and the Death of "Defective" Babies in American Medicine and Motion Pictures since 1915*. New York: Oxford University Press, 1996.

Schor, Naomi. "Blindness as Metaphor." *Differences* 11/2 (1999): 76–105.

Scotch, Richard K. *From Goodwill to Civil Rights: Transforming Federal Disability Policy*. 2nd ed. Philadelphia: Temple University Press, 2001.

Shapiro, Joseph P. *No Pity: People with Disabilities Forging a New Civil Rights Movement*. New York: Random House, 1993.

Snyder, Sharon L., and David T. Mitchell. "Out of the Ashes of Eugenics: Diagnostic Regimes in the United States and the Making of a Disability Minority." *Patterns of Prejudice* 36/1 (2002): 79–103.

Snyder, Sharon L., Brenda Jo Brueggemann, and Rosemarie Garland-Thomson, eds., *Disability Studies: Enabling the Humanities*. New York: Modern Language Association, 2002.

Trent, James W., Jr. *Inventing the Feeble Mind: A History of Mental Retardation in the United States*. Berkeley: University of California Press, 1994.

Van Cleve, John Vickery, and Barry A. Crouch. *A Place of Their Own: Creating the Deaf Community in U.S.* Washington, D.C.: Gallaudet University Press, 1989.

Wait, Gary E. "Julia Brace." *Dartmouth College Library Bulletin* 33/1 (November 1992).

Watcrhouse, Edward J. "Education of the Deaf-Blind in the United States of America, 1837–1967." In Edgar Lowell and Carole Rouin, eds., *State of the Art: Perspectives on Serving Deaf-Blind Children*. Washington, D.C.: United States Department of Education, 1977: 5–17.

Wendell, Susan. *The Rejected Body: Feminist Philosophical Reflections on Disability*. New York: Routledge, 1996.

Wright, Mary Herring. *Sounds Like Home: Growing Up Black and Deaf in the South*. Washington, D.C.: Gallaudet University Press, 1999.

INDEX

190, 192, 195, 200, 201, 227, 258, 260, 267, 270, 274; Keller's ancestors, 28; Keller's deafness, 54, 55–56, 71, 72, 120, 123

Deliverance, 101, 103, 104–106

Democracy, 52, 222, 231, 235, 240, 256, 257, 280

Dickens, Charles, 23

Disabled veterans, 4, 184–185, 186, 230, 247, 248, 279; hospital visits, 234, 235, 237, 239–240

Dogs, 5, 209; Keller's dogs, 9, 34, 77, 101, 102, 132–135, 159, 212–213, 214, 215, 216, 223, 262, 292; dogs of others, 9, 103, 153, 155, 161, 258, 262, 291

Dulles, John Foster, 271

Economic analyses, 51–55, 58–65, 69–70, 73–74, 99, 100, 142, 183

Egypt, 5, 263, 267–268, 269

Emerson, Ralph Waldo, 69, 148, 215, 232

England. *See* Great Britain

Fagan, Peter, 94, 95, 96, 126, 142–145

Fairbanks, Douglas, 104

Finger-spelling, 1, 3, 76, 94, 117, 126, 217, 227; Keller's descriptions of, 2, 236, 246

Finley, John H., 189–193, 198–201

Flaherty, Robert, 228, 229

Flynn, Elizabeth Gurley, 67, 69–71

Ford, Henry, 99, 112–114

Forest Hills, New York, 101, 104, 114, 117, 199, 208, 213

Foster, Mrs. Elliot, 44–47

Foundation for the Overseas Blind. *See* American Foundation for the Overseas Blind

France, 5, 68, 219, 247, 277, 285, 292, 293; Keller's descriptions of, 263–266, 287–289. *See also* Becheron, France; Paris, France

Fundraising, 210, 213, 249, 253, 278

Germany, and World War I, 68, 69. *See also* Nazi Germany

Giovannitti, Arturo, 67, 69–71, 94, 95

Gordon, Ruth, 223

Gray, Ethel, 10

Great Britain, 22, 51, 150, 214, 238, 247, 250, 276, 277, 278, 285, 293, 294

Greece, 5, 247–250, 277

Grew, Joseph C., 194

Grummons, Stuart, 233, 279

Haas, Herbert, 159, 181, 185, 215, 216, 220, 225, 234, 255, 290, 293

Hale, Dr. Edward Everett, 20, 28, 81, 84, 130, 131

Hamilton, Nancy, 223, 266, 295

Harding, Warren G., 55

Hawaii, 196

Haywood, Big Bill, 54

Helen Keller's Journal, 4, 147–168

Heineman, Clare, 184–187, 224–227

Henney, Nella Braddy, 205, 219, 222, 224, 243, 273, 274, 286, 291; Keller's editor, 3, 117, 126; Keller's letters to, 230–234, 251–256, 262–271, 277–283

Hiroshima, Japan, 251, 252–254, 256–257

Hitler, Adolph. *See* Nazi Germany

Hitz, John, 2, 21, 97, 121–124, 127, 140; Keller's letters to, 10–11, 16–17, 19–20, 23–24, 75

Holmes, Ned, 101, 103, 108, 109, 161, 173

Holmes, Walter, 180–182, 198

Holocaust, 271. *See also* Nazi Germany

Hopkins, Sophia, 15, 108

Howe, Samuel Gridley, 23, 41

Hugo, Victor, 264

Humason, Thomas, 12

Hunter, Robert, 56

Hutton, Eleanor, 19, 22

India, 5, 203, 273, 274–276, 293

Industrial Workers of the World, 53–54, 67–71, 94, 99

ABOUT THE EDITOR

KIM E. NIELSEN is Associate Professor of History and Women's Studies in the Department of Social Change and Development at the University of Wisconsin–Green Bay. She is the author of *The Radical Lives of Helen Keller* (also available from NYU Press) and *Un-American Womanhood: Antiradicalism, Antifeminism, and the First Red Scare.*

7-3-14